AUDREY HEPBURN

AUDREY HEPBURN

A Bio-Bibliography

David Hofstede

Bio-Bibliographies in the Performing Arts, Number 55
James Robert Parish, *Series Adviser*

Greenwood Press
Westport, Connecticut • London

Library of Congress Cataloging-in-Publication Data

Hofstede, David.
      Audrey Hepburn : a bio-bibliography / David Hofstede.
         p. cm.—(Bio-bibliographies in the performing arts, ISSN 0892–5550 ; no.
55)
      Includes index.
      ISBN 0–313–28909–3
      1. Hepburn, Audrey, 1929– . 2. Hepburn, Audrey, 1929– —
Bibliography. 3. Motion picture actors and actresses—United
States—Biography. I. Title. II. Series.
PN2287.H43H64 1994
791.43′028′092—dc20   94–5823
  [B]

British Library Cataloguing in Publication Data is available.

Library of Congress Catalog Card Number: 94–5823
ISBN: 0–313–28909–3
ISSN: 0892–5550

First published in 1994

Greenwood Press, 88 Post Road West, Westport, CT 06881
An imprint of Greenwood Publishing Group, Inc.

Printed in the United States of America

The paper used in this book complies with the
Permanent Paper Standard issued by the National
Information Standards Organization (Z39.48-1984).

10 9 8 7 6 5 4 3 2 1

Copyright Acknowledgment

All photographs courtesy of Photofest.

For Audrey

Contents

Illustrations

Preface

In July of 1992, Alistair Cooke announced his departure as host of *Masterpiece Theater*. Speculation over his successor commenced, and on July 31 *USA Today* television critic Matt Roush nominated Audrey Hepburn: "The only adequate pick. Epitomizes class. She could convince me that any old masterpiece is a jewel in the crown."

At this time Audrey Hepburn had made only three feature film appearances in the past sixteen years. She kept the lowest of low profiles, devoting most of her time to the type of on location charity work for UNICEF that is not covered on starstruck television shows like *Entertainment Tonight*. And yet the image of Audrey as the epitome of class, style and elegance remained, unassailable by time, age or absence from the public eye.

With some Hollywood stars image is just that; but critics and audiences sensed that Audrey's noblesse image was not the creation of a clever publicist. "She's a *lady*," said actor Van Johnson. "When she participates in the Academy Awards, she makes all those starlets look like tramps." Audrey's breakthrough role as a European princess in *Roman Holiday* (1953) showcased her regal bearing, aristocratic voice and chic fashion sense in a way that further blurred the distinction between actress and role.

Audrey Hepburn, like Marilyn Monroe, captured the public's attention in the early 1950's, and no two actresses ever progressed from unknown to celebrity to icon so quickly. Their physical appearances and screen personae could not be further apart, but both Marilyn and Audrey were ranked among the most beautiful women in motion pictures, and both had a profound influence on the style of the day. The difference is that Audrey also received acclaim for her skills as an actress which Marilyn, unfairly, did not.

"That face could have excused a lot of bad movies--it didn't have to," wrote critic Frank Thompson in *American Film*. With a mere twenty starring roles in film and two engagements on Broadway, Audrey Hepburn's career was exemplified by quality more than quantity, but her place in the pantheon is secure; she won an Academy Award and a Tony Award three days apart in 1954 and would later receive Oscar nominations for playing both a nun and a prostitute. Her portrayals of Princess Anne, Sabrina Fairchild, Sister Luke, Holly Golightly and Eliza Doolittle are treasured by generations of audiences.

Audrey Hepburn's achievements in show business are surpassed only by her achievements away from the spotlight. As a child growing up in the Dutch city of Arnhem, she experienced the horrors of war and hunger first hand when the Nazis invaded Holland. She would never forget those feelings of despair or her gratitude toward the relief workers who brought food and supplies after Arnhem was liberated by the Allies. In 1988 she expressed a desire to repay those workers and joined UNICEF as a Special Ambassador. In the next four years she would visit thousands of children in Ethiopia, El Salvador, The Sudan, Somalia and other strife-torn nations, bringing food and hope to people who would never know the Audrey of movies.

The choice to leave Hollywood in the 1980's for more humanitarian pursuits was not difficult. Audrey was never driven by her career, as her relatively sparse filmography illustrates. A precedent was set when Paramount Studios held up production of *Roman Holiday* for a still-unknown Audrey Hepburn, rather than recast the role. At a time when the stringent studio system was not yet a thing of the past, Audrey worked when she wanted to, talked to the press when she wanted to, and would take years off between movies to spend time with her family. The audience would never stop waiting, though a decade passed between *Wait Until Dark* (1967) and *Robin and Marian* (1976), and she would appear in just three more films in the last seventeen years of her life.

Despite searching hundreds of magazine articles, newspaper interviews and references in the biographies of co-workers, it is next to impossible to find a negative word written about Audrey Hepburn. Such sentiment tends to transform any attempt at objective biography into a fan letter. "To say anything against Audrey is like talking against the church," wrote *Hollywood Reporter* columnist Radie Harris in her book *Radie's World* (1975). *Good Housekeeping* asked, "Can anybody be as perfect as Audrey Hepburn?" in a 1962 article, certain that no one could really be "so noble, so thoughtful, so perennially 'good'?"

The reason for this image is not that Audrey Hepburn was without flaw, but that she was always careful to conduct herself in public with the utmost grace. In interviews she would rather express her thanks for the blessings she has received from earliest childhood. During World War II she witnessed the execution of relatives by the Nazis and the internment of her stepbrothers in German work camps. Her father abandoned his family when Audrey was six years old. As an adult she endured two failed marriages, five miscarriages and uncommon agony in her first successful delivery. But to Audrey these matters were not the concern of the general public, and reporters who were charmed by her affectionate manner and her smile would only later realize that she had deftly avoided every question about her private life.

Audrey Hepburn's death from cancer in 1993 was mourned around the globe, from North America and Europe where she is cinema royalty to Japan where her almost cult-like following began with *Roman Holiday* and never subsided, to South America and Africa, where her missions for UNICEF helped focus the world's attention on the needs of the less fortunate. *Audrey Hepburn: A Bio-Bibliography* is primarily a reference guide to her distinguished career, but it will also, inevitably, pay tribute to her philanthropic achievements.

The book is divided into nine sections:

1. A short biography.

2. A chronology of important events in her career and personal life.

3. A list of her stage appearances.

4. A filmography, including complete cast and credits for each film plus a synopsis, review summary and commentary.

5. Appearances in radio.

6. Appearances on television, including guest appearances and awards show presentations.

7. A discography of song recordings and books-on-tape.

8. An annotated bibliography of magazine articles, newspaper articles and books about her or referring to her.

9. A complete index of names and titles.

There are also two appendices: (1) a list of movie roles offered to her throughout her career that she was unable or unwilling to play, and (2) a list of awards, honors and tributes.

Acknowledgments

The author wishes to express his appreciation, for their assistance and encouragement, to the staff and librarians of the University of California at Los Angeles, the University of Southern California, California State University at Northridge, the Center for Motion Picture Study at the Academy of Motion Picture Arts and Sciences, the New York Public Library for the Performing Arts, and the University of Nevada, Las Vegas. Also, thanks to James Robert Parish and George Butler for their support when we agreed and their patience when we did not, to Wendy Bousman at Video Park for supplying tapes of Audrey Hepburn films, to Teresa Rogers, Jeri Johnson at *McCall's*, Gabriella Pura at *Parade*, Darryl Williams at *Dance* magazine and Karin Kaplan at *Seventeen* for sending articles, to Larry Billman, and at the Westminister Research Library Miss Katharine Oxenham for their help with Audrey's early stage credits, and to Helen Sanders at Carson Productions and Louis Spitzler, Jane Klain and Alvin H. Marill for their help in researching Audrey Hepburn's television appearances.

1

Biography: Once a Princess . . .

Audrey Hepburn's name appeared above the title of only twenty films from 1953 to 1993, but she will forever be ranked among the legendary actresses of the industry, most of whom have three times as many screen credits. She did not earn this status by a noblesse image alone, though it is impossible to describe Audrey Hepburn without some reference to aristocracy, nobility or class. But image can only create celebrities, not actresses, and there is a remarkable consistency to the quality of her regrettably sparse filmography that, along with five Academy Award nominations, verifies Hepburn's accomplishments as an actress. To use a baseball analogy, her batting average was worthy of the Hall of Fame.

She always believed it was luck, all her success and good fortune, and luck certainly played a role near the beginning of her career. In 1951 Hepburn received both the title role in the Broadway show *Gigi* and the female lead opposite Gregory Peck in *Roman Holiday*, when her resume` contained only limited experience in both media. It was her performance that would make or break both projects, and she deserves the credit for their respective success, just as she certainly would have been held responsible had they failed. It is still widely believed that Audrey's Oscar-winning performance in *Roman Holiday* (1953) was her film debut, which it was not. However, it was her first starring role, and that is no less impressive of an achievement.

Audrey was never comfortable with her looks, though her unique gamine beauty was undoubtedly persuasive in securing early acting jobs. She thought her nose was too big, and her teeth were too crooked, and that she was too skinny, but critics and audiences disagreed. In an era when Marilyn Monroe, Jayne Mansfield and Sophia Loren reigned as goddesses of the silver screen, Audrey was able to be just as alluring with much less apparent effort. Writers looked into her resplendent eyes and didn't need to look any lower before falling in love. Words like "elfin," "ethereal" and "pixie" were among the most frequently-offered descriptions, and were sprinkled liberally in the reviews that put Audrey's name above the title within a week of *Gigi*'s opening night.

She never lost the devotion and (it often seemed) outright support of the press, despite her lack of cooperation in granting interviews and supplying details about her personal life. Of her relatively few films that were not successful, many critics expressed sympathy instead of unleashing a venomous jeer. Once a princess, always a princess.

Audrey Hepburn may have been destined to portray royalty in her breakthrough role; the aristocratic Dutch heritage of her family can be traced back to the 12th century. Her maternal grandfather, Baron Aernoud van Heemstra, was at one time Governor of Surinam (Dutch Guiana), and a familiar figure at the court of Queen Wilhelmina. The family home had once been the Castle of Doorn, where the exiled German Kaiser spent his declining years. Her mother Ella was commonly addressed as Baroness van Heemstra. The Baroness was already twice divorced and raising two sons, Alexander and Jan, when she met and married an Anglo-Irish banker named John Victor Anthony Hepburn-Ruston in September of 1926. Their union produced one child, a daughter born on May 4, 1929 on John's old estate near Brussels.

Edda Kathleen Hepburn van Heemstra was a quiet and shy little girl who developed a strong affection for music and dance at a very early age. Ballet held a special enchantment, but the influence of her stepbrothers also turned young Edda into a tomboy who preferred climbing trees to dressing dolls. The dogs, cats, rabbits and other animals that roamed their Belgian estate were her next closest companions, but she also enjoyed finding a secluded corner on the grounds to draw pictures or daydream for hours. It was a convenient world in which to escape from her parents' marital problems; both Hepburn and the Baroness were strong-willed, domineering personalities, whose stormy relationship ended when Edda was six years old. After the divorce Hepburn walked out on his family. Though the sight and sound of her parents' frequent bickering was heartbreaking to Edda, she worshiped her father and was far more distressed when he disappeared, only to surface later as a member of Sir Oswald Mosley's Blackshirts (aka the British Union of Fascists).

In 1989, Audrey looked back on her father's departure as "the most traumatic event in my life." "I remember my mother's reaction. You look into your mother's face, and it's covered with tears, and you're terrified. You say to yourself, 'What's going to happen to me?' The ground has gone out from under you." (see B094). Audrey never lost the need to know her father, and when she was thirty she tracked down his whereabouts through the Red Cross. She wrote first and then visited John Hepburn's tiny Dublin apartment, accompanied by her then-husband Mel Ferrer. John had remarried, to a woman almost the same age as his daughter. The reunion was at first tentative, but it quickly became obvious that Hepburn had followed his daughter's career when he asked how she was feeling after her fall from a horse while filming *The Unforgiven* (1960). "Of course you were a fool to ride that gray stallion," he said, and the ice was broken. Audrey never revealed if they saw each other again, but she took care of her father's every need until his death at age 94. "It helped me to lay the ghost," she told *Parade* Magazine, "I went on suffering as long as I didn't see him."

The divorce of Edda's parents was triggered not only by clashing temperament but also by disagreement over the management of the van Heemstra money. Audrey's mother moved the family back to Arnhem, in the Netherlands, only to discover that her fortune had been squandered by her ex-husband. Considering this circumstance, it is surprising that the Baroness would agree to a custody settlement stipulating that Edda attend a girls' school near London, so that her father could exercise his visitation privileges. But when war broke out on September 1, 1939, the Baroness arranged for her daughter's return to Holland, which she presumed would be safer. This would not prove to be the case.

The Germans invaded Arnhem in May of 1940, and Edda temporarily took her mother's name to cover her English identity. Since she spoke English and French too fluently for comfort in a German-occupied city, she went to elementary school to learn Dutch. Hardship followed hardship; the family was stripped of nearly all of their material possessions. Edda's step-brother Alexander joined the Dutch army, and ended up in a German labor camp. She watched as her uncle, a prominent Arnhem lawyer, was gunned down by the Nazis for plotting to blow up a German train. One of her cousins was also executed, and several friends of her mother began to disappear under mysterious circumstances.

The Baroness, like her ill-fated brother, was active in the Dutch underground, a cause she had begun to organize long before the occupation began. The children helped however they could--Edda would frequently carry messages to other operatives in her shoes on the way to school. She had more than one close call with German soldiers, but always managed to smile and charm her way past the patrols. Meanwhile, she managed to continue her ballet studies at the Arnhem Conservatory of Music, near the famous bridge where the British were defeated in one of the bloodiest battles of the war. "People don't realize that during a war of this kind nothing basically changes inside of you.

Conditions and habits change but the human doesn't. If you wanted to be a dancer before, you want to be one just as much despite the war." she would later tell *Dance* magazine (see B072).

The dream of becoming a ballerina sustained Edda through many difficult times, but it was not an easy dream to pursue. The Baroness, however, was determined that her daughter be allowed to dance. When she was younger The Baroness and her sister both wanted to study for the opera, but at that time the stage was forbidden to girls of good breeding. So instead both daughters married and gave up their career ideas, but the Baroness vowed that if she ever had a talented child, especially a daughter, she would do everything possible to encourage her.

When tights and slippers became impossible to buy they would make their own, using curtains and old sheets for dresses and felt to make slippers. Edda danced for hours on end in toe shoes worn to shreds, and worn-out boxes hardened with furniture varnish. For a while even ordinary shoes were rationed, and the black market became the only remaining source. Finally only wooden shoes were available, which obviously were not ideal for ballet! But not only did Edda continue dancing, she taught classes for children of all ages at a dime a lesson. The village carpenter put up a barre in one of their rooms, and a wind-up gramophone provided the music.

The money Edda raised through dancing lessons was used to fund the Underground. Behind closed doors, and with lookouts posted to watch for German soldiers, Edda would play piano and dance in clandestine "blackout" performances for other Dutch patriots. It was against Nazi regulations for more than a handful of people to gather in any one place, but the 100 or more who turned out to watch the petite young ballerina were always careful, and the Nazis never found out. In 1954 the now internationally famous Audrey Hepburn remembered those private recitals in a *Coronet* Magazine interview; "The best audience I ever had made not a single sound at the end of my performance." (see B147).

For Edda, the worst was still yet to come. In the fourth year of occupation, the family had no milk, no butter, no eggs and no sugar. For days on end, the only food the van Heemstras had was endive. By the end of the war, without water or electricity in their home, the malnourished family was eating tulip bulbs to stay alive. Shortly before the Allied invasion of the continent, German police began rounding up all available Dutch women to work in their military kitchens. Edda was seized in the street but managed to break away and hide in a cellar. There she remained for a month, in darkness and silence, suffering from yellow jaundice and hepatitis.

The liberation of Arnhem on May 5, 1945 came none too soon. Edda ran up from the cellar when she heard men speaking English, and into the arms of British troops. The van Heemstra home had been occupied by a German army squad, who set up a radio transmitter on the upper floor. They departed when the allies entered the city, but not before bombing the house into rubble. Now fifteen years old, Edda had missed four years of formal schooling but received a harrowing education in survival and self-control. The Baroness and Edda worked for a time in a rest home for Dutch soldiers and then moved to Amsterdam, where they would try over the next three years to put their lives back together.

Edda still had thoughts of a career in ballet, but dance training required money, and her mother had lost everything she had in the war. The Baroness remained determined to keep her daughter's artistic pursuits alive, and somehow the money was found for Edda to attend classes with a Russian teacher named Olga Tarassova, who was the organizer of the still-functioning Netherlands Ballet. Edda gradually began to recover the strength in her limbs that was lost during the war, but despite spending hours every day in practice it was becoming clear that she would never be as good a dancer as she wanted to be.

Her studies never culminated with the lead in *Swan Lake*, but they were directly responsible for her introduction to movies. One day in 1948 her class was visited by Dutch film director Charles Huguenot van der Linden and producer H.M. Josephson, who were about to begin work on a travelogue called *Nederlands in 7 Lessen*. The two men were looking for an attractive young girl with an aristocratic dignity and sophistication to play a KLM air stewardess, who would introduce and conclude the film. Edda's captivating looks--short black hair cut Joan of Arc-style, large, almond-shaped eyes, a swanlike neck, long shapely legs and a waist size (20 inches) that was smaller than her hat size (22 inches)-- had already won her a job modeling in a fashion house, and had now captured the attention of van der Linden and Josephson, who offered her the part when the class was over. Edda was thrilled with the idea, and eagerly accepted. She was eighteen years old when she made her film debut, which amounted to a few minutes on screen that took all of three days to shoot.

In 1949, the following year, Alexander and Jan left home to work in the Dutch East Indies, and Edda was offered a scholarship to the Rambert School of Ballet in London. The Baroness decided that her daughter had seen too many unhappy things in Holland anyway, so with the equivalent of ten dollars in their possession they set sail for England. With the war over there was no longer a reason for Edda to not use her father's surname, and somewhere during the English Channel crossing Edda van Heemstra became Audrey Hepburn.

Marie Rambert was a stern taskmaster who would not hesitate to whack her pupils' knuckles with a stick for being caught with folded arms or slouched shoulders. Audrey was eager to begin her studies, but there were more immediate concerns--the money they had would only cover the cost of food and a cheap hotel for three days. Madame Rambert, who was only stern in the classroom, recognized both Audrey's talent and her desperate situation. She took her new student into her home, and housed and fed her free of charge for six months.

The Baroness, meanwhile, worked for a short time in a florist's shop and then as an interior decorator, before being appointed manager of a block of flats in Mayfair. She was then able to leave her decrepit hotel and move into a small apartment. Audrey later moved in, and wasted no time in finding a job that would help support her mother and pay back Madame Rambert. Once again she turned to modeling, and her face soon graced the advertising for Lacto-Calomine, a popular beauty preparation. The moment her classes were over with Rambert, she would make the rounds of West End auditions for musical stage shows. This she did only for hope of another paycheck--still thinking herself a ballerina, Audrey looked down on the less classical forms of entertainment. As time went on, however, she was forced to face the hard reality of her limited future on the classical stage.

"I was eighteen, an adult, but my technique didn't compare with that of the girls who had had five years of Sadler's Wells teaching, paid for by their families, and who had always had good food and bomb shelters. Reason made me see that I just couldn't be so square as to go on studying ballet. Still, I thought it was way below my dignity to go into a musical." (see B072).

It was just six months after her arrival in London that Audrey faced a career crossroads; she was offered two jobs in the same week. One of which represented the fulfillment of a childhood dream; a troupe of Madame Rambert's students were invited to embark upon a government-sponsored tour of South America. The day before, Audrey had been one of ten girls chosen from 3000 applicants to dance in the chorus of *High Button Shoes*. The London production of the Broadway musical hit was scheduled to open on December 22 at the London Hippodrome Theatre.

Had she followed her emotions Audrey would have certainly headed south of the border. But she was pragmatic enough to realize that ballet now represented her past, while the musical stage, with luck, just might provide a future. She turned down Madame Rambert and accepted the eight pound-a-week role in *High Button Shoes*.

Jerome Robbins' high-speed choreography, typified in *High Button Shoes* by the frenetic "Bathing Beauty Ballet," required a style of dancing that Audrey wasn't very familiar with, or that she was particularly good at. But her beauty and dedication were noticed by Cecil Landeau, a stage producer in the audience, and after the show closed he offered her a part in his musical-comedy revue *Sauce Tartare*. The show, featuring an international cast of singers, dancers and comedians, opened on May 18, 1949 at the Cambridge Theatre and ran 437 performances. Audrey then went immediately into *Sauce Piquante*, which Landeau had prepared before *Tartare* had even closed.

Sauce Piquante lasted less than two months at the Cambridge Theatre after its April 27, 1950 debut, but during its brief run Landeau observed the attention Audrey received from male audience members, and promoted her from the chorus. She was given a solo dance number and a supporting role in two comedy skits. Although the producer and director of *Nederlands in 7 Lessen* can rightly claim to have first discovered Audrey's show business potential, it was Cecil Landeau who was chiefly responsible for the launch of her career. Audrey's solo was spotted by director Thorold Dickinson, who would later cast her in *The Secret People*. When *Piquante* closed Audrey remained with Landeau and performed in the revue *Summer Nights* at the famed Ciro's nightclub. There she was noticed by director Mario Zampi, who would use Audrey in the film *Laughter in Paradise* (1951). Though her role lasted just twenty seconds, it was enough to convince a Paramount Pictures executive that she might be right for a film being developed by the studio called *Roman Holiday*.

It was also Landeau who realized, perhaps even before Audrey herself, that his discovery had a promising future in show business, but not as a dancer. He sent Audrey to acting classes conducted by Felix Aylmer, a veteran character actor who had once coached Charles Laughton, and was knighted by the empire in 1965. Aylmer worked on her diction and the timbre and resonance of her voice, which Landeau believed needed help to reach the cheap seats in the theater. Aylmer refined but thankfully did not (or could not) remove the Continental lilt in Audrey's voice that would later distinguish her from the Hollywood galaxy of stars. "He taught me to concentrate intelligently on what I was doing," she said later, "and made me aware that all actors need a 'method' of sorts to be even vaguely professional." (see B186).

Audrey registered with the casting offices of Britain's film studios in the hope of getting work as an "extra." Instead she received an offer to play a leading role in the comedy *Laughter in Paradise*. But she was still under contract to Cecil Landeau, and although he probably would have let her go she turned it down. The role went to Beatrice Campbell, but Audrey does appear briefly in the film as a cigarette girl. Almost immediately she landed another bit part in the film *One Wild Oat* (1951), the film adaptation of a popular British stage farce. Her appearance as a hotel receptionist could not be considered memorable, but the paycheck, combined with those from Landeau's revues and the occasional modeling assignment, was enough for Audrey to pay back her mother and become more or less financially independent.

Audrey's next film was *Young Wives Tale* (1951), another comedy adapted from a West End play. Once again her role was insignificant, but she made many friends among the distinguished cast which included Joan Greenwood, Nigel Patrick and Guy Middleton. It was at a party in 1950 that followed the completion of the film that Audrey first met James Hanson, the twenty-eight-year-old son and heir of a wealthy British trucking executive. The debonair Hanson had already acquired the "playboy" reputation that inevitably follows when youth, looks and money are mixed. He made the nightclub rounds in luxury cars that comfortably accommodated his six-foot-four frame. One of his steady girlfriends was the actress Jean Simmons, but after that night he and Audrey became inseparable.

The relationship became more serious, but Hanson's hectic work schedule, which involved frequent trips to Canada, made any long-range plans difficult. Audrey continued to land small movie parts, and next up was a film that became a classic--Ealing's *The Lavender Hill Mob* (1951), directed by Charles Crichton and starring Alec Guinness as a timid bank clerk who masterminds an elaborate gold heist. The film won an Oscar for its screenplay and a nomination for Guinness, who shared Audrey's only scene. Although her role as a hat-check girl named Chiquita was typically undistinguished, Guinness was impressed with Audrey and introduced her to director Mervyn LeRoy, who was then casting the film *Quo Vadis?* (1951).

For the second time during her career as an extra, Audrey was considered for a featured role in a film; LeRoy approached MGM about casting the talented unknown for the lead role of Lygia. But the studio wanted a star, and the role was later given to Deborah Kerr. As a result, she was free to accept a role in Ealing's *The Secret People* (1952), a political melodrama which clearly demonstrated why the studio is best remembered for its comedy offerings. Director Thorold Dickinson gave Audrey her best part to date--as Nora, the younger sister of the protagonist, she was third-billed behind Valentina Cortesa and Serge Reggiani, and for the first time her name went above the title.

During production of *The Secret People* Hepburn and Hanson became engaged, but marriage plans would have to wait; Hanson was off to Canada once again, and Audrey had won a role in the lame musical comedy *Monte Carlo Baby* (1953). The part was a definite step back from her supporting work in *The Secret People*, but the free trip to Monte Carlo was a delightful compensation. Audrey left for the French Riviera looking forward to enjoying a month in the sun, wearing the Dior dress that was designed for her character and cashing another respectable paycheck. But the film would provide another bonus beyond any of her expectations--the definitive "big break" that would catapult Audrey Hepburn from bit player to star.

The story, which is told in nearly every article about Hepburn because it sounds almost too cliched' to have actually happened, begins in the lobby of the Hotel de Paris, where preparations were being made to shoot one of Audrey's scenes. The French novelist Colette was a guest in the hotel and stopped to watch the filming. The 78-year-old woman in the wheelchair was not known to Audrey, and the feeling was certainly mutual, but during a break Audrey received word that the spectator wished to see her. One of Colette's novels, *Gigi*, was being adapted for the Broadway stage by writer Anita Loos and producer Gilbert Miller. It was the story of an adolescent maiden in Paris at the dawn of the 20th century, who is brought up to be a mistress. The lead role had not yet been cast, but now the author was certain the problem was solved. When she first saw Audrey, she told her husband "Voila`, there's your Gigi."

Audrey wasn't quite so sure. "When Colette proposed it I replied that I wasn't equipped to play a leading role since I'd never said more than one or two lines on stage. But she said, 'You've been a dancer, you've worked hard, and you can do this, too.' " (see B186). Back in London she read the part for Gilbert Miller and Anita Loos, both of whom had flown from New York to meet Colette's discovery. "I tried to explain to all of them that I wasn't ready to do a lead," she said later, "but they didn't agree, and I certainly wasn't going to argue with them." (see B 210).

Signing the contract with Gilbert Miller meant postponing for a second time her marriage to James Hanson. "When I marry James, I want to give up at least a year to just being a wife to him," she told *Hollywood Reporter* columnist Radie Harris the following year. "He knows it would be impossible for me to give up my career completely. I just can't. I've worked too long to achieve something. And so many people have helped me along the way, I don't want to let them down." (see B068). In December of 1952, the engagement was officially broken. They would remain friends, and in 1954 when Audrey married Mel Ferrer, Hanson was one of the very few in her exclusive circle to receive an invitation.

While Audrey studied her lines for *Gigi*, which she was under orders to have memorized before her arrival in New York, she received a call from Paramount Pictures. They had become interested in her as a candidate for the lead role of Princess Anne in William Wyler's next film, *Roman Holiday*. A screen test was arranged in London. The test was conducted by Thorold Dickinson, who was instructed by Wyler to keep the cameras running after the scene was over. Wyler hoped for some unrehearsed footage of the actress, and he got it. When the director yelled "Cut!" Audrey sat up in the royal bed from which she said her dialogue, clasped her hands around her knees and grinned delightedly at the praise she was receiving from those in attendance. "The test began with a wink and ended with a giggle, neither of which were in the script," reported the *Los Angeles Times* later (see B118), and it was Audrey's natural ebullience as much as her line reading that won her the coveted role.

Paramount had their Princess, and signed Audrey to a short-term, two picture deal. They also agreed to wait six months for her while she fulfilled her prior commitment to *Gigi*. With Wyler and Gregory Peck already signed, the postponement of a project to accommodate a former chorus girl and extra was practically unheard of, but the decision set a precedent that remained throughout Audrey's film career; at a time when the studio system was not yet entirely a thing of the past, Audrey Hepburn worked when she wanted to.

In November of 1951, Broadway publicist Arthur Cantor sent the following message to the New York newspapers and press services; "New British actress named Hepburn arriving this morning at Pier 90 to appear in Broadway play. She is a great find. Suggest you send reporters and photographers." The announcement was disregarded by every recipient, and Audrey's ship arrived to an empty dock. The publicist was there, and he managed to track down one ship-news reporter and begged him to ask the new starlet a few questions. "Nah," the reporter told him. "I'd rather go have a cup of coffee." (see B001).

Perhaps it was just as well. During the voyage across the Atlantic, Audrey had gained fifteen pounds after gorging on the rich ocean liner food. The war still wasn't all that long ago, and after five years of near starvation the temptation of several free meals a day proved too great. At first rehearsal she was ordered to begin a diet, which made the eighteen-hour workdays all the more taxing. At the end of every rehearsal she was given additional acting lessons in her hotel suite. It seemed clear that the confidence of Gilbert Miller and Anita Loos in Colette's discovery was not exactly overwhelming. And then the play opened.

The company was still in previews in Philadelphia when reviews began proclaiming Audrey as "the acting find of the year." Broadway was a tougher room, but the notices were exactly the same--good play; glorious new star. "Miss Hepburn is the one fresh element in the performance," raved the *New York Times*. "She is an actress; and as Gigi she develops a full-length character from artless gaucheries in the first act to a stirring emotional climax in the last scene. It is a fine piece of sustained acting that is spontaneous, lucid and captivating."

Audrey's name went up in lights on the marquee of the FultonTheatre one week after the play opened on November 24, 1951. Audrey darted across the street to have a look, and then sighed: "Oh dear, and I've still got to learn how to act." (see B210). British film studios finally woke up and sent Audrey a selection of movies, but their timing was late, as it was with Charlie Chaplin, Vivien Leigh and a host of others. The girl they could only find room for as a cigarette girl now belonged to

Broadway and Hollywood. When *Gigi* closed in June, Audrey flew to Italy to begin filming *Roman Holiday*.

"Whether Audrey Hepburn was chosen for *Roman Holiday* or it was chosen for her, is a moot point, " writes Ian Woodward in his Hepburn biography (see B367), "But the result was an alliance made in some cinematic heaven." The story, of a pretty young princess who escapes her regimented life for 24 hours of fun with an American newspaperman, was not intended to be a showcase for its neophyte star. But after the first few days of shooting, it became obvious that this would be Audrey's movie. Gregory Peck asked Paramount to give her co-star billing, and the studio reluctantly granted his request. They became close friends on the set and remained so until Audrey's death in 1993. William Wyler nurtured his newcomer with patience and genuine affection; in 1983 Audrey still referred to herself as "Willy's baby," and blushed when asked if the director was in love with her (see B127).

When the movie opened in 1953, film critics and audiences made their Broadway counterparts look like rank amateurs when it came to rapturous praise. "Paramount's new star sparkles and glows with the fire of a finely cut diamond," wrote *Time* magazine; "Impertinence, hauteur, sudden repentance, happiness, rebellion and fatigue supplant each other with lightning speed on her mobile, adolescent face." (see B210). "It was the lusciousness of Hepburn's voice and speech, in addition to the accent itself, in addition to the girlish-impish charm of the face, that ravished us," echoed Stanley Kauffmann. "'Do you know,' she says near the beginning to the lady-in-waiting who is tucking her primly into bed in her nightgown, 'I've heard that there are people who sleep with *nothing* on.' If you have ever heard that 'nothing,' you have a little treasure of sound in your memory." (see B301). Some of the adoration was downright embarrassing, such as *Photoplay*'s hyperbolic tribute; "The girl is so alive, every sense so aware, that not even the worst cynic could come away from an hour with her without smelling spring in the air, hearing faraway music from the heavens."

Audrey's reaction was appreciative, but she refused to buy into the ballyhoo. "Success," she said, "is like reaching an important birthday and finding out you're exactly the same. All I feel is the responsibility to live up to it. And even, with luck, to survive it." (see B076). However, she was very moved by a phone call from Jean Simmons, the early favorite for the role of Princess Anne. "Miss Hepburn, I've just seen *Roman Holiday* and although I wanted to hate you, I have to tell you that I wouldn't have been half as good. You were wonderful." (see B277). Joan Crawford was also a fan; "Everybody in the film industry should open his arms to this child and ask her to come in and help us. She has that magic spark that pictures need." (see B081).

After completing *Roman Holiday* and the American tour of *Gigi* that followed, Audrey returned to London for a well-deserved rest. In May of 1953 she attended a dinner party at the Grosvenor Square flat of Gregory Peck, and was introduced to Peck's friend and temporary roommate Mel Ferrer, who was then filming MGM's *Knights of the Round Table* (1953). She expressed admiration for his performance in *Lili* (1953), one of her favorite films. Since *Roman Holiday* was not yet released Ferrer couldn't return the compliment, but he was immediately taken with Audrey.

Melchor Gaston Ferrer was born on August 25, 1917 in Elberon, New Jersey, the son of a Cuban Spaniard who became a New York physician. While attending Princeton University he wrote, produced, directed and acted. He left college after two years and went to Mexico to write books. Within six months he was in Vermont working for a book publisher, and dancing in the Broadway musical *Everywhere I Roam*. He was then forced to abandon it all when he was partially paralyzed by polio. A couple of years later, completely recovered, he became a producer in radio, then left for Hollywood in 1943 to take a job as a talent scout. He progressed from screen-test director to producer-director, and would take acting jobs in exchange for the chance to direct. His mercurial approach to life and career prompted one wag to ask "what Mel finds to keep himself busy while he's asleep."

Ferrer married socialite sculptress Frances Pilchard, had two children, then divorced her in 1943 to marry a woman named Barbara Tripp. He later divorced Tripp and remarried Pilchard. At the time he met Audrey, the relationship was again on the rocks. During their first conversation Audrey said she'd like to do a play with Ferrer one day, and he sensed that her statement was not just hollow cocktail party chatter. After escorting her to the theater the following week, Ferrer began looking for a project in which they could appear together.

Meanwhile Audrey returned to Hollywood to start her next film, an adaptation of the Samuel Taylor play *Sabrina Fair*, to be directed by Billy Wilder. The film, entitled simply *Sabrina* (1954) was a frothy romantic comedy filmed in an atmosphere that was more appropriate to a war movie. The role of Linus Larrabee, the wealthy executive who falls for his chauffeur's daughter, was written for Cary Grant but went to Humphrey Bogart, who was none too happy about it. He disliked the movie, he disliked co-star William Holden, he disliked Billy Wilder and after the first week of production he came to dislike Audrey as well (see F9).

Holden and Wilder both became infatuated with Audrey, which drove Bogart further into his pique. "After so many drive-in waitresses in movies, here is class, somebody who went to school, can spell and possibly play the piano," said Wilder. The director was also responsible for what may be the most memorable quote about Audrey Hepburn the actress; "She may make bazooms a thing of the past." (see B348).

Holden flat out fell in love with his leading lady, and this time when the romance rumors began in the press (as they had with Audrey and Gregory Peck) there was some basis for their conjecture. Audrey eventually got over the flirtation; Holden did not.

Moments of levity were rare, but everyone had a much-needed laugh when the King and Queen of Greece visited the set, and were presented to the cast by Wilder. As the stars executed all the proper requirements of protocol, an electrician working above yelled "Hey Queen! Where were you last night when I needed to fill a straight?" The film's subsequent success when it was released in 1954 hopefully soothed any lingering ill will.

Sabrina also marked the beginning of Audrey's forty-year collaboration with designer Hubert de Givenchy. When Givenchy first heard that a Miss Hepburn was coming to view his collection, he expected Katharine. "When this thin young woman entered, I was very disappointed," he said. But since that first meeting "she became the most loyal of friends, almost a sister." (see B002). Together in such films as *Funny Face, Charade, Paris When it Sizzles* and most notably with the famous sleeveless black dress and lampshade hat Audrey wore in *Breakfast at Tiffany's*, they created a style--the gamine look--that is still emulated around the world.

Givenchy also designed Hepburn's off-screen wardrobe and developed his perfume with her in mind. "I continue to think of Audrey when I design" he said in 1992, while Audrey expressed her thanks for the confidence she gained by wearing his clothes. "All those fund-raising trips, cocktails and galas---I don't think I could have done it without Hubert's love and kindness." (see B187).

Cecil Beaton, who would later design Audrey's gowns for *My Fair Lady*, was among the first to define the "Hepburn look." "Nobody," he wrote in *Vogue*, "ever looked like her before World War II. The lively, spare, unfussed good looks of Audrey Hepburn have become the good looks of the era, the yardstick for contemporary shapes and faces." Her hair is "neat, but not symmetrical;" her head is usually tilted "with an appealing, characteristic perk that focuses on the gazelle eyes, the exalted neck, [which] minimizes some minor faults in the nose." The eyes are "charcoaled, heavy with lashes; the face, pale-lipped and 'natural' although it takes her an hour and a half to make up; the extraordinary grace of the body, clearly revealing that she started her career as a dancer;" arms "that have a delicate roundness; legs ditto, both assets for the narrow, faintly curved sheaths (Givenchy and otherwise) that have been cult symbols for the looks in fashion now; the black pants and outsize schoolboy pullover Hepburn has helped make famous; the crisp immaculate simplicity; the absence of jewelry--two tiny pearl earrings seem to be the maximum." (see B009).

While Audrey was dodging Bogart's wrath on the set of *Sabrina*, an envelope arrived for her from Mel Ferrer. It contained a copy of the romantic fantasy play *Ondine*, by Jean Giraudoux, with a note from Ferrer suggesting that this could be the project they had discussed earlier. Audrey loved the play when she read it, and agreed to return to Broadway as soon as *Sabrina* was in the can. It was during rehearsals in New York that the relationship between Mel and Audrey blossomed into love.

As with *Gigi*, it was clear from the first preview performance that *Ondine* was a hit, and equally clear who was getting the credit. "This show will probably be known from now on as *The Audrey Hepburn Show*," wrote the *Boston Globe*. "Audrey Hepburn is all magic in her ballet dancer's body and in the music of her voice." The play opened at New York's Forty-Sixth Street Theatre on February 18, 1954, and *Hollywood Reporter* columnist Radie Harris was there; "The audience cheered and bravoed, hoping that Audrey would take one curtain call alone. But with every bow, there was Mel, always at her side. Finally, when the house lights were on, and the audience still applauding madly for Audrey, Mel held up his hand to hush the house for a curtain speech. An acknowledgement to his lovely co-star, we all assumed. Instead, we heard a flowery expression of thanks to (director) Alfred Lunt, and since this audience was well aware of the backstage differences between Ferrer and Lunt, this public recapitulation was received with slightly raised eyebrows!" (see B068).

This was the first of many articles to chronicle what was perceived as Ferrer's attempt to share, or perhaps even steal, the spotlight that always followed Audrey. And after every such article there would be a defensive response from Audrey--"Why shouldn't Mel share my curtain calls? After all, it's his play too, isn't it?" Though the New York notices were unanimously favorable, nearly all the praise was centered on Audrey's performance as the water-nymph who ascends from the sea and falls in love with a handsome German knight. The consensus was that when she left the stage, the play dragged.

All of the critical raves and audience cheers of the previous year were consummated during the week of March 25, 1954, in which Audrey received both the Academy Award for *Roman Holiday* and the Tony Award for *Ondine*. Such an achievement was rare but not unprecedented--Shirley Booth had managed it just one year earlier (for the play *Time of the Cuckoo* and the film *Come Back, Little Sheba*), and in 1975 Ellen Burstyn won an Oscar for *Alice Doesn't Live Here Anymore* and a Tony for *Same Time Next Year*. Audrey's response was characteristically humble; "It's like when somebody gives you something to wear that's too big, and you have to grow into it. I'm truly happy." The Baroness was more succinct-- "Considering that you have no talent it's really extraordinary where you've gotten."

"She said it in the middle of all the lovely successes I was having," Audrey told an interviewer in 1989. "She wasn't putting me down. She was saying how fortunate I was. Oh, I think she was right. I don't have this huge talent. I landed in this business because I had to earn a living." (see B235).

Just two months into the run of *Ondine*, newspaper headlines were describing Audrey as "a very sick girl." She was suffering from anemia, loss of weight and severe emotional exhaustion, and under doctor's orders she canceled every professional commitment except for the play. Audrey never missed a performance, but when *Ondine* closed in June she proposed to alter her priorities. After *Roman Holiday* was released she was already telling the press that she planned to keep her career in perspective. "I don't like the idea of a telephone jangling, then rushing off to Hollywood. I like the thought of working at a certain time, and having the rest of the time to call your own. I might like to do a play, to travel, to study, maybe to marry. That is the pattern for my life--the way I can be happy." (see B093). But the pattern had become clouded by a volume of professional demands she could not possibly foresee. After trying and failing to satisfy all of them, Audrey put her career on hold and left for Gstaad, Switzerland, where she would spend one month under strict medical care away from all visitors, reporters and telephones.

When the secret of her arrival was discovered, Audrey retreated to a two-bedroom chalet on top of Burgenstock, a mountain overlooking Lake Lucerne. Mel Ferrer flew in for a visit after Audrey's health had improved, and the following week they were married. The civil service was conducted by the local mayor in his home, and the religious ceremony followed on September 25 at a tiny thirteenth-century chapel below Burgenstock. Among the 25 guests were the Baroness, members of Mel's family and the former British ambassador to the Netherlands, Sir Nevile Bland.

The couple honeymooned for four days in Italy, before Mel was forced to return to work on his next film, *La Madre*. Audrey too was ready to get back to work, but she was determined to maintain a balance between career and family. She and Mel had settled into a third-floor flat in London's Portman Square, and from there she perused several script submissions, including Otto Preminger's *Saint Joan* and *L'Aiglon*, to be directed by William Wyler. She finally reached a decision in the summer of 1955, and signed to play Natasha in King Vidor's lavish, $6 million film adaptation of Leo Tolstoy's gargantuan novel *War and Peace*. Two factors helped sway her decision; the casting of Mel Ferrer as Prince Andrei, and her salary of $350,000, quite a raise from the $12,500 she received for *Roman Holiday*.

The events in Europe that led to Napoleon's downfall provide the

P.4039-95

Audrey and Mel Ferrer prior to their marriage in 1954.

backdrop to the story of *War and Peace*, which chronicles the changing fortunes of the Rostov family and their friends in St. Petersburg. Three years of war have the affect of aging Natasha considerably, and Audrey told *Newsweek* that making that transition was "the toughest job I've ever had to do." Fortunately, the magazine pointed out, "she had a five-year wartime experience of her own to draw upon." (see B144). The *New York Herald-Tribune* hailed Audrey's Natasha as "the best feminine performance of the year," and other reviews were nearly as flattering, but the film turned out to be a bigger hit with critics than audiences.

She went next into *Funny Face* (1957) her first musical and the realization of a lifelong dream to dance with the legendary Fred Astaire. For his part, Astaire also looked forward to meeting his new leading lady. "I knew that Audrey wanted to make the picture and that sooner or later the studio would come around...So I told my agents to forget all other projects for me. I was waiting for Audrey Hepburn. She asked for me, and I was ready. This could be the last and only opportunity I'd have to work with the great and lovely Audrey, and I was not missing it. Period." (see B348).

Director Stanley Donen, who confessed that he was in love with Audrey from the first time he saw her in *Roman Holiday*, (see B367) remarked that "you had to earn her respect and trust, and they were slow in coming." Donen did so when he clashed with her over a costume change; "There was a scene in which we agreed she would wear a black sweater, black slacks, and black shoes. But I wanted her to wear white socks to draw a tiny bit of attention to her feet. She was shocked. 'It has to be black socks,' she said. 'White socks will break the line and completely ruin the number.'" They screen-tested both versions, and still disagreed on which was preferable. Donen recalled that she almost burst into tears when he forced her to film the scene his way. "She felt miserable for the three or four days it took to shoot the sequence, but she went through with it without a whimper."

After the film was completed and Audrey watched the picture in its entirety for the first time, she wrote Donen a short and sweet note. It simply said, "You were right about the socks." *Funny Face* was a resounding success, and won Audrey praise for her dancing and her vocal rendition of George Gershwin's "How Long Has This Been Goin' On?"

Between films Audrey sought solace at Burgenstock whenever possible. Her determination to preserve a semblance of a domestic life had already begun to manifest itself in a rather unique homemaking observance, which was described by The *Los Angeles Examiner* in 1957; "Whenever the Ferrers move into a hotel suite, Audrey promptly calls the bellboy and housekeeper and hands over to them the traditional dull furnishings. Then out of the trunks come the silver candlesticks, books, pictures, flower vases, records, linens, ashtrays, lamps, two hand-knit blankets, cushions and a set of china. 'It's nice to be able to carry your prized possessions with you," she said." (see B232). To accommodate this ritual, Audrey and Mel would often travel with over fifty pieces of luggage.

That year their bags were unpacked in Paris, where Audrey began filming *Love in the Afternoon* with Gary Cooper and Maurice Chevalier. Billy Wilder produced, directed and co-wrote this story of a pretty teenage cello student, Ariane, who falls in love with a middle-aged, American millionaire playboy. As she invents imaginary lovers to make the ladies' man jealous, Ariane's detective father is hired to investigate the American's activities, and he makes a surprising discovery.

Audrey was at this point used to being cast opposite leading men who were old enough to be her father--both Humphrey Bogart in *Sabrina* and Fred Astaire in *Funny Face* were thirty years her senior. But for the public and reviewers, the most disturbing example of this tendency was *Love in the Afternoon*, according to Molly Haskell. Haskell describes the film as "sublimely wistful and beautifully acted," but observed that viewers were troubled by "the portrait of Gary Cooper, all-American hero, as an aging Lothario, his eyes hauntingly empty, the beautiful face lined with age and depravity...he is on automatic pilot until he is brought back to life by a woman. A woman who in essence is older and wiser than he is." (see B071).

Reception for the picture was mild, but over the years its reputation has improved to the point where it is now considered one of the best romantic-comedies of the 1950's (see B209). For her part Audrey was delighted to be working with Billy Wilder again, and gained another friend and fan in Gary Cooper. "I've been in pictures over thirty years," he said, "but I've never had a more exciting leading lady than Audrey. She puts more life and energy into her acting than anyone I've ever met." (see B274).

Funny Face and *Love in the Afternoon* were both released in 1957, which kept Audrey's public profile high throughout the year. But Audrey herself had decided to take 1957 off, and once again she retreated to the serenity of Burgenstock. There she hoped to start a family with her husband, and enjoy a few months out of the limelight. Throughout her career she would not only insist on spending the majority of her time away from show business, she would also defend her private life while she worked by turning down as many interviews as her agents would allow.

Part of her reluctance to talk to the press on a film set stemmed from a chronic insecurity over her ability as an actress. "Acting doesn't come easily to me," she confessed. "I put a tremendous amount of effort into every morsel that comes out. Many of my reactions stem from instinct rather than knowing. So I must work very hard to achieve what I'm after. That's why any kind of diversion throws me off the track. Can you imagine," she said in 1956, "doing a play, for instance, and someone during one of the acts says 'Just a moment, please,' and you stop? A stranger wanders on the stage, you shake hands, and then you all sit down and you chat. Then after a while he leaves, and you are expected to go on with the play exactly as if nothing had happened?" (see B090).

It was this attitude that made Audrey the delight and despair of her publicists. "She is our nicest and most difficult client," one of them said (see B007). "She has politely turned down more than ninety percent of the publicity ideas we've dreamed up for her. Interviewers are enchanted with Audrey, as long as the talk is about acting. But when the questions get personal, she changes the subject. Her private life is private. Period."

A few years later, in 1962, NBC television began a biographical series on popular contemporary figures, entitled *The World of---*. After seeing *The World of Bob Hope* and *The World of Sophia Loren*, Audrey's representatives tried to convince their client to do *The World of Audrey Hepburn*. NBC agreed, enthusiastically. Audrey didn't. "Absolutely not! There is no 'world of Audrey Hepburn.' I live a narrow, confined, uninteresting life. I have a job, a baby, a husband and a house to take care of. But don't millions of other wives? What could be duller than to foist this on the public for a full hour?" (see B007).

Another reason for Audrey's reticence was her upbringing, which she described as typically Anglo-Saxon; "You don't fuss about yourself, you don't talk about yourself and you don't make a spectacle of yourself." (see B235). She was naturally shy as a child, and the traumatic experience of growing up under Nazi occupation certainly heightened her need for solitude and security. Her icy self-control, and what has been perceived as aloofness toward people she didn't know well (observed by Stanley Donen during production of *Funny Face*), were all characteristics developed during the time in her life when a wrong word or an impulsive gesture could cost somebody's life.

Audrey's preoccupation with financial as well as personal security can also be traced back to the war years, when the bare necessities of life were sometimes out of reach. She invested her earnings wisely, so that if she became ill and could no longer work, or if she decided to retire completely from movies, money would never be a worry. There were other lingering effects, including an aversion to endive, which she found in her dressing room one day on the set of *Funny Face*. " Never in her life will she again eat endive. As a child during World War II she once survived for days on nothing but endive. Just the thought of it now turns her stomach." (see B129).

Audrey wasn't getting along with the press for another reason during the early years of her marriage, and that was the proliferation of stories that branded Mel Ferrer as a Svengali who controlled every aspect of his wife's life and career. This led to such articles as *Photoplay's* "My Husband Doesn't Run Me," in which she responded to the accusations with uncharacteristic outrage; "How can people say that Mel makes all my decisions, that he decides what I am going to play, and with whom, and where! It so infuriates me. I know how scrupulously correct he is, and how he loathes to give an opinion unless I ask for it. This is *because* we want so badly to keep our careers separate. We *don't want* to interfere with each other." (see B090).

And yet, the only professional endeavor Audrey completed in 1957 was a television production of *Mayerling*, in which she appeared as Maria Vetsera opposite her husband as Prince Rudolph. It wasn't all that long ago that the Ferrers co-starred in *War and Peace* (and it was speculated that Mel was cast only at Audrey's insistence), and before that it was *Ondine*, and the furor over Mel's being at his wife's side for every curtain call. Two years later Audrey starred in *Green Mansions*, her first bomb, which was Mel's attempt to join the first string of Hollywood directors. With the hindsight that followed their divorce in 1968, it becomes clear that some of the charges were probably accurate.

One should not imply from this, however, that Audrey wasn't often correct in following Mel's career guidance. The following year, it was Mr. Ferrer who had read Kathryn C. Hulme's best-selling novel *The Nun's Story*, and suggested that Mrs. Ferrer say yes when director Fred Zinnemann called about doing a movie based on the book. *The Nun's Story*, released in 1959, brought Audrey more awards and critical acclaim than any film since *Roman Holiday*, and put to rest any remaining suspicion that she was only capable of playing wide-eyed, Givenchy-clad gamines.

"The change from star to actress was made almost without our noticing," observed *Films and Filming* (see B017). "The chief characteristic of her skill is an apparent absence. The distinction between Hepburn and the character she is playing is almost impossible to draw...this lack of apparent acting, of histrionics, is perhaps the reason many critics can say so little about her. They return to the same words every time, such as 'charming' and 'delicate', and to images such as 'gazelle-like.'"

To prepare for the role of Sister Luke, a nun who serves as a nurse in the Congo before breaking her vows, Audrey spent two days and nights in a convent in Paris. She never once made a move that the actual nuns, her advisers, felt was out of character. Later, during location shooting in the steaming heat of the Congo, Audrey seemed to be playing the role of the selfless nun whether the cameras were rolling or not. She never mentioned that the air conditioner shipped to her apartment by Warner Bros. had, by mistake, been replaced by a humidifier. During one particularly hot and humid day she was without drinking water for several hours. When it arrived, she poured cupfuls for thirty natives, leaving none for herself.

The Nun's Story co-starred Peter Finch, Peggy Ashcroft, Dean Jagger, Beatrice Straight and Colleen Dewhurst. When it was released the film made more money for Warner Bros. than any film in the studio's history. Audrey received her third Oscar nomination in six films, and won Best Actress honors from the New York film critics and the British Film Academy.

Her follow-up, the jungle love story Green Mansions (1959) was not as well-received. Audiences weren't sure what to make of Audrey as the supernatural bird-girl Rima created by author W.H. Hudson, who helps a political refugee (played by Anthony Perkins) track down his father's assassins. "If any film star could play Rima, Audrey Hepburn is she," wrote Films and Filming, "but Rima has an 'animal purity no actress could ever project.' Like many another classic heroine she is 'all things to all men' and part of the brilliance of Hudson's creation of her is that he never describes her physically in any great detail, and when he does it is in terms of translucence and change, the play of light and shade across her skin." (see B017).

The public stayed away in droves, and in doing so effectively put the kibosh on Mel Ferrer's career as a director. He would be at the helm of only one more film, the forgettable Every Day is a Holiday (1966), though he would continue to work successfully as an actor. As would Audrey, who next appeared opposite Burt Lancaster in the John Huston western The Unforgiven (1960). She played Rachel Zachary, the adopted daughter of a frontier family whose Indian heritage leads to friction among the prejudiced neighbors.

Filming was well underway in Mexico when Audrey was thrown from a horse, suffering two fractured vertebrae. Production was suspended when she was flown back to Los Angeles for six weeks to recuperate. One of her nurses was the real Sister Luke, who had met Audrey on the set of The Nun's Story. Audrey returned to Mexico, still in pain but determined to ride the same horse. She succeeded, but the film did not.

It was during production in Mexico that Audrey learned that she was pregnant. She and Mel had hoped to have children almost from the day they were married, but their first two attempts ended in miscarriages. Biographer Ian Woodward writes that she suffered a total of six miscarriages over twenty years, but the actual number has never been established. In two separate interviews in the 1990s Audrey herself disputed the number; she acknowledged two to one reporter, and four to another. The pregnancy she discovered in Mexico turned out to be another miscarriage, though the event was unrelated to her fall from the horse.

Once again devastated by the news, Audrey went back to doting on her Yorkshire terrier, Famous, and a fawn named Ip who became her constant companion on the set of *Green Mansions.* The animals were surrogates for the maternal feelings she wanted so desperately to bestow upon a child. Seven months after the miscarriage, she was again expecting a baby. This time, every precaution would be taken, and Audrey wouldn't even think about working. Among the projects that were turned down because of her decision was the epic remake of *Cleopatra* (1963), and the proposed Alfred Hitchcock film *No Bail for the Judge.* The latter film was later discarded completely by the Master of Suspense, who was outraged at Audrey's change of heart and refused to recast her role.

On January 17, 1960, at the Municipal Maternity Clinic in Lucerne, Switzerland, Audrey gave birth to a healthy, nine and a half pound son. The boy was named Sean, an Irish variation on the name of Audrey's brother Ian, which meant "gift from God." If she was reluctant to work before the birth, she was even more firm in her resolve to savor her first few months of motherhood. She spent the spring and summer at Burgenstock, changing diapers and turning down the role of Maria in *West Side Story* (1961).

It was October of 1960 when she at last emerged from her chalet and flew to New York to begin essaying what would become one of her signature roles--Holly Golightly in *Breakfast at Tiffany's* (1961). Blake Edwards directed this serio-comic story of love among Manhattan's Bohemian set, which co-starred George Peppard, Patricia Neal and Mickey Rooney, and introduced the song "Moon River," performed by Audrey. The mercurial Holly, a former country bumpkin turned chic $50-a-trick call girl, was one of the most memorable film characters of the sixties, and inspired what may have been Audrey's best screen performance. About the only negative review she received came from Truman Capote, who wrote the novella on which the film was based. "I knew Truman and was very fond of him," said Audrey. "It wasn't until later that I learned he was astounded that I was cast. He wanted Marilyn Monroe, so I can see how he would have been surprised when I showed up." (see B238).

Breakfast at Tiffany's brought Audrey her fourth Oscar nomination. She flew to Los Angeles from Switzerland to attend the ceremony, but was confined to her hotel room with a severe sore throat. "It was a long way to come to watch a television show," she said later.

Audrey was then reunited with her *Roman Holiday* director William Wyler for *The Children's Hour* (1962), the second film based on Lillian Hellman's play about two teachers at a private school for girls who are falsely accused of lesbianism. Wyler had hoped to be more explicit in portraying homosexuality than he was in *These Three*, his 1936 attempt at the same material, but he still ends up tiptoeing around the subject rather than confronting it head on. The result, despite four Oscar nominations and some favorable notices, now seems antiquated and oppressive.

Demure Audrey and brassy Shirley MacLaine got along famously on the set, and together they found ways to relax from the intense scenes they had to play. "Audrey and I had a running gag all through the picture," said MacLaine. "She was teaching me how to dress and I was teaching her how to cuss." Co-star James Garner also had kind words for his two leading ladies; "It was a happy set, because of Audrey and Shirley. I remember that toward the end of the shooting a bunch of the crew were following the National League pennant race on the radio. What does Audrey do? She reads up on baseball and sits with the crew every chance she gets, listening and debating the Dodgers' chances against Cincinnati." (see B007).

The early sixties were Audrey's busiest years as an actress. She worked on seven films between 1960 and 1965, and still managed to devote the majority of each year to Mel and Sean in their Swiss alpine home. Although tabloid articles hinted at trouble in the Ferrer marriage, there was no evidence in their public appearances together of any truth in the accusations.

In 1962 Audrey began filming *Paris When it Sizzles* with William Holden, who had loved Audrey since they met on the set of *Sabrina*. Liquor softened the intensity of his unrequited love, but didn't do much for his performance. The script may have been beyond redemption anyway--Holden played a screenwriter who becomes inspired by his pretty typist Gabrielle (Audrey), and finishes a script in 48 hours. While composing he envisions himself and Gabrielle as the lovers whose story he is writing. The film was shelved by Paramount for two years before being released to dreadful reviews.

Audrey remained in Paris to film *Charade* (1963) with Cary Grant, a pairing that seemed long overdue. Peter Stone's script, a Hitchcock pastiche played for laughs, perfectly suited its sophisticated stars, who delivered their expertly-crafted lines with effortless style. The director was Stanley Donen, who would not have any disagreements with Audrey this time about socks or anything else; "By then," he said years later, "she realized I appreciated her gifts and would do anything to make her as good as possible, no matter what it took in effort, time, and cost." (see B367) The film returned Audrey to the top of the list of bankable box office attractions, and propelled her into the then-very limited ranks of stars who earned one million dollars per movie.

The only film role that Audrey genuinely desired before it was offered to her was that of Eliza Doolittle, the cockney flower girl who is transformed into a gentlewoman by Professor Henry Higgins in the Lerner and Loewe musical *My Fair Lady*. But when she got it, she began to wish that she didn't. The consensus of public opinion among the Hollywood community was that the role belonged to Julie Andrews, whose interpretation of Eliza was a triumph on Broadway. When Andrews's co-star Rex Harrison was cast for the film and Julie was not, Audrey received some of the worst press of her career.

It didn't seem to matter that Hollywood had been recasting Broadway stage hits without critical hostility as far back as 1928, when Mary Pickford copped the first talking picture Oscar for Helen Hayes's stage role in *Coquette*. Or that Julie Andrews was not left destitute by the snub; that same year she landed the title role in Disney's *Mary Poppins*, which turned out to be the other big musical to open in 1964. Or that this was not a case of Audrey doing a big star turn and demanding that the role be snatched from Julie's grasp and given to her; the decision rested solely with Warner Bros. boss Jack Warner, who publicly stated his refusal to gamble a film with a $17 million budget on an unknown stage actress. If Audrey did not take the role, it would have been given to another movie star.

"It's strange," she mused. "There have been so many fine actresses who played Eliza. Do you remember Wendy Hiller in the film *Pygmalion*? You can't let yourself worry when you play a classic role. If I had stopped to think about comparison with my predecessors as Eliza, I'd have frozen completely. But I loved this part. Eliza is vulnerable, but she has a beautiful inner strength. I made myself forget the problems. I threw myself into it and tried to make it me." (see B005).

But there were more problems to come. Audrey studied singing with vocal coach Susan Seton for five weeks, eight hours a day. A reporter was on the set when filming commenced on the "Wouldn't it be Loverly?" sequence, and he noted that Audrey was visibly upset. "Twice, she herself broke off the takes, dissatisfied with her performance, annoyed because the going was not good. She stamped her foot, groaned, wiped real tears out of her eyes; she bullied herself through some dozen tries at the song. Audrey Hepburn does show anger. Audrey Hepburn is temperamental. The hitch is that she takes out emotion only on herself." (see B191).

Although she would eventually complete the vocal tracks for all of Eliza's songs, the decision was made to bring in a musical pinch-hitter; Marni Nixon, the most famous and oft-used vocal understudy in the business, was hired to dub Audrey's songs. Audrey was devastated by the decision, but director George Cukor remarked that she "carried on with her dignity intact, her chin up," (see B315), all the while withstanding derision from the press about the "half a performance" she was reduced to giving.

She received more supportive treatment from Rex Harrison, who would always remain diplomatic when asked to compare his leading *Lady*s, and Stanley Holloway, whom Audrey had known since her brief appearance in *One Wild Oat*. The crew she won over from the moment she spurned a limousine on the lot to ride a bicycle called Eliza. Consciously or not, she was pedaling show business democracy. The extent of their affection was discovered by a reporter from *McCall's*; "Standard call sheet form is for the female star to be listed by her first and last names, followed by the male star and supporting players. But from August to December, the Call Sheet for *My Fair Lady* began: MISS Audrey Hepburn.

"I asked the proper authorities to find out whether this was a request, from Hepburn ego agents or a front office. No, came back the answer; the MISS was a grace note, a love note if you will, from the sheet-writers themselves. They had hoped that nobody but Audrey would notice, especially since such luminous ladies as Geraldine Page, Bette Davis and Polly Bergen were working at the same time and were listed the old Miss-minus way." (see B191). Two crew members cried at her goodbye party at which Audrey passed out individual gifts, including a puppy named Henry Higgins to her hairdresser Frank McCoy.

It was front-page news in Los Angeles when Audrey did not receive an Academy Award nomination for Best Actress, while *My Fair Lady* was remembered in twelve other categories. Julie Andrews was nominated for *Mary Poppins*. Although the reviews for *My Fair Lady* were overwhelmingly favorable, and Audrey's performance won over most of the critics, the Hollywood community was not ready to forgive. "I think Audrey should have been nominated," said Julie, "I'm very sorry she wasn't." (see B365). "She did the acting," wrote *Daily Variety*, "but Marni Nixon subbed for her in the singing department, and this is what undoubtedly led to her erasure." "If that 's true," countered one Warner Bros. executive, "next time we have some star-dubbing to do out here we'll hire Maria Callas!"

Patricia Neal, the previous year's Best Actress winner, suffered three strokes the week before the nominations were revealed. So the Academy, in a classic display of gall, asked Audrey to present the award. She accepted, and the *Hollywood Reporter* ran her acceptance as its headline, noting that "her sportsmanship has captured this town's imagination like nothing since Mary Pickford said yes to Douglas Fairbanks." Audrey was introduced by Bob Hope and received the longest ovation of the night, accompanied by a shot of Julie Andrews clapping for her. To her obvious delight, Rex Harrison was the winner, and he kept his arm around Audrey throughout his acceptance. "I feel in a way I should split it in half between us," he said (see B365).

Julie Andrews won Best Actress honors, and even Jack Warner later admitted that he voted for her. Audrey skipped the post-Awards parties and returned to Europe the following day, but not before sending Julie Andrews a bouquet of flowers.

Later that year the Ferrers purchased a picturesque old farmhouse at Tolochenaz-sur-Morges, above Lake Geneva. The sleepy little village of Tolochenaz, population 500, offered the comfort, security and quiet they desired, as well as a good non-German language school for Sean. They kept the Burgenstock chalet for sentimental reasons, but Tolochenaz and the home she would christen "La Paisible" (the Peaceful) would remain Audrey's home until her final days.

How to Steal a Million (1966) was a decidedly less controversial film for Audrey than *My Fair Lady*, and found her back in familiar territory-- Paris, Givenchy, William Wyler at the helm and light romantic comedy with more than a touch of class. Audrey and co-star Peter O'Toole got along so well that their frivolity often held up production, but their gaiety is visible in the finished product. Critics had seen it all before, but applauded the performances and the film's centerpiece, a meticulously-choreographed museum break-in.

Audrey was again in high spirits during production of *Two for the Road* (1967), her most ambitious stretch as an actress since *The Nun's Story*. In the past, Audrey told reporters how hard it was to be sincere in an on-set interview; "I want to be home and with my family. Now, how does that look in print? But I really do. I am quite a simple person." (see B191). Now, for the first time, she may have been happier on the set, especially in the company of her handsome young co-star Albert Finney. Rumors of unhappiness in the Ferrer marriage persisted, and were aggravated by reports that Hepburn and Finney had become more than friends.

"She and Albie have this wonderful thing together, like a pair of kids with a perfect understanding and a shorthand of jokes and references that close out everybody else," observed novelist Irwin Shaw, a visitor to the set and a friend of Audrey's for twelve years. "It's like a brother-sister in their teens. Very attractive and very appealing. When Mel was there it was funny. Audrey and Albie got rather formal and a little awkward, as if now they had to behave like grownups." (see B097). "I love Albie, I really do. He's so terribly, terribly funny. He makes me laugh like no one else can," said Audrey. "And you can talk to him. Really *talk*. He's serious, too, completely so about acting. And that's wonderful. Albie's just plain wonderful, that's all there is to it."

Stanley Donen, back to direct Audrey for a third time, also noticed a change in her personality. "The Audrey of the last few weeks on this film I didn't even know. She overwhelmed me. She was so free, so happy. I never saw her like that. So young! I don't think *I* was responsible, flattering as that thought would be. I guess it was Albie." (see B097). Donen would later describe Audrey's performance as Joanna Wallace, a woman trapped in a boring and unfaithful marriage, as the best of her career.

"The role was a departure for her. It required a depth of emotion, care, yearning, and maturity that Audrey had never played before," said Donen. "She had to go very deep into herself for the part, and she did." (see B367). The public's reaction to Audrey, as Joanna, uttering the word "bastard" in the film reveals the Hepburn image for what it is-- elegance, mixed with a childlike innocence. Editorials were written about Audrey's profanity, and her first swimsuit scene, also in *Two for the Road*, generated articles that equated Audrey with Annette Funicello, graduating from the Mickey Mouse Club to *Beach Blanket Bingo*. Never mind the fact that Audrey was 37 years old at the time; all of a sudden the pure, ingenuous, dignified little princess had become a woman. Audrey herself admitted that "it is inconceivable that [the film] could have been submitted to me ten years ago, even five," (see B097) but she laughed about shocking the masses. "People seem to have this fixed image of me. In a way I think it's very sweet, but it's also a little sad. After all, I'm a human being. When I get angry, I sometimes swear." (see B237).

It seems extraordinary now that Audrey did not receive her fifth Academy Award nomination for this performance, but she did earn one for her other 1967 film, *Wait Until Dark*. The Academy always was a sucker for a performance that incorporated a disability, and Audrey's portrayal of a blind housewife who is attacked by a gang of narcotics smugglers had all the right elements. Alan Arkin, who played the gang leader, was humorously chided for brutalizing our fair lady on screen, and confessed: "I've tried to wipe out the memory with a number of heartwarming performances on public television." (see B131).

The film was produced by Mel Ferrer, which was meant to be another sign to the world that Audrey and Mel's marriage, now in its thirteenth year, was still solid. It is conceivable, then, that the news of their divorce on September 1, 1968 was a bewildering surprise to anyone who was not among the Ferrers' inner circle of friends, or who did not read the tabloids. It was not the twelve-year difference in their ages, which early articles singled out as a sign of trouble; it was not the two miscarriages Audrey suffered between 1966 and 1968, though they certainly put an additional strain on a relationship that was already floundering.

According to Audrey's publicist Henry Rogers, it was a case of differing priorities; "she wanted to work less and spend more time in private with Mel and Sean. She was filled with love. Mel was filled with ambition, for his wife and for himself." (see B339). Additionally, according to Ian Woodward's Hepburn biography, "those closest to the couple held

Audrey Hepburn in 1976.

the belief that the changes which Mel masterminded for his wife's new screen image, first in *Two for the Road*, then in *Wait Until Dark*, turned Audrey into two women--both of them Audrey; both of them different-- and that two women broke up her marriage." (see B339).

Whatever the cause, their separation gave the impression of being one of the most amicable in Hollywood history. After their divorce was announced, Audrey and Mel flew back to Tolochenaz together and spent a week strolling together through the gardens and the nearby village. But then Mel left, and Audrey remained, in near-total self-imposed isolation, for weeks. Mel Ferrer continued to act in European-based films throughout the 1970's and '80's, and appeared for a time as Jane Wyman's lawyer on the television series *Falcon Crest*. In February of 1971 he married Elizabeth Soukutine, a 34-year-old Belgian editor of children's books.

No one could have guessed, however, that Audrey would be remarried before her ex-husband. In June of 1968, after her separation from Mel, Audrey accepted an invitation to cruise the Greek islands on a yacht chartered by French industrialist Paul Annik and his wife, Princess Olympia Torlonia. Also on board was Dr. Andrea Dotti, a handsome, energetic and outgoing Italian psychologist, nine years Audrey's junior. "We became fast friends and I found I liked him very much, more than I would admit to him," said Audrey later. "I was afraid of that age difference, that it might be a big handicap to a new relationship, let alone to a possible marriage." (see B061).

Dotti had met Audrey twice before; once as a teenager who came up to her during a break in production of *Roman Holiday* and shook her hand, and again in the mid-1960's, at a party thrown by mutual friends. "I know I should," said Audrey, and it broke my heart to have to admit to Andrea that I couldn't, honestly, remember either meeting!" (see B061). This time the doctor made a more profound impression--on January 18, 1969, Audrey and Andrea were married in a simple, private ceremony in the town hall of Morges, a Swiss lakeside village near La Paisible. The couple would settle in a villa near Rome that was owned by Andrea's mother.

"When we married, everyone assumed I was marrying my own psychiatrist. Actually, I've never been psychoanalyzed, and I don't think we analyze each other more than the average husband and wife," Audrey said (see B237). She had other concerns as well; "I asked [if] the fact that I'm an actress would in any way hurt his career in medicine. I said it would bring him publicity and all kinds of things he should not have as a serious doctor." (see B162). But it was the memory of her first marriage, the failure of which she blamed on herself, that caused Audrey the most trepidation. "It was terrible. More than that, it was a keen disappointment. I thought a marriage between two good, loving people, had to last until one of them died," she said. "I can't tell you how disillusioned I was. I'd tried and tried. I knew how difficult it had to be, to be married to a world celebrity, [and] believe me, I put my career second.

"Finally, when it was clear it was ending, I still couldn't let go. I was devastated, and I decided that if and when there was a second marriage, I would not let my fame or anything at all get in the way of personal happiness--for myself, for my son and for the second child I hoped for." (see B061).

Four months after the wedding Audrey learned she was pregnant. Determined not to lose another child, she spent the last two trimesters in bed or on a couch. Dr. Dotti, meanwhile, was photographed at nightclubs with other women. "My husband and I had what you could call an open arrangement," she said later. "It's inevitable, when the man is younger. I wanted the marriage to last. Not just for our own sake, but for that of the son we had together." It was the first sign of trouble in the marriage (see B061).

Luca, Audrey's second child, was born on February 8, 1970 in Lausanne. The seven pound-eight ounce boy was delivered by Caesarian section, with Andrea by Audrey's side. Audrey now had one more reason not to resume her career, and was content to play the role of a doctor's wife for the next five years. "I don't care anymore if I don't go around the world, if I don't see more than I've seen," she said in a 1976 interview. "I feel very saturated--in the good sense, not in boredom. I haven't enough time to think about everything I've done and seen. Living is like tearing through a museum. Not until later do you really start absorbing what you saw, thinking about it, looking it up in a book and remembering."

Friends would say that a "new Audrey" emerged since the marriage; "she is gay and outright careless. She is young and seems to have lots of fun. Her phone number is listed in the Roman telephone book; she shops around Via Frattina or Via Condotti; she lunches with lady friends at the popular Trattoria Bolognese at Piazza del Popolo and every once in a while, on a sleepy afternoon, one can bump into her and Andrea holding hands like newlyweds in a small cinema in the center of town." (see B162). The credit is given to Andrea Dotti, who is described as a gentlespoken man with an unhurried manner, a man of great maturity, a man of great stability, and a good listener.

Audrey would briefly emerge twice from her semi-retirement after *Wait Until Dark*; in 1970, she appeared on the U.S. television special *A World of Love* to help raise money for UNICEF. It would be her first involvement with the United Nations' charity which benefited needy children around the world, and that would occupy much of her time in the next decade. And in 1971, Audrey filmed four commercials for a Tokyo wig manufacturer, which were broadcast only in Japan. For some reason, the following she attained in Japan with *Roman Holiday* never subsided, and twenty years later Audrey remained firmly entrenched in the box office top ten. "It's curious," she mused. "Maybe I look Japanese." (see B367).

When she finally did return to the silver screen in 1976, Audrey was bemused at the amount of attention her "comeback" received. "How can it be a comeback when I never really left?" she told columnist Liz Smith. "I had no intention of staying away so long--it happened mainly because I felt my family needed me, and I, them, more than I needed to make movies. My life today is guided by my husband's free time."

The project that brought her out of retirement was *Robin and Marian*, a serio-comic update of the Robin Hood legend. Directed by Richard Lester and starring Sean Connery as Robin and Audrey as Maid Marian, the film received mixed reviews but was cheered by Hepburn fans around the world. "No other movie--not even Robert Redford's *All the President's Men* or Alfred Hitchcock's *Family Plot*--has provoked so many advance calls to this department," wrote the critic for the *Dallas Morning News*. "Most of the questions center on Hepburn's return to the screen." (see B236). At the Radio City Music Hall opening, Audrey was given a standing ovation from 6,200 fans, whose shouts of "We love you!" moved her to tears.

Back in Rome, Audrey received a fearful reminder of the dangers of celebrity when she learned that Sean and Luca were being stalked. The children were flown to La Paisible before the prospective kidnappers could make their move, but weeks later Andrea was almost abducted by four gunmen just after leaving his clinic in the Roman suburb of Parioli. He was nearly knocked unconscious by a pistol butt, but managed to create enough commotion to ward off his attackers.

Fortunately, the scare did not persuade Audrey to again retreat from the spotlight. Her next film was *Bloodline* (1979), a tawdry, globe-hopping murder-mystery based on a novel by Sidney Sheldon. Audrey played Elizabeth Roffe, the head of a pharmaceutical empire who is targeted for elimination by one of her relatives, after refusing to let the company go public. Despite an all-star cast (James Mason, Omar Sharif, Michelle Phillips) and the usually-reliable Terence Young (*Wait Until Dark*) directing, the film was a bomb both critically and commercially. Audrey received more pity than blame for her involvement, with *Variety* noting that "it would take several pictures on the level of *Bloodline* to seriously damage her stature," but adding "it's a shame she picks something like this, now that she works so seldom."

The following year she accepted a supporting role (though she was top-billed) in *They All Laughed* (1981), a quirky romantic comedy directed by Peter Bogdanovich. As with *Bloodline*, she apparently chose the film more out of affection for its director than any real attachment to the material. "He [Bogdanovich] adores old movies, as do I, and he calls our film a modern variation on *Roman Holiday*, though it's definitely not a remake." (see B061). There was added incentive for Audrey in the time she was afforded with Sean; not only was her eldest son hired as a production assistant on the film, he also played a small role and shared one scene with his mother.

"But would audiences have not even a glimpse of the Hepburn of yesterday?" the *Los Angeles Times* asked. "Ah, well, they can't have that," she said, "Time goes by; times change. But I think there's more fun in this film than in the (recent) things I've done, and people have a great need for that now." (see B133). The result, however, did not live up to such lofty promotion; *They All Laughed* was lauded in such highbrow venues as the Venice Film Festival for its non-linear narrative style, but was ignored everywhere else. The film had about as much in common with *Roman Holiday* as *Deliverance*.

In September of 1980, Andrea Dotti's stepfather Vero Roberti disclosed to the press that the marriage of Audrey and Andrea was over, though the actual divorce would not become final until 1982. Audrey could no longer look the other way while the paparazzi snapped photo after photo of her husband with a variety of other women. His love for Audrey was genuine, but his observance of "marriage--Italian style" did not agree with Audrey's more traditional philosophy.

Besides, Audrey had also met someone else, though unlike her soon-to-be ex-husband she would not pursue the relationship publicly until her separation was official. It was at a party in Los Angeles that Audrey was first introduced to Robert Wolders, a handsome Dutch actor and producer who had been in the *Laredo* series on television. He abandoned his career after marrying actress Merle Oberon in 1975, and was still mourning her death in 1979 when he met Audrey. Their rapport was instant, and the two Netherlanders talked for hours about old neighborhoods and surviving Nazi occupation.

Six months went by before they met again, this time on the set of *They All Laughed*. From then on they were in frequent contact by telephone, and friendship grew into love. "We love to live the same way-- the country life," Audrey said. "If I'd met him when I was 18, I wouldn't have appreciated him. I would have thought, 'That's the way everyone is.'" (see B094). When her divorce from Dr. Dotti came through everyone expected Audrey to tie the knot once again, but it never happened. "Why bother? It's lovely this way," she said. "The idea is, sort of, more romantic, because it does mean we're together because we want to be. Not because now we have to be. It's a slight, very small difference, but maybe it's a very good one." (see B037).

On March 9, 1988, a few weeks after Audrey completed the Made-For-TV movie *Love Among Thieves* with Robert Wagner, she was appointed a UNICEF Special Ambassador. Before this appointment she had already participated in fund-raising and advocacy activities, and appeared at benefit events in Tokyo and Macao. In 1989 she joined a distinguished group of celebrity supporters (Liv Ullman, Peter Ustinov, Sir Richard Attenborough, Harry Belafonte) as an official Goodwill Ambassador. "UNICEF saved me as a child," she said. "When they approached me I jumped at the chance. To save a child is a blessing. To save one million is a God-given opportunity. I've seen children so weak they didn't have the energy to move or even talk. I've seen mothers and their children who had walked for ten days, even three weeks, looking for food. That image is too much for me!" (see B235).

Following her appointment as UNICEF Ambassador, Audrey's first mission was to drought-stricken Ethiopia. From the capital city she flew with UNICEF officials to the provinces of Eritrea and Tigray, which were among the worst-affected by the drought of the early 1980s. Immediately she became determined to prove that her title was not just ceremonial; after visiting a food distribution center, an orphanage and a food-for-work dam building project, she held a series of press conferences around the world to call attention to Ethiopia. "Drought in Ethiopia is recurrent; famine need not be," she said.

Just one month later Audrey was in Turkey, administering oral polio vaccine to infants and representing UNICEF at the International Children's Day celebration. In October she traveled to South America to visit Venezuela and Ecuador. Then in February of 1989 she visited Guatemala, Honduras, El Salvador and Mexico. Later she was invited to Washington D.C. to testify at the Hearings of the House Foreign Operations Sub-Committee and the House Select Sub-Committee on Hunger. She also met President and Mrs. Bush, as well as several senators and representatives.

Audrey then departed for the Sudan in April, where she greeted the first barge of food and medical supplies before their journey into Kosti. In October, she completed an extensive UNICEF mission which began with an advocacy and fund-raising trip throughout Australia to assist the National Committee. Then she traveled to Thailand and Bangladesh, visiting UNICEF-assisted projects in immunization, education, slum improvement and women's programs. Her 1990 activities included a visit to Vietnam, and a series of fund raising concerts with Michael Tilson-Thomas and the New World Symphony, in which Audrey read passages from *The Diary of Anne Frank*.

There was little time for stardom during these busy years, except for how it could be used by Audrey to raise money at fundraisers, and gain the ear of government officials around the world. "If people are still interested in me, if my name makes them listen to what I want to say, than that is wonderful," said Audrey at a UNICEF press conference. "But I am not interested in promoting Audrey Hepburn these days. I am interested in telling the world about how they can help in Ethiopia." She was, however, delighted to participate in the many tributes to actors and directors who helped distinguish her career; when the Kennedy Center honored Cary Grant and Gregory Peck, Audrey was there. She also attended the American Film Institute salutes to Fred Astaire, William Wyler and Billy Wilder.

Audrey, now a member of Hollywood royalty herself, received her share of tributes as well. The Hollywood Foreign Press Association bestowed its lifetime achievement award, the Cecil B. DeMille Prize, to Audrey in 1990. On April 22, 1991 the Film Society of Lincoln Center paid tribute to her career in a gala at New York's Avery Fisher Hall. Tickets sold out months before the event, and the Society was forced to return hundreds of checks to disappointed worshipers. Said one representative: "We could have done this in Shea Stadium." (see B131). Among her friends and colleagues in attendance were Billy Wilder, Gregory Peck, Harry Belafonte, Stanley Donen, Anthony Perkins, Alan Arkin and Hubert de Givenchy. "They jammed the steps just to catch a glimpse of her," wrote the *Detroit News*, "to check out the cheekbones and noble bearing, to wonder at the clean swirls of dark chestnut hair and white silk, to witness, once before they die, the spectacle of her alighting from a limo, as only Audrey Hepburn can." (see B131).

"If they feel the body of my work is enough to be given an evening like this, well, it's absolutely marvelous, but it's also absolutely terrifying," said Audrey (see B185). After the testimonials and 18 excerpts from her films, Audrey took the stage and marveled aloud to the reverentially silent audience at the fact that this "skinny broad," as she called herself, had been turned into a "marketable commodity."

After signing on with UNICEF, Audrey Hepburn the actress would return only once. In 1989 she accepted Steven Spielberg's invitation to play a small role in *Always*, the director's remake of the 1943 tearjerker *A Guy Named Joe*. Audrey played an angel--perfect casting according to most reviews--who helped fallen pilot Richard Dreyfuss adjust to the afterlife. It was an old-fashioned, squeaky-clean romance of the kind that most Golden Age stars complain aren't made anymore, though Audrey herself was not bothered by the new "permissiveness" in contemporary film; "We're all quite freer now than we were years ago." (see B050).

Such occasional forays in the fantasy world of show business were a welcome and necessary balance to the hunger and decimation Audrey saw in the all-too-real world during her travels for UNICEF. Her two beloved sons were now grown up; Sean became a fledgling film producer, Luca studied graphic arts in Rome, and in Robert Wolders she found a companion who would preside over her schedule, make sure she gets nine to ten hours of sleep every day and accompany her where she goes, from the Academy Awards ceremony in Los Angeles to a relief center in the remote mountain villages of Guatemala. "Robby has no ego, that's for sure," she said. "It took me a long time to find someone like him, but sometimes it is better late than never." (see B094).

The year 1992 began as the previous three years had, with Audrey back on the road for UNICEF. In January and February she conducted a major fundraising and media tour in the United States. In March she participated at the Summit of First Ladies in Geneva and in April she gave the keynote speeches at a nurses ceremony in Indianapolis and at Brown University. In between she received special honors from the British Academy of Film and Television Arts in March and from the Variety Clubs International at a gala in New York.

In September she visited war-ravaged, drought-stricken Somalia and refugee camps in Northern Kenya. "I walked right into a nightmare," she told reporters. "No media report could have prepared me for the unspeakable agony I felt seeing countless little, fragile, emaciated children sitting under the trees, waiting to be fed, most of them ill. I'll never forget their huge eyes and tiny faces and the terrible silence." (see B161). Audrey began to feel pain of another kind during the tour, but she completed the scheduled itinerary before returning to the United States to seek treatment.

Doctors found cancer in her colon. On November 1 Audrey underwent surgery at Cedars-Sinai Medical Center in Los Angeles. A piece of the colon was removed, and there was confidence among her physicians that the cancer had not spread. A statement released to the press from the hospital expressed their expectation that she would recover completely, noting that the cure rate for her condition was 85-90 percent. Audrey, reported to be in "excellent spirits," left the hospital and quietly returned to Tolochenaz.

Despite the doctors' optimistic forecast, ominous rumors began to emerge from Switzerland. The tabloids reported that Audrey was dying, and Hollywood's sudden renewed recognition of her career seemed to serve as a macabre confirmation that the end was near; in the waning days of 1992 Audrey received the Screen Actors Guild Award for lifetime achievement and the Medal of Freedom, the United States's highest civilian honor, from President George Bush. The Academy for Motion Picture Arts & Sciences announced that Audrey had also been chosen to receive the Jean Hersholt Humanitarian Award, to be presented at the Oscars ceremony in June of 1993. It would have been her fourteenth appearance at an Academy Awards, but sadly it was not to be.

Audrey Hepburn died on January 20, 1993 of colon cancer. She was 63. She died at her beloved La Paisible, with Sean and Luca at her bedside. The news made headlines around the world--in the United States, even the inauguration of President Bill Clinton could not displace it from the front page. "God has a most beautiful new angel," said Elizabeth Taylor after hearing the news. Critic Rex Reed was likewise moved; "In a cruel and imperfect world, she was living proof that God could still create perfection."

The funeral, on January 24, was attended by 120 invited guests, including Mel Ferrer, Andrea Dotti, Robert Wolders, Hubert de Givenchy, Roger Moore, and Alain Delon, as well as Audrey's two sons and her brother Jan. Another 700 onlookers, mostly friends and admirers from the area, gathered outside the tiny stone church in Tolochenaz and listened to the service on loudspeakers. Flower arrangements were sent from Elizabeth Taylor, Gregory Peck and the Dutch royal family. "She was an angel in the biblical sense," said Pastor Maurice Eindiguer, the retired minister who had married Hepburn and Ferrer in 1954. "Even in her illness, she visited those children of Somalia, and in their faces was a light reflected from her smile."

Sean spoke next. "Last Christmas Eve, Mummy read a letter to us written by a writer she admired...'Remember if you ever need a helping hand, it's at the end of your arm. As you get older, you must remember that you have a second hand. The first one is to help yourself, the second one is to help others." "She believed in one thing above all." he concluded, "She believed in love." (see B161).

Audrey Hepburn was buried in a small cemetery 200 yards from La Paisible, atop a knoll, facing the Alps she loved. A single white Audrey Hepburn tulip (so named by its creator years earlier) was placed on her simple oak coffin. Remembrances of friends, colleagues and co-workers filled the world's newspapers for the next seven days. "Anyone who knew Audrey is, I'm sure, drowning in memories this week," wrote columnist Robert Osborne in the *Hollywood Reporter*. "The way she classed up Hollywood's image was incalculable, though she always discounted her own importance as a star...Lest anyone has ever been cynical enough to question it, that selflessness she displayed for UNICEF was absolutely genuine. She'd never agree but it was work she really shouldn't have been doing. Of all people, Audrey Hepburn was not a person who could see bloated babies and ever forget it; she could not look into the eyes of suffering people and ever sleep peacefully again. She was a brilliant, irreplaceable image for UNICEF, but that affiliation mightily took its toll on her." (see B150).

People magazine paid tribute to Audrey with the cover story of its February 8, 1993 issue. One week later, *People* published its first ever special issue to commemorate a single movie star. The first $100,000 from newsstand sales was donated to UNICEF, which had already set up an Audrey Hepburn fund. "It was soon apparent to the staff that even a cover story couldn't do full justice to this extraordinary woman," wrote publisher Ann Moore. "The actress--ethereal, mischievous and inherently wise--was the princess of all our fairy tales, the deserving Cinderella, the swan who never forgot what it was like to be an ugly duckling." (see B161).

The definitive Audrey Hepburn story, the one that could only be told by the lady herself, was never written. In 1989 Audrey said she had received requests from seven different publishers for an autobiography, but she predictably turned them all down. It was thus left to others to attempt an explanation of what made Audrey Hepburn special: "She was a magical combination of high chic and high spirits." (Gregory Peck); "There was a modesty and a sadness about her." (Peter O'Toole); "She does not think of herself as a particularly good actress, but she is a consummate one, whether she likes it or not." (Alan Arkin); "Every gesture was gracious, every word. She wasn't ever trying to impress you. She was just like that." (Princess Catherine Aga Khan).

One of the best summations emerged from Audrey herself, who rarely analyzed her popularity in print. But in a 1991 interview (see B126) she looked back on her stellar career and offered her own hypothesis about its fruition; "I myself was born with an enormous need for affection and a terrible need to give it. That's what I'd like to think has been the appeal. People have recognized something in me they have themselves--the need to receive affection and the need to give it. Does that sound soppy?"

2

Chronology

1929   **May 4**--Edda Kathleen Hepburn van Heemstra born to Baroness van Heemstra and John Victor Anthony Hepburn-Ruston on the Hepburn estate near Brussels.

1935   Edda's parents divorce; the Baroness moves Edda and her two brothers to Arnhem, in the Netherlands.

1939   **September 1**--World War II erupts in Europe.

       Winter--Edda begins studying ballet at the Conservatory of Music and Dance.

1940   **May 18**--the German army invades Arnhem. The van Heemstra family joins the Dutch underground.

1945   **May 5**--Arnhem is liberated by British troops.

       Autumn--the van Heemstras move to Amsterdam.

1948   **Spring**--appears in Dutch travelogue film *Nederland in 7 Lessen*.

       June--Edda and her mother move to London; Edda changes her name to Audrey Hepburn, begins ballet study at the Rambert School of Ballet.

       December 22--opens as chorus girl in London production of *High Button Shoes* at the London Hippodrome Theatre (291 performances).

1949   **May 18**--*Sauce Tartare* opens at London's Cambridge Theatre (437 performances).

1950   **April 27**--*Sauce Piquante* opens at London's Cambridge Theatre (67 performances). Audrey is promoted from chorus to bit parts in sketches.

1951   **May**--movie *One Wild Oat* is released (bit part).

   Spring--meets author Colette during production of the film *Monte Carlo Baby*, offered the title role in *Gigi* on Broadway.

   June--film *Laughter in Paradise* is released (bit part).

   Summer--screen tests in London for *Roman Holiday*.

   October--movie *The Lavender Hill Mob* is released (bit part).

   November 24--opens in *Gigi* at Broadway's Fulton Theatre (219 performances).

1952   **February**--film *The Secret People* premieres (supporting role).

   May--film *Monte Carlo Baby* is released (bit part).

   November--film *Young Wives' Tale* premieres (bit part).

   December--breaks engagement to London businessman James Hanson.

1953   **May**--meets actor Mel Ferrer at a London party hosted by Gregory Peck.

   August--film *Roman Holiday* premieres.

1954   **February 14**--opens in the title role of the play *Ondine* at Broadway's Forty-Sixth Street Theatre (157 performances).

   March--receives Tony Award for *Ondine*.

   March 24-- Audrey receives the Academy Award for Best Actress (*Roman Holiday*).

   July--moves into chalet at Burgenstock, Switzerland.

September--film *Sabrina* opens. Audrey first wears the designs of Hubert de Givenchy.

September 25--marries Mel Ferrer in Burgenstock.

1955 **March**--Academy Award nomination for Best Actress (*Sabrina*).

1956 **August**--film *War and Peace* premieres.

1957 **February 4**--appears in live television drama *Mayerling*, opposite Mel Ferrer.

March--film *Funny Face* premieres.

July--film *Love in the Afternoon* opens.

1959 **April**--film *Green Mansions* opens.

June--film *The Nun's Story* opens.

1960 **January 17**--birth of first son, Sean, to Audrey and Mel Ferrer at Lucerne, Switzerland.

April--film *The Unforgiven* opens.

April--Audrey receives her third Oscar nomination for *The Nun's Story*.

1961 **October**--premiere of film *Breakfast at Tiffany's*.

1962 **February**--film *The Children's Hour* opens.

April--Oscar nomination number four, for *Breakfast at Tiffany's*.

1963 **November**--Premiere of film *Charade*.

1964 **October**--film *My Fair Lady* opens.

1965 **April**--film *Paris When it Sizzles* opens, after being shelved for two years by Paramount Pictures.

April--Audrey presents the Academy Award for Best Actor to Rex Harrison (*My Fair Lady*).

Autumn--Audrey and Mel move into "La Paisible," a farmhouse at Tolochenaz-sur-Morges, Switzerland.

1966 **July**--Premiere of film *How to Steal a Million.*

1967 **May**--film *Two for the Road* opens.

October--film *Wait Until Dark* opens.

1968 **April**--Audrey receives her fifth and final Oscar nomination (*Wait Until Dark*).

June--meets Dr. Andrea Dotti on Greek island cruise.

June--receives special Tony Award.

September 1--Audrey and Mel Ferrer divorce.

1969 **January 18**--wedding of Audrey and Andrea Dotti in the town hall of Morges near La Paisible.

1970 **February 8**--Son Luca is born to Audrey and Andrea in Lausanne.

December 22--Audrey appears on U.S. television special *A World of Love*, her first involvement with UNICEF.

1971 **February 4**--Mel Ferrer marries Elizabeth Soukutine.

Summer--Audrey films four commercials for a Tokyo wig manufacturer.

1976 **April**--Premiere of film *Robin and Marian.*

1979 **June**--film *Bloodline* opens.

1980 **Summer**--Audrey meets Dutch actor Robert Wolders at a Los Angeles party.

September--Audrey and Andrea Dotti separate.

1981 **November**--Premiere of film *They All Laughed.*

1982 Divorce of Audrey and Andrea Dotti becomes final.

1987   **February 23**--airdate of television movie *Love Among Thieves*.

1988   **March 9**--Audrey is appointed a UNICEF Special Ambassador.

      March 14--begins five-day visit to Ethiopia, her first mission for UNICEF.

      April 23--four-day visit to Turkey, represents UNICEF at celebration of International Children's Day.

      October 15--fourteen-day visit to Venezuela and Ecuador.

1989   **January**--named official Goodwill Ambassador for UNICEF.

      February 5--seven-day visit to Guatemala, Honduras, El Salvador and Mexico.

      April 12--three-day visit to The Sudan.

      October 15--begins nine-day visit to Thailand and Bangladesh.

      October 31--four day visit to Vietnam.

      December--*Always*, Audrey's final film appearance, is released.

1990   **January 20**--receives the Cecil B. DeMille Prize from the Hollywood Foreign Press Association.

      March 19--in Philadelphia, Audrey first performs the Concert for Life with Michael Tilson-Thomas and the New World Symphony.

1991   **April 22**--tribute to Audrey Hepburn at the Film Society of Lincoln Center.

1992   **September**--Audrey visits Somalia for UNICEF.

      November 1--undergoes surgery for colon cancer at Cedars-Sinai Medical Center in Los Angeles.

1993   **January 20**--succumbs to colon cancer at the age of 63.

      January 24--funeral at Tolochenaz. Audrey is buried in a small cemetery 200 yards from La Paisible.

February--subject of *People* Magazine's first special issue to commemorate a single movie star.

March 29--Sean Ferrer accepts the Jean Hersholt Humanitarian Award on behalf of his mother at the 65th Academy Awards ceremony in Los Angeles.

3

Stage Work

S 1 HIGH BUTTON SHOES

London Hippodrome Theatre, December 22, 1948.
291 performances.

Credits
Produced by Robert Nesbitt; Book by Stephen Longstreet;
Music and lyrics by Jule Styne and Sammy Cahn; Choreography
by Jerome Robbins and Fred Hearn; Scenic design by Alick
Johnstone; Stage direction by Tommy Hayes; Costume design
by Alec Shanks and Slade Lucas; Music directed by Freddie
Bretherton

Cast
Lew Parker (Harrison Floy), Tommy Godfrey (Mr. Pontdue), Peter
Felgate (Uncle Willie), Sidney James (Henry Longstreet), Jack
Cooper (Hubert Ogglethorpe), Michael Nicholls (Stevie
Longstreet), Trevor Hill (Elmer Simpkins, Jr.), James Ramsay
(Elmer Simpkins), James Dixon (Police Captain), Robin Ford (Mr.
Anderson), Hermene French (Fran), Kay Kimber (Sara
Longstreet), Joan Heal (Nancy), Louisa Lewis (Shirley Simpkins),
Nick Dana, Denny Bettis, Harry Ashton, Maurice Boyle, Andre
Cordova, Peter Glover, John Bleasdale, George Barron, Keith
Beckett, Raymond Farrell, Stephen Warwick, Daphne Johnson,
AUDREY HEPBURN, Diana Monks, June Wheeler, Jean Allison,
Mary Maxfield, Lola Derrol, Gillian Roma, Bubbly Rogers, Noreen
Lee, Louisa Lewis (Dancers), M. Ryan, B. Moskalyk, D. Taylor, R.
Morris, J. Vicars, B. Jay, G. Jenkins, G. Cornwall, A. Cogan, S.

Veitch, P. Hall, H. McGalddery, M. Diana, Margot Brett, G. Mars, F. Grace (Singers)

Synopsis
The setting is Atlantic City in the 1920's. Harrison Floy, a fast-talking con man, launches a series of scams on a parade of pigeons, and is forced to run for his life from an earnest but clueless police force.

Reviews
"It is a lively American show. We can understand its American popularity, even while we wonder if it is a ginger pop which has traveled well." (*London Times*, December 23, 1948)

"This new musical has already enjoyed a big success in New York. Jack Hylton's production over here [follows] the original closely, and will be remembered particularly for the delightful dance sequences." (*Theatre World*, March 1949)

Additional Reviews
Illustrated London News (January 15, 1949); *The Observer* (February 1, 1949); *The Stage* (December 31, 1948); *Sunday Times* (January 2, 1949)

Commentary
Stephen Longstreet's recollections of growing up in New Brunswick circa 1913 formed the basis for *High Button Shoes*, which also owed a great debt to the Keystone Kops films of Mack Sennett. The original production opened on September 10, 1947 with Phil Silvers and Nanette Fabray, and ran for 727 performances at Broadway's Century Theatre. When the show moved from New York to London changes were made in the story to avoid a plagiarism lawsuit from Sennett. Ten chorus girls were needed to maneuver their way through Jerome Robbins frenetic production numbers, and Audrey was one of three thousand applicants who auditioned for the positions, which paid 8 pounds a week. Also among the dancers was Kay Kendall, who would later star in the film classic *Genevieve* (1953) and marry Audrey's future on-screen diction coach in *My Fair Lady* (1964), Rex Harrison. The show's most famous sequence, the "Bathing Beauty Ballet," was revived for the 1990 Tony Award winning musical, *Jerome Robbins' Broadway*.

S 2   SAUCE TARTARE

Cambridge Theatre (London),   May 18, 1949.

437 performances.

Credits
Produced by Cecil Landeau; Sketches and songs by Geoffrey Parsons, Matt Brooks and Berkeley Fase; Additional music by Allan Gray; Sketches directed by Audrey Cameron; Choreography by Buddy Bradley and Andree' Howard; Music arranged anddirected by Phil Cardew; Scenic design by Alick Johnstone; Costume design by Honoria Plesch; Sound by R.G. Jones

Cast
Renee Houston, Claude Hulbert, Ronald Frankau, Jack Melford, Muriel Smith, Zoe Gail, Harold Holness, Dudley Heslop, Terence Theobald, David Keller, Ray Browne, Roy Byfield-Riches, Chris Grainger, Patricia Dare, Charlotte Bidmead, Marlana, Jean Bayless, Enid Smeedon, Nina Tarakanova, Aud Johannsen, Jan Muzurus, Peter Glover, Bernard Eastoe, AUDREY HEPBURN, Sara Luzita, Miguelita

Synopsis
A vaudevillian series of sketches set in different parts of the world. Among the 27 scenes that comprise the revue are "The Psychiatrist," a Sigmund Freud parody; a musical featuring the "prima donna of the Amalgamated Dairies' Operatic Society," and an exotic jungle extravaganza entitled "Babalu."

Reviews
"Gay, topical and tuneful." (*Daily Telegraph*, May 19, 1949)

"Inventive, tasteful and witty for far more of the time than we have come to expect in such shows." (*Evening Standard*, May 19, 1949)

"A fine glancing wit and considerable style distinguish this revue from its humbler fellows. Everyone in the company can do something and has the chance to do it. " (*London Times*, May 19, 1949)

Additional Reviews
The New Statesman (May 28, 1949); *The Observer* (May 22, 1949); *The Spectator* (May 27, 1949); *The Stage* (May 26, 1949)

Commentary
Producer Cecil Landeau   glimpsed Audrey in the chorus of *High Button*

Shoes, and offered her a job in this musical-comic revue. This time she was one of five dancers in a show that brought together talented performers from around the world; other chorus girls were from Russia, Norway and Spain. Two individual performers were from Holland and Belgium. Comedienne Renee' Houston was from Scotland, and the music was provided by a calypso band from Trinidad led by a Portuguese singer named Miguelita. The United States was represented by singer Muriel Smith, who starred on Broadway in *Carmen Jones* (1943). After Audrey became an international star, several tabloid magazines unearthed photos of her from *Sauce Tartare* wearing a short, swimsuit-like costume, and ran them as evidence of her "scandalous" past. Her water-nymph costume in *Ondine* (1954) was actually a great deal more revealing.

S 3 SAUCE PIQUANTE

Cambridge Theatre (London), April 27, 1950.
67 performances.

Produced and directed by Cecil Landeau; Sketches and songs written by Geoffrey Parsons and Berkeley Fase; Choreography by Andree` Howard, Harold Turner, Elsa Brunelleschi and Buddy Bradley

Cast
David Hurst, Moira Lister, Douglas Byng, Peter Dimuanlis, Joan Heal, Norman Wisdom, Muriel Smith, Marcel le Bon, Bob Monkhouse, Aud Johanssen, Diana Monks, Enid Smeeden, Patricia Dare, AUDREY HEPBURN, Richard Inger, Sara Luzita

Synopsis
A follow-up to *Sauce Tartare*, featuring thirty satiric sketches and musical numbers lampooning the films and popular entertainment of the day. In one scene, the finance minister tries to receive a revitalization that would avoid the necessity of a subsidy to his Comedie Francaise, via permitting his musical producer to amend his repertory of classics by turning them into light musicals. In another, a French radio station stages a round table forum, but when only one man shows up he handles all parts by altering his voice. A peasant becomes King For A Day through a radio giveaway in the final skit, with outrageous results.

Reviews
"We are agreeably entertained, even though what we remember of our

entertainment is almost nothing." (*London Times*, April 28, 1950)

"By the second night, when this reviewer was present, Cecil Landeau's new revue had been pruned, with the happiest of results. Highlight of the sketches was "A Tramcar Called Culture," whose origin needs no naming." (*Theatre World*, June 1950)

"Cecil Landeau's successor to *Sauce Tartare* is a lavish, mixed grill served without adequate seasoning. Gay production numbers, bright lyrics and eye-filling scenes cannot gloss over the fact that the show lacks the essentials of a good revue. There is hardly a trace of satire and only a modicum of wit." (*Variety*, May 3, 1950)

Additional Reviews
Variety (November 6, 1950)

Commentary
Cecil Landeau had already begun planning *Sauce Piquante* before *Sauce Tartare* ended its successful run. Muriel Smith also returned, and she was joined by impersonator Douglas Byng, Latin heartthrob Marcel le Bon (who dated Audrey on and off during the show's run) and comedic actress Moira Lister, whose parody of Vivien Leigh in *A Streetcar Named Desire* (1951) was the show's highlight. Choreographer Buddy Bradley was the first African-American to receive program credit for his contribution. The American-born Bradley had earlier taught Fred and Adele Astaire, and worked on several Broadway shows without recognition.

     Landeau noticed that Audrey was attracting the attention of male audience members, and included her in some of the comedy routines. In one sketch, entitled "Non Compos Mentis," she appeared in a brief "French waitress" costume. According to Ian Woodward's biography of Audrey Hepburn (see B367), other dancers in the show were jealous of the attention she received from both Landeau, who raised her salary to fifteen pounds a week, and from audiences. "They're all looking at bloody Audrey," lamented principal dancer Diana Monks, "We don't stand a chance. We might just as well stay in our dressing-rooms." Audrey's appeal was not enough to save the show, however, which closed early and in debt. Landeau retained Audrey's services for a floor show he would later produce for the famous nightclub Ciro's.

S 4   GIGI

Previews at Walnut Street Theatre in Philadelphia, November 8-

22, 1951. Opened in New York at the Fulton Theatre on
November 24, 1951.
219 performances.

Credits
Directed by Raymond Rouleau; Produced by Gilbert Miller;
Written by Anita Loos, based on the novel by Colette; Settings
by Raymond Sovey; scenery designed by Lila De Nobili

Cast
AUDREY HEPBURN (GIGI), Josephine Brown (Mme. Alvarez, her
grandmother), Cathleen Nesbitt (Alicia de St. Ephlam, her aunt),
Doris Patston (her mother), Michael Evans (Gaston Lachaille),
Francis Compton (Victor), Bertha Belmore (Sidonie)

Synopsis
Paris,1900. Sixteen-year-old Gigi is trained to be a mistress by her
mother, grandmother and aunt, all of whom have first-hand experience in
the position. Gaston Lachaille, a wealthy young gentleman, falls in love
with Gigi. She refuses to become his mistress, but her objections drop
when he proposes marriage.

Reviews
"Miss Hepburn is as frisky as a puppy out of a tub. She brings a candid
innocence and a tomboy intelligence to a part that might have gone
sticky, and her performance comes like a breath of fresh air in a stifling
season." (*New York Herald-Tribune*, November 26, 1951)

"Among other things, [Gigi] introduces us to Audrey Hepburn, a young
actress of charm, honesty and talent who ought to be interned in America
and trapped into appearing in a fine play." (*New York Times*, November
26, 1951)

"Audrey Hepburn in the title role has unquestionable beauty and talent.
[She] acts with grace and authority, if in this case without much
relaxation." (*New York World-Telegram and Sun*, November 26, 1951)

Additional Reviews
Catholic World (January 1952); *Commonweal* (December 14, 1951);
Nation (December 15, 1951); *New Yorker* (December 1, 1951);
Newsweek (December 3, 1951); *Saturday Review* (December 15, 1951);
School and Society (February 16, 1952); *Theatre Arts* (February 1952);
Time (December 3, 1951)

Commentary

It's one of those stories that sound too perfect to be true; a bit player, doing a nothing part in a nothing movie, is pulled from the crowd and offered the title role in a Broadway show. On opening night, the bit player becomes the toast of New York.

In 1951 Audrey Hepburn was on location in the French Riviera, filming her brief appearance in the forgettable comedy *Monte Carlo Baby* (see F9). She was spotted by the author Colette, who was vacationing in Nice while her novel *Gigi* was being adapted for Broadway. "The moment I saw her I could not take my eyes away," Colette recalled. "There, ' I said to myself incredulously, 'is Gigi.'" "On stage," wrote Bernard Kalb in the *New York Times* on August 30, 1953, "it took Audrey Hepburn exactly 120 minutes...to make the long journey from obscurity to stardom."

Still more impressive was the fact that she made the journey while fighting a bad case of influenza, not to mention stagefright. Despite the cheers after the final curtain, Audrey was certain she had ruined the play and derailed her career, despite the kind words from dressing room visitors Marlene Dietrich and Helen Hayes. The next morning, she bumped into David Niven, who was staying in the hotel room next to hers. Niven had already bought all the papers, and was the first to give Audrey the good news. The reviews were unanimously favorable, and one week later Audrey's name was moved above the title of the play on the Fulton Theatre marquee.

Co-star Cathleen Nesbitt knew Audrey would be successful. She recalled her as being frightened, and having no idea how to project, "but she had that rare thing--audience authority," Nesbitt remembered, "the thing that makes everybody look at you when you are on the stage." When the show closed Audrey flew to Rome to make *Roman Holiday*, and then returned to the United States for an extensive road tour of *Gigi*.

The London production of *Gigi* opened on May 23, 1956 at the New Theatre with Leslie Caron in the title role. It ran for ten months. Caron also starred in the movie musical adaptation, released by MGM in 1958 (see Appendix A). This was actually the second film based on the Colette novel--the first, almost forgotten now, was made in France in 1950 and starred Daniele Delorme. *Gigi* later returned to the New York stage as a musical in 1973, with Karin Wolfe as Gigi supported by Agnes Moorehead, Alfred Drake and Daniel Massey. It closed after thirteen weeks.

S5 ONDINE

Previews at Colonial Theatre in Boston, February 1-14, 1954.
Opened in New York at the Forty-Sixth Street Theatre on

February 18, 1954.
157 performances.

Credits
Directed by Alfred Lunt; Produced by the Playwright's Company (Maxwell Anderson, Robert Anderson, Elmer Rice, Robert E. Sherwood, Roger L. Stevens, John F. Wharton); Written by JeanGiraudoux, adapted by Maurice Valency; Settings by Peter Larkin; Music by Virgil Thomson; Costumes by Richard Whorf; Lighting by Jean Rosenthal

Cast
John Alexander (Auguste), Edith King (Eugenie), Mel Ferrer (Ritter Hans), AUDREY HEPBURN (ONDINE), Dran Seitz, Tani Seitz, Sonia Torgeson (Ondines), Robert Middleton (Old One), Alan Hewitt (Lord Chamberlain), Lloyd Gough (Superintendent of theatre), James Lanphier (Trainer of seals), Marian Seldes ((Bertha), Peter Brandon (Bertram), Anne Meacham (Violante), Gaye Jordan (Angelique), Jan Sherwood (Venus), Barry O'Hara (Matho), Lily Paget (Salammbo), William Le Massina (A lord), Stacy Graham (A lady), William Podmore (The king), Robert Crawley (Executioner)

Synopsis
In a magical realm in the Middle Ages, a water sprite named Ondine falls for the dashing knight errant Ritter Hans. As creatures of two different worlds, however, their love is doomed from the start. After proving unable to adjust to life on the surface, Ondine returns to the sea.

Reviews
"Miss Hepburn gives a magical performance as Ondine. She is a rapturously beautiful young woman, but there is no self-consciousnessor vanity in her acting...She gives a pulsing performance that is all grace and enchantment, disciplined by an instinct for the realities of the stage." (*New York Times*, February 19 and 28, 1954)

"During the times when Audrey Hepburn was absent from the stage, it occurred to me that *Ondine* had the makings of a quite majestic bore. On each of her entrances, however, Miss Hepburn set about creating a queer, personal miracle...Miss Hepburn's gift is such that everything she says and does has an almost irresistible charm. The frailest joke takes on an extra dimension of personality and becomes hilarious; the most perfunctory and obvious bit of business seems at the moment a brilliant acting inspiration." (*New Yorker*, February 27, 1954)

"What Miss Hepburn gives us is in every sense of the word a performance and not a piece of acting. This is not to discredit Miss Hepburn, who has earned the superlatives heaped on her by all the daily critics, but rather to clarify what it is this clever youngster does. Her angular boyish stance, her tall erect posture, and her nimble leaps and scurryings about the stage are joyous and refreshing. Her speeches, while overarticulated and delivered with too much help from the eyebrows, are well-projected and stated with veteran poise." (*Saturday Review*, March 13, 1954)

Additional Reviews

America (March 20, 1954); *Catholic World* (April 2, 1954); *Commonweal* (April 2, 1954); *Life* (March 8, 1954); *Look* (April 20, 1954); *Nation* (March 6, 1954); *New Republic* (March 8, 1954); *Newsweek* (March 1, 1954); *Theatre Arts* (May 1954); *Time* (March 1, 1954)

Commentary

Ondine was first performed in Paris at the Theatre Athenee' on April 27, 1939. Madeline Ozeray played the title role, and Louis Jouvet played Ritter Hans. It was Mel Ferrer's idea to bring the Jean Giraudoux romance to Broadway as a vehicle for himself and his future wife. With great difficulty, Audrey convinced Paramount Pictures to delay any new movie projects so she could appear in the play. The distinguished actor and director Alfred Lunt agreed to helm the play, on the sole condition that Audrey play the lead.

The romance between Audrey and Mel was in full bloom, though they continued to deny the relationship to the press. Even before their engagement was official, however, there was already talk that Ferrer was becoming Mr. Hepburn when they were together, and would overcompensate by asserting his professional authority over her. Arguments between Lunt and Ferrer were frequent, with Audrey, not wishing to offend either side, trapped in the middle.

She dyed her hair blond for the role, but was disappointed with the result. "I'm not a blonde, inside or out," she told the *New York Times*. "I'm going to dye it back and get a wig--one can't change the basic things. Considering the brevity of her costume, it is doubtful that male audience members even noticed her hair color. Strategically placed synthetic seaweed provided the only covering on her green fishnet garb, which prompted one Paramount executive to observe that Audrey's aristocratic image had already become formidable; "Any other actress would have been censored from here to Timbuctoo for that Minsky outfit. But what censor would dare point a finger at Audrey Hepburn?"

In her Tony Award Winning performance as the water sprite *Ondine*, from 1954. Mel Ferrer (left) co-starred as the knight Ritter Hans.

The critics raved on opening night, but were hostile toward Ferrer for not allowing Audrey a solo curtain call. One month later, after being described as "churlish" by more than one Gotham newspaper, Ferrer stepped back and let Audrey accept the cheers alone.   In April of 1954, just days after receiving the Academy Award for *Roman Holiday*, Audrey received the Tony Award for "Distinguished Performance In a Dramatic Play By a Female Star."

The London Royal Shakespeare Company production of *Ondine* opened on January 12, 1961 at the Aldwych Theatre. As in *Gigi*, Leslie Caron   inherited Audrey's role, and Richard Johnson played Ritter Hans. Mel Ferrer tried unsuccessfully to talk Hollywood into a film adaptation of the story.

S 6   CONCERT FOR LIFE

Performed March 19, 1990 at the Academy of Music in Philadelphia, March 21 at Orchestra Hall in Chicago, March 23 at the Cullen Theater in Houston and March 25 at the United Nations General Assembly Hall in New York.

Credits
Music composed by Michael Tilson-Thomas, and performed by the New World Symphony Orchestra, conducted by Tilson-Thomas. Sponsored by the U.S Committee for UNICEF.

Reviews

"He [Tilson-Thomas] is a gifted musician, and one would have been surprised at anything less than the expert craftsmanship shown in this piece...A couple of false entries did not diminish Miss Hepburn's moving contribution." (*New York Times*, March 29, 1990)

Commentary
This concert tour was one of Audrey's most unique fundraising activities for UNICEF. She chose and narrated passages from *The Diary of Anne Frank*, accompanied by original music performed by the New World Symphony Orchestra. The program began with Mozart's Symphony #35, which was followed by Audrey's appearance. The evening concluded with Prokofiev's Symphony #5. In New York, Brahms Academic Festival Overture was also performed.

4

Filmography

F 1   NEDERLANDS IN 7 LESSEN
(Dutch Independent, 1948; 48 minutes; black and white)

Credits
Directed, written and produced by Charles Hugenot van der Linden and H.M. Josephson

Cast
AUDREY HEPBURN (KLM AIR HOSTESS), Wam Heskes, Han Bents van den Berg, Koos Koon

Synopsis
A travelogue of the Netherlands, filmed at various locations around the country.

Commentary
Dutch director Charles Hugenot van der Linden was about to begin work on a British-Dutch travelogue, and was looking for an attractive and sophisticated young woman to play a KLM stewardess, who would introduce and conclude the movie. Accompanied by co-producer H.M. Josephson, van der Linden visited the ballet class of Madame Olga Tarassova, hoping that one of her students would possess the combined qualities of beauty, charm and refinement they were seeking. Both men singled out eighteen-year-old Audrey, "the tall, thin girl with the eyes," as van der Linden recalled describing her, as the ideal choice. Audrey happily accepted their offer, and completed her part in just three days. It was the only film she appeared in prior to changing her name from Edda van Heemstra. It is unknown as to whether any copies still exist.

F2   ONE WILD OAT
(Coronet/Eros, 1951; 78 minutes; black and white)

Credits
Directed by Charles Saunders; Written by Vernon Sylvaine and
Lawrence Huntington, based on the play by Sylvaine; Produced
by John Croydon; Photography by Robert Navarro; Music by
Stanley Black; Edited by Marjorie Saunders

Cast
Robertson Hare (Humphrey Proudfoot), Stanley Holloway (Alfred
Gilbey), Sam Costa (Mr. Pepys), Andrew Crawford (Fred Gilbey),
Vera Pearce (Mrs. Gilbey), June Sylvaine (Cherrie Proudfoot),
Robert Moreton (Throstle), Constance Lorne (Mrs. Proudfoot),
Gwen Cherrill (Audrey Cuttle No. 1), Irene Handl (Audrey Cuttle
No. 2), Ingeborg Wells (Gloria Samson), Charles Groves
(Charles), Joan Rice (Annie, Maid), AUDREY HEPBURN, Fred
Berger, William (James) Fox

Synopsis
The story is set in London, where Cherrie Proudfoot, the daughter of
prominent attorney Humprhrey Proudfoot, announces her engagement
to Fred Gilbey, the son of Humphrey's old enemy Alfred Gilbey. The
children hope to unite the families through their marriage, but instead
Humphrey hires a detective to dig up dirt on the Gilbeys. In retaliation,
Alfred concocts a scheme to place Humphrey in a compromising position
with a pretty young hotel receptionist.

Reviews
"A successful British stage farce of last season, *One Wild Oat* has been
transferred to the screen with the minimum of adjustment. It is given the
broad laughter treatment that invariably rates high with British audiences,
but it cannot expect to make anything of an impact on the U.S. market."
(*Variety*, May 16, 1951)

Commentary
Audrey plays the "wild oat" referred to in the title of this bedroom farce in
the classic British tradition, which reached the screen via a successful run
in London's West End. However, the suggestive double-entendres and
misunderstood overtures that propel such farces on stage were deemed
too risque by motion picture censors, and as a result most of Audrey's
role as a hotel receptionist was edited out. In the final cut she appears
briefly in two scenes. Stanley Holloway, one of the film's stars,

would work with Audrey again both in *The Lavender Hill Mob* (1951) and most memorably in *My Fair Lady* (1964), playing Eliza's father.

F3 YOUNG WIVES' TALE

(Associated British Pictures/Allied Artists, 1951; 78 minutes; black and white)

Credits
Directed by Henry Cass; Written by Ann Burnaby, based on the play by Ronald Jeans; Produced by Victor Skutetzky; Photographed by Erwin Hillier; Music by Phillip Green; Edited by E. Jarvis; Musical Direction by Louis Levy; Art Direction by Terence Verity; Makeup by Bob Clark

Cast
Joan Greenwood (Sabina Pennant), Nigel Patrick (Rodney Pennant), Derek Farr (Bruce Banning), Guy Middleton (Victor Manifold), Athene Seyler (Nanny Gallop), Helen Cherry (Mary Banning), AUDREY HEPBURN (EVE LESTER), Fabia Drake (Nurse Blott), Irene Handl, Joan Sanderson (Nurses--Regents Park), Selma Vaz Dias (Ayah), Jack McNaughton (Taxi Driver), Brian Oulton (Man in Pub), Carol James (Elizabeth)

Synopsis
In World War II Britain, two couples, Sabina and Rodney and Bruce and Mary, live together in a large house with their children and an unwed boarder named Eve. Complications from this forced arrangement are frequent, and the quartet's inability to keep a nanny leads to further increased tensions.

Reviews
"To say that this nonsense is witless and foolish is putting it mildly. It is empty of inspiration, humor and even professional shame. And no matter how hard Joan Greenwood, Nigel Patrick, Derek Farr and others try-- including that pretty Audrey Hepburn as the unwed boarder--it stays on the ground." (*New York Times*, November 4, 1952)

"By a fluke a main box office value for U.S. is the fact Audrey Hepburn occupies fourth feature (not star) spot in the billing...Miss Hepburn was then an unknown. She appears in this in only seven scenes, mostly inconsequential." (*Variety*, June 21, 1954)

Additional Reviews

Film Daily (June 25, 1954); *Hollywood Reporter* (June 21, 1954); *Motion Picture Herald Product Digest* (November 29, 1952)

Commentary
Audrey's second feature film is very similar to her first in its tone and distinctly "British" quality. An *Odd Couple*-like premise, in which a meticulous, organized couple is forced by a wartime housing shortage to share space with a more slovenly husband and wife, is exploited to the fullest. Audrey had more screen time but remained primarily in the background. Thirty years later, she recalled the film as one of her most unpleasant working experiences, a result of director Henry Cass' abusive nature; "I was his whipping boy, that was for sure. Half the time I was in tears, but adorable Joan Greenwood and Nigel Patrick were very sweet and protective."

F4   LAUGHTER IN PARADISE
(Transocean/Associated British Films-Pathe, 1951; 94 minutes; black and white)

Credits
Directed and produced by Mario Zampi; Written by Michael Pertwee and Jack Davies; Photographed by William McLeod; Music by Stanley Black; Edited by Giulio Zampi; Art Direction by Ivan King

Cast
Alastair Sim (Deniston Russell), Fay Compton (Agnes Russell), Beatrice Campbell (Lucille Grayson), Veronica Hurst (Joan Webb), Guy Middleton(Simon Russell), George Cole (Herbert Russell), A.E. Matthews (Sir Charles Robson), Joyce Grenfell (Elizabeth Robson), Anthony Steel (Roger Godfrey), John Laurie (Gordon Webb), Eleanor Summerfield (Sheila Wilcott), Ronald Adam (Mr. Wagstaffe), Leslie Dwyer (Police Sergeant), Ernest Thesiger (Endicott), Hugh Griffith (Henry Russell), Michael Pertwee (Stuart), AUDREY HEPBURN (CIGARETTE GIRL), Mackenzie Ward (Benson), Charlotte Mitchell (Ethel), Colin Gordon, Mary Germaine, Noel Howlett, Martin Boddey

Synopsis
Henry Russell, England's No. 1 practical joker, leaves 50,000 pounds to each of his four nearest relatives, on the condition that they each carry out a last request. Henry's haughty sister Agnes must work as a maid for 28 days, which delights the many servants she treated rudely for years. Cousin Deniston, a writer of sleazy pulp detective stories, must spend 28

days in jail to collect his share. Docile bank teller Herbert Russell is instructed to hold up his place of employment, and Simon Russell, a notorious skirt-chaser, is ordered to marry the first single girl he meets. All four relatives attempt to carry out Henry's wishes, but the joker still has the last laugh.

Reviews
"It is, at best, an extended antic that only occasionally is inventive. Despite a truly surprising ending, *Laughter in Paradise* is merely pleasant, not especially surprising, comedy." (*New York Times*, November 12, 1951)

"Producer-director Mario Zampi very nearly succeeds in bringing off an outstanding comedy with *Laughter in Paradise*...an excellent cast has been lined in support, and each role is filled with finesse." (*Variety*, June 14, 1951)

Additional Reviews
BFI/Monthly Film Bulletin (June 1951); *Christian Century* (January 2, 1952); *Motion Picture Herald Product Digest* (December 1, 1951); *The New Republic* (December 3, 1951); *New Statesman* (June 9, 1951)

Commentary
A cast rich in veteran film talents helped make *Laughter in Paradise* Britain's top moneymaker in 1951. Alastair Sim, Guy Middleton and George Cole may be best known to American audiences for their work in *The Belles of St. Trinian's* (1955); Fay Compton's career dates back to the silent era, and includes performances in the classics *Odd Man Out* (1947) and *Nicholas Nickleby* (1947). Audrey can take very little credit for the film's success--she makes one appearance as a cigarette girl. Director Mario Zampi liked the way she fluttered her eyelashes, however, and doubled the length of her part--it lasts twenty seconds. Richard Mealand, the head of production at Paramount Pictures' London office, noticed those twenty seconds and confirmed director William Wyler's decision to add Audrey's name to the list of candidates for the role of Princess Anne in *Roman Holiday*.

F5   THE LAVENDER HILL MOB
(Ealing/Universal, 1951; 82 minutes; black and white)
Available on Videocassette (Thorn EMI) and Laserdisc (IEI)
<u>Awards</u>: Academy Award for Best Screenplay; nomination for Best Actor (Alec Guinness)

Credits
Directed by Charles Crichton; Written by T.E.B. Clarke; Produced by Michael Balcon; Photographed by Douglas Slocombe; Music by Georges Auric; Edited by Seth Holt; Musical Direction by Ernest Irving; Art Direction by William Kellner

Cast
Alec Guinness (Henry Holland), Stanley Holloway (Pendlebury), Sidney James   (Lackery), Alfie Bass (Shorty), Marjorie Fielding (Mrs. Chalk), John Gregson (Farrow), Edie Martin (Miss Evesham), Clive Morton (Station Sergeant), Ronald Adam (Turner), Sydney Tafler (Clayton), Jacques Brunius (Official), Meredith Edwards (P.C. Edwards), Gibb McLaughlin (Godwin), Patrick Barr (Inspector), Marie Burke (Senora Gallardo), AUDREY HEPBURN (CHIQUITA), John Salew (Parkin), Arthur Hambling (Wallis), Frederick Piper (Cafe Proprietor), Peter Bull (Joe the Gab), Patric Doonan (Craggs), Alanna Boyce (Schoolgirl with Paperweight), William (James) Fox (Gregory), Michael Trubshawe (Ambassador), Ann Heffeman, Eugene Deckers, Paul Demel, Andrea Malandrinos, Cyril Chamberlain, Tony Quinn, Moutrie Kelsall, Christopher Hewitt, David Davies, Joe Clarke, Charles Lamb, Archie Duncan, Fred Griffiths, Frank Forsyth, Arthur Mullard, Jacques Cey, Marie Ney, John Warwick, Robert Shaw

Synopsis
For twenty years, mild-mannered courier Henry Holland supervises armored car shipments of gold bullion, ignored and even ridiculed by the bank where he works. Angered by his employer's indifference and tempted by the bars of gold he has counted year after year, he begins to form a plan to steal enough for an early and luxurious retirement. He enlists the aid of a paperweight manufacturer, who creates a mold in the shape of the Eiffel Tower. The plan is to hijack the next gold shipment, melt it down into Eiffel Tower paperweights, and ship the lot to Paris as souvenirs. Two professional crooks are recruited to help, but the meticulously plotted heist goes awry almost immediately. But, as Henry recalls from his hotel in South America, the "Lavender Hill Mob" managed to correct their mistakes and complete the caper. The man listening to his story turns out to be a lawman, who then takes him into custody.

Reviews
"There is no hilarity in *The Lavender Hill Mob*, but its humors are so ingenious and persistent that it is one big chuckle from beginning to end." (*The New York Times*, October 16, 1951)

"A superior British-made thriller, divided into almost equal parts of high comedy and farce." (*Time*, October 15, 1951)

"With *The Lavender Hill Mob*, Ealing clicks with another comedy winner. It's almost in the same class as the succession of hits from this studio a year or two back, and puts the outfit back in the top rung of laugh-makers." (*Variety*, June 26, 1951)

Additional Reviews

BFI/Monthly Film Bulletin (July 1951); *Catholic World* (November 1951); *Christian Century* (December 5, 1951); *Commonweal* (October 26, 1951); *Film Daily* (October 15, 1951); *Films in Review* (December 1951); *Hollywood Reporter* (January 10, 1952); *The London Times* (July 2, 1951); *Motion Picture Herald Product Digest* (October 21, 1951); *The New Republic* (October 22, 1951); *The New Statesman and Nation* (July 7, 1951); *The New Yorker* (October 20, 1951); *Newsweek* (October 22, 1951; *Saturday Review* (October 13, 1951); *Senior Scholastic* (November 14, 1951); *Sight and Sound* (August-September 1951); *The Spectator* (June 29, 1951); *Theatre Arts* (November 1951)

Commentary

Throughout the 1940's and 1950's, Britain's Ealing Studios produced a series of comedies that are now considered classics, including *Passport to Pimlico* (1949), *Kind Hearts and Coronets* (1949) and *The Titfield Thunderbolt* (1953). *The Lavender Hill Mob* is one of Ealing's best, earning an Oscar for its screenplay and a Best Actor nomination for Alec Guinness as unlikely criminal mastermind Henry Holland. Audrey's bit part occurs early, before Guinness begins relating the film's story in flashback. As Chiquita, she greets Henry affectionately, and he hands her some money to buy a gift. She thanks him and exits, never to return. Producer Michael Balcon and writer Tibby Clarke both paid no particular attention to her, but Alec Guinness spotted something special in Audrey, and introduced her to director Mervyn LeRoy. "I don't know if she can act, but a real film star has just been wafted on to the set. Someone should get her under contract before we lose her to the Americans." LeRoy also recognized Audrey's potential and hoped to cast her as the female lead in his next film, *Quo Vadis?* (1951). The studio, MGM, intervened and demanded that a more famous actress receive the role, which ultimately went to Deborah Kerr.

F6 THE SECRET PEOPLE (Ealing/Lippert, 1952; 96 minutes; black and white)

Credits
Directed by Thorold Dickinson; Written by Thorald Dickinson, Wolfgang Wilhelm and Christianna Brand, based on a story by Dickinson and Joyce Carey); Produced by Sidney Cole; Photographed by Gordon Dines; Music by Roberto Gerhard; Edited by Peter Tanner; Art Direction by William Kellner; Costumes by Anthony Mendleson

Cast
Valentina Cortesa (Maria Brentano), Serge Reggiani (Louis), AUDREY HEPBURN (NORA BRENTANO), Charles Goldner (Anselmo), Angela Fouldes (Nora as a child), Megs Jenkins (Penny), Irene Worth (Miss Jackson), Reginald Tate (Inspector Eliot), Norman Williams (Sgt. Newcome), Michael Shepley (Pavillion Manager), Athene Seyler (Mrs. Reginald Kellick), Sydney Tafler (Syd Burnett), Geoffrey Hibbert (Steenie), John Ruddock (Daly), Michael Allan (Rodd), John Field (Fedor Luki), Bob Monkhouse (Barber), Hugo Schuster (Gen. Galbern), Charlie Cairoli & Paul (Speciality), Lionel Harris, Rollo Gamble, John Penrose, John Chandos, Michael Ripper, Yvonne Coulette, John Mansi, John Gabriel, Olga Landiak, Frederick Schiller, Phaedros Antonio, Gaston Richer, Derek Elphinstone, Edward Evans, Ingeborg Wells, Helen Ford, Ann Lancaster, Grace Draper, Bertram Shuttleworth, Pamela Harrington, John Allen, Joe Linnane, Bay White, Sam Kydd, Simone Silva

Synopsis
In 1930, Maria Brentano and her younger sister Nora flee to London after their father is murdered by a European dictator. Seven years later, during a weekend trip to Paris, Maria unexpectedly meets Louis, her former lover who is now plotting the assassination of the dictator. Maria and Nora become involved in the plan, which goes tragically amiss when the time bomb they plant kills an innocent bystander. Maria confesses to the police, managing to keep Nora out of the picture.

Reviews
"The film I found stylish, thoughtful and just a little disappointing." (*The New Statesman and Nation*, February 16, 1952)

"Here is one of the most disappointing efforts to come from the Ealing Studios in some time. The sinister backroom plotting against the dictator is handled with an over-heavy touch. Audrey Hepburn, in a minor role as the kid sister, combines beauty with skill, shining particularly in two short dance sequences." (*Variety*, February 5, 1952)

Additional Reviews
BFI/Monthly Film Bulletin (March 1952); *Hollywood Reporter* (August 22, 1952); *The London Times* (February 11, 1951); *Motion Picture Herald Product Digest* (August 30, 1952);*Sight and Sound* (April-June 1952); *The Spectator* (February 8, 1952)

Commentary
The Secret People offered Audrey the most substantial of her pre-*Roman Holiday* roles, her first dramatic role, her first above-the-title credit and the only opportunity she had to utilize her ballet training on film. Third-billed with her name above the title, she earned good notices, though the film was less well-received. Director Thorold Dickinson, like *Laughter in Paradise*'s director Mario Zampi, first spotted Audrey in the stage revue *Sauce Piquante* (1950--see S3). For the ballet sequences, Audrey was paired with John Field, a lead dancer from London's Royal Ballet.

F7 MONTE CARLO BABY (General Films
Distributors/Favorite Pictures, 1953; 79 minutes; black and white)
AKA Nous Irons a Monte Carlo

Credits
Directed by Jean Boyer and Lester Fuller; Written by Jean Boyer, Lester Fuller and Alex Joffe; Produced by Ray Ventura; Music by Paul Misraki, lyrics by Geoffrey Parsons; Edited by Franchette Mazin; Art Direction by Robert Giordani

Cast
Jules Munshin (Antoine), Michele Farmer (Jacqueline), Cara Williams (Marinette), Philippe Lemaire (Philippe), Russell Collins (Max), AUDREY HEPBURN (LINDA FARREL), Ray Ventura and His Orchestra

Synopsis
The baby son of an estranged Hollywood couple is mistakenly left with the drummer of Ray Ventura's Band, who in turn leaves the baby in Ventura's cabin with a note stating that it belongs to one of the musicians. The confusing scene is made moreso when the band tries to learn the identity of the father, while the real parents frantically search the entire French Riviera. The conclusion reunites mother, father and baby, while a

subplot involving the band's singer and his lady love also ends happily.

Reviews
"As witless a film exercise as ever was spewed from an ingenuous camera...Audrey Hepburn appears in it occasionally, playing a movie star. She made this film before she became one in reality. It is rather astonishing how she stands out in that seared desert of mediocrity. Miss Hepburn saves *Monte Carlo Baby* from being completely worthless." (*New York Times*, May 29, 1954)

"...a contrived comedy of errors." (*Variety*, February 12, 1952)

Additional Reviews
BFI/Monthly Film Bulletin (April 1954); *Motion Picture Herald Product Digest* (June 19, 1954)

Commentary
Monte Carlo Baby is a series of strained comedy skits loosely linked together by the recurring appearance of Ray Ventura's Orchestra. The film was a sequel of sorts to *Nous Irons a Paris*, a very successful film from the previous year. It was shot in both British and French, but by all accounts failed to recapture the charm of its predecessor, and was disappointing in either language. It is ironic that what is arguably the worst film in which Audrey appeared also turned out to be the most beneficial to her career.

Producer Ray Ventura was looking for an unknown to play the role of Linda Farrel, a famous actress on her honeymoon. A 1955 article in *Cosmopolitan* reported that Ventura auditioned "an endless line of hopefuls, spotted Audrey and sent everybody else home" (see B001). The part was nothing special, which Audrey was getting used to by now, but at least this film had the fringe benefit of a location shoot in Monte Carlo. At the Hotel de Paris, while preparations were made to shoot a scene, the French author Colette paused to watch the filming. She saw Audrey, and immediately decided that this was the girl to star in the Broadway adaptation of her novel *Gigi*. Though her stage experience at this point was limited to the chorus (see S1-S3), Audrey won the role which launched her career. After subsequent triumphs in *Roman Holiday* and *Sabrina*, *Monte Carlo Baby* was released in the United States with Audrey top-billed, though in reality she was on screen for less than fifteen minutes. According to *Films in Review*, the film "made those who had not seen *Gigi* wonder what all the fuss was about" (see B186). They would not have to wait much longer to find out.

F8 **ROMAN HOLIDAY** (Paramount, 1953; 119 minutes; black and white)

Available on Videocassette and Laserdisc (Paramount)
Awards: Academy Awards for Best Actress (Audrey Hepburn), Best Story, Best Costume Design; nominations for Best Picture, Best Supporting Actor (Eddie Albert), Best Director, Best Screenplay, Best Cinematography, Best Art Direction, Best Editing

Credits
Directed and produced by William Wyler; Written by Ian McLellan Hunter (Dalton Trumbo) and John Dighton, based on a story by Hunter (Trumbo); Photographed by Frank F. Planer and Henri Alekan; Music by Georges Auric; Edited by Robert Swink; Art Direction by Hal Pereira and Walter Tyler; Costumes by Edith Head; Makeup by Wally Westmore

Cast
Gregory Peck (Joe Bradley), AUDREY HEPBURN (PRINCESS ANNE), Eddie Albert (Irving Radovich), Hartley Power (Mr. Hennessy), Laura Solari (Hennessy's Secretary), Harcourt Williams (Ambassador), Margaret Rawlings (Countess Vereberg), Tullio Carminati (Gen. Provno), Paolo Carlini (Mario Delani), Claudio Ermelli (Giovanni), Paolo Borboni (Chairwoman), Heinz Hindrich (Dr. Bonnachoven), Gorella Gori (Shoe Seller), Alfredo Rizzo (Taxi Driver), John Horne (Master of Ceremonies), Count Andre Eszterhazy, Col. Ugo Ballerini, Ugo de Pascale, Bruno Baschiera (Embassy Aides), Princess Alma Cattaneo, Diane Lante (Ladies-in-Waiting), Giacomo Penza (H.E. the Papal Nuncio, Monsignor Altomonto), Eric Oulton (Sir Hugo Macy de Farmington), Rapindranath Mitter, Princess Lilamani (H. R.R. The Maharajah and The Raikuuari of Khanipur), Cesare Viori (Prince Istvan Barossy Nagyavaros), Col. Nichola Kohopleff, Baroness Teresa Gauthier (Ihre Hoheit der Furst und die Furstin von und zu Luchtenstichenholz), Hari Singh, Kmark Singh (Themselves), Luigi Bocchi, Helen Fondra (Count and Countess Von Marstrand), Mario Lucinni, Gherdo Fehrer (Senor y Senora Joaquin de Capoes), Luis Marino (Hasaan El Din Pasha), Armando Annuale (Admiral Dancing with Princess), Luigi Moneta (Old Man Dancing with Princess), Marco Tulli (Pallid Youg Man Dancing with Princess), Maurizio Arena (Young Boy with Motorcar), John Fostini, George Higgins, Alfred Browne, John

Cortay, Richard McNamara, Sidney Gordon (Correspondents at Poker Game), Richard Neuhaus (Embassy Guard Reporting), Alcide Tico (Sculptor), Tania Weber (Irving's Model), Armando Ambrogi (Man at the Telephone), Patricia Varner (Schoolmarm at Fontana de Trevi), Gildo Bocci (Flower Seller), Giustino Olivieri (Cafe Waiter), Dianora Veiga, Dominique Rika (Girls at Cafe), Gianna Segale (Girl With Irving), Carlo Rizzo (Police Official), Mimmo Poli (Workman Hugging Three outside Police Station), Octave Senoret, Pietro Pastore (Faceless Men on Barge), Giuliano Raffaelli (Faceless Man on Gangplank), Hank Werbe, Adam Jannette, Jan Dijkgraaf (Correspondents), Piero Scanziani, Kurt Klinger, Maurice Montabre, Sytske Galema, Jacques Ferrier, Otto Gross, J. Cortes Cavanillas, Friedrich Lampe, Julio Moriones, Stephen House, Ferdinando De Aldisio (Themselves), Edward Hitchcock (Head of Foreign Correspondents), Desiderio Nobile (Embassy Official at Press Conference)

Synopsis

Princess Anne embarks on a highly publicized tour of European capitals. When she and her royal entourage arrive in Rome, she begins to rebel against her restricted, regimented schedule. One night Anne sneaks out of her room, hops into the back of a delivery truck and escapes her luxurious confinement. However, a sedative she was forced to take earlier starts to take effect, and the princess is soon fast asleep on a public bench. She is found by Joe Bradley, an American newspaper reporter stationed in Rome. He takes her back to his apartment. The next morning Joe dashes off to cover the Princess Anne press conference, unaware that she is sleeping on his couch!

Once he realizes his good fortune, Joe promises his editor an exclusive interview with the princess. Anne starts to return to her guardians but is quickly distracted by the sights of the city. She spends a delightful day with Joe and his friend Irving, who is surreptitiously snapping photos of the princess to accompany Joe's story. But by day's end, the reporter and the princess have fallen in love, and Joe cannot bring himself to betray her. At a press conference the following day, Anne is shocked to see Joe and Irving among the press corps. He conveys the message that her secret is safe. When asked to name her favorite stop on the tour, Anne begins to give the standard "each in its own way" reply, but then looks at Joe again. "Rome." she states with conviction. "I shall cherish my visit here in memory as long as I live."

Reviews

"It is a contrived fable but a bittersweet legend with laughs that leaves the spirit soaring. Although she is not precisely a newcomer to films, Audrey Hepburn, the British actress who is being starred for the first time as Princess Anne, is a slender, elfin and wistful beauty, alternately regal and childlike in her profound appreciation of newly-found, simple pleasures and love." (*New York Times*, August 28, 1953)

"Any summary of the plot of *Roman Holiday* is unfair to the picture. Actually, it struck me as a delight, thanks mostly to Audrey Hepburn, the Princess, who through some private magic raises the enterprise to the level of high comedy. Miss Hepburn is an actress of considerable eminence." (*New Yorker*, August 29, 1953)

"One of the gayest, most original, and endearing comedies to be credited to Hollywood in recent years...Audrey Hepburn, making her American film debut after her 1951 hit in the Broadway version of Colette's *Gigi* is a darling to remember (nor will Hollywood easily forget her) as the charming envoy that some identify with Princess Margaret." (*Newsweek*, September 7, 1953)

"The aged face of the Eternal City provides a contrast to the picture's introduction of a new face, Audrey Hepburn, British ingenue who already has made an impression with legit-goers in *Gigi*. The young lady has talent, plus a personality that wears well on film. She has a delightful affectation in voice and delivery that is controlled just enough to have charm and serve as a trademark, as well as the looks and poise to make her role of a princess of a not-too-mythical country come over strongly." (*Variety*, June 30, 1953)

Additional Reviews
America (September 5, 1953); *BFI/Monthly Film Bulletin* (September 1953); *Catholic World* (September 1953); *Commonweal* (September 18, 1953); *Film Daily* (July 1, 1953); *Films in Review* (August-September 1953); *Hollywood Reporter* (June 30, 1953); *Life* (August 24, 1953); *Look* (August 11, 1953); *The Nation* (September 12, 1953); *Saturday Review* (September 5, 1953); *Sight and Sound* (October-December 1953); *Time* (September 7, 1953)

Commentary
The day after *Gigi* closed on Broadway, Audrey flew to Rome to begin filming *Roman Holiday*. Frank Capra had originally conceived the idea for the film after seeing a photograph of England's Princess Margaret on holiday in Capri. A script was written with Cary Grant and Elizabeth Taylor as the original choices for Joe Bradley and Princess Anne. The project fell through, and Capra later released the story to William Wyler, who

expressed a desire to make the film on location in Rome. Gregory Peck was quickly signed, but when Elizabeth Taylor and then Jean Simmons became unavailable the search was on for Princess Anne. Audrey's bit part in *Laughter in Paradise* (1951) was spotted by a Paramount representative in London, who suggested she test for the role. Wyler set up the test, with instructions that the cameras be left rolling after the actual test was over. Thus in addition to her impressive performance Wyler captured a charming, unrehearsed moment that contributed greatly to her earning the role.

The film's carefree ambience was a remarkable achievement considering the difficulty of the shoot. The task of clearing crowded streets and public monuments required reams of paperwork and more than a few bribes to the proper officials. The motor scooter chase alone, in which Audrey and Peck are pursued by the police through the center of town, was a miracle of logistics. Watching the film now it is hard to believe that at the Baths of Caracalla, the Pantheon and every other location there were scores of tourists just out of camera range watching the action and clamoring for autographs. If that weren't enough to try the patience of a film crew, the political situation in Italy at the time was a powderkeg waiting to explode. Communists and fascists were fighting in the streets, and the sound of gunfire was heard more than once. There was a close call when the police discovered explosives underneath a bridge just 24 hours before the crew arrived for a day's shooting.

When filming began Gregory Peck, who was among the first to be impressed by Audrey's test, told the studio it would be " pretentious" of him to take top billing alone, because "the real star of this picture is Audrey Hepburn." Reluctantly, Paramount agreed to allow a still-unknown actress to be billed on the same line as one of Hollywood's leading men. When the film opened no one questioned the decision; Audrey achieved worldwide acclaim and a trophy case full of awards for her performance, including the Oscar and the Golden Globe. The film itself was also a huge critical and popular success, and remains one of the most delightful romantic-comedies ever made. Since it was Frank Capra who first conceived the project, it is appropriate that the finished product is strongly reminiscent of Capra's own nobility-on-the-run story, *It Happened One Night*.

Audrey's unique gamine beauty was unlike anything Hollywood had ever seen before, and sent reviewers scurrying for a thesaurus. "Audrey Hepburn fits none of the chiches` and none of the cliches fit her," wrote *Time* (see B210). "Even hard-boiled Hollywood personages who have seen new dames come and go are hard put to find words to describe Audrey." Some, like famed columnist Louella Parsons, resorted to comparing her to actresses who created a similar splash in their first starring role--"Audrey Hepburn, tall, blue-eyed, and twenty-four, becomes the kind of star I haven't seen since the young Bergman, or, much too long ago, the twenty-two year-old Garbo in *The Torrent.* (see B 155).

In many ways *Roman Holiday* defined Audrey Hepburn in the eyes of the moviegoing public. Though it would be merely the first of many memorable performances in subsequent films, the image of Audrey as a European princess--regal and elegant in a formal white gown and diamond tiara--would prove indelible. It helped that most of the world met Audrey and Princess Anne at the same time, forging an identification between actor and role that remained long after the film was over.

Princess Anne was indeed a character worth remembering--a beautiful, sexy young woman, with equal parts sophistication and naivete`, whose guileless charm encourages the nobler instincts in the men she meets, whatever their initial intentions may have been. When Gregory Peck as reporter Joe Bradley finds himself alone in his room with the drugged Anne, unaware that she is a princess, he does not take advantage of the situation even after she asks Joe to help her undress. Later, after promising all the dirt on Anne's day off to his editor, the desire to protect her becomes predominant, and Joe forfeits the story and a hefty paycheck.

Audrey brought out similarly protective, caring qualities in her co-star--Gregory Peck remained a close friend until her death. "That girl is going to be the biggest star in Hollywood" he predicted as filming progressed, and in interviews he would often praise her comedic skills. Her timing and delivery are indeed flawless, as evidenced in her line on entering Joe's apartment--"Is this the elevator?"--and the famous scene at the "mouth of truth." Peck matches her stride for stride in one of the very few comedies in his filmography. Eddie Albert earned an Oscar nomination as Joe's engaging sidekick.

Although *Roman Holiday* is remembered as Audrey's first American film, it was actually shot entirely in Rome at Cinecitta Studios. Wyler made superb use of several locations throughout the Eternal City, with an evening dance in the shadow of the Castel Sant'Angelo particularly memorable.

Roman Holiday was remade as a film for television in 1987 with Catherine Oxenberg, Tom Conti and Ed Begley, Jr. Oxenberg, best-known for her work on the TV series *Dynasty*, is a blond beauty who, like Audrey, has the regal bearing that emerges from genuine blue-blooded stock, but the story's near-perfect rendering the first time made this version superfluous. Critic Leonard Maltin described it as falling neatly into the "'If it ain't broke, don't fix it' category of moviemaking."

On May 10, 1993, the Academy of Motion Picture Arts and Sciences presented an Oscar to the widow of Dalton Trumbo, the writer of *Roman Holiday*. In 1953 Trumbo was a member of the Hollywood Ten, who were blacklisted during the McCarthy era. Trumbo's friend, fellow screenwriter Ian McClellan Hunter, acted as a front for him as the credited writer. In 1992 the Writer's Guild officially changed the film's credits to reflect Trumbo's authorship.

F9   SABRINA (Paramount, 1954; 112 minutes; black and white)

Available on Videocassette (Paramount) and Laserdisc (Pioneer Artists, Inc.)
Awards: Academy Award for Best Costume Design; nominations for Best Actress (Audrey Hepburn), Best Direction, Best Screenplay, Best Cinematography, Best Art Direction

Credits
Directed and produced by Billy Wilder; Written by Billy Wilder, Samuel Taylor and Ernest Lehman, based on the play *Sabrina Fair* by Taylor; Photographed by Charles Lang, Jr.; Music by Frederick Hollander, songs by Wilson Stone, Richard Rodgers, Lorenz Hart, Harold Lewis and John Cope; Edited by Arthur Schmidt; Art Direction by Hal Pereira, Walter Tyler, Sam Comer and Ray Moyer; Costumes by Edith Head, gowns by Hubert de Givenchy

Cast
Humphrey Bogart (Linus Larrabee), AUDREY HEPBURN (SABRINA FAIRCHILD), William Holden (David Larrabee), Walter Hampden (Oliver Larrabee), John Williams (Thomas Fairchild), Martha Hyer (Elizabeth Tyson),   Joan Vohs (Gretchen Van Horn), Marcel Dalio (Baron), Marcel Hillaire (The Professor), Nella Walker (Maude Larrabee), Francis X. Bushman (Mr. Tyson), Ellen Corby (Miss McCardle), Marjorie Bennett (Margaret the Cook), Emory Parnell (Charles the Butler), Kay Riehl (Mrs. Tyson), Nancy Kulp (Jenny the Maid), Kay Kuter (Houseman), Paul Harvey (Doctor), Emmett Vogan, Colin Campbell (Board Members), Harvey Dunn (Man with Tray), Marion Ross (Spiller's Girl), Charles Harvey (Spiller), Greg Stafford (Man with David), Bill Neff (Man with Linus), Otto Forrest (Elevator Operator), David Ahdar (Ship Steward), Rand Harper

Synopsis
Sabrina, a chauffeur's daughter, has a crush on David Larrabee, the playboy son of a New York plastics magnate, who is also her father's employer. Unable to take his indifference anymore, she attempts suicide

by carbon monoxide poisoning, but is rescued by David's brother Linus, an all-work no-play bachelor with less interest in Sabrina than David. She leaves the next day to attend cooking school in Paris. Linus tries to railroad David into marriage with a sugar cane heiress, a match that would be beneficial to the family business. Sabrina, now a stunning young woman, returns after two years and David falls in love with her at first sight. After an embarrassing accident takes him out of commission for awhile, Linus begins to court Sabrina, ostensibly to get her mind off David. The plan fails when he falls for her as well.

Reviews
"*Sabrina* is, in our wistful estimation, the most delightful comedy-romance in years...One might guess this is Miss Hepburn's picture, since she has the title role and has come to it trailing her triumph from last year's *Roman Holiday*. And, indeed, she is wonderful in it--a young lady of extraordinary range of sensitive and moving expressions within such a frail and slender frame. She is even more luminous as the daughter and pet of the servants' hall than she was as a princess last year, and no more than that can be said." (*New York Times*, September 23, 1954)

"While my admiration for Audrey Hepburn, who plays the heroine, is considerable, I'm afraid there are times here when her gamine charm gets a trifle out of hand, and dissipates into coyness. But when she is right, she is very, very right." (*The New Yorker*, October 2, 1954)

"Bogart is sock...[William Holden] sells his comedy strongly, wrapping up a character somewhat offbeat for him. Miss Hepburn again demonstrates a winning talent for being "Miss Cinderella" and will have audiences rooting for her all the way." (*Variety*, August 4, 1954)

Additional Reviews
Film Daily (August 2, 1954); *Films and Filming* (October 1954); *Films in Review* (August-September 1954); *Hollywood Reporter* (August 2, 1954); *Library Journal* (September 1, 1954); *Life* (October 4, 1954); *The London Times* (September 13, 1954); *Motion Picture Herald Product Digest* (August 7, 1954); *National Parent-Teacher* (September 1954); *Newsweek* (August 30, 1954); *Saturday Review* (August 28, 1954); *Senior Scholastic* (September 15, 1954); *Sight and Sound* (October-December 1954); *The Spectator* (September 10, 1954); *The Tattler* (September 22, 1954); *Time* (September 13, 1954); *Woman's Home Companion* (September 1954)

Commentary
Samuel Taylor's play *Sabrina Fair* was a 1953 hit on Broadway at the

A publicity still from *Sabrina* (1954).

National Theatre with Margaret Sullivan in the title role. The London production, also well-received, opened in 1954 starring Marjorie Steel. Romance stories between the privileged wealthy and their hired help, however, date back to Samuel Richardson's 1740 novel *Pamela* and probably well before that. *Sabrina* added little to the steadfast formula. As Sabrina Fairchild in the film version Audrey moves from "Upstairs" to "Downstairs," exchanging her *Roman Holiday* crown for the cap of a chauffeur's daughter, but the class drop could not conceal her radiance.

Billy Wilder proved that the story was not as important as the telling; even the most tired cliches will work when dressed up by Givenchy and delivered by three Academy Award winners. Wilder had his hands full throughout the production, particularly with Humphrey Bogart. Bogie was a last-minute substitute for Cary Grant, the director's first choice for Linus. Grant was a natural in light romantic comedy, but Bogart was sailing in uncharted waters, and did not enjoy the voyage.

He was frustrated with the script, impatient with Audrey's need for multiple takes, and would mock Wilder's Austrian accent by calling him a "Nazi." The insult was even more profound since Wilder was in fact Jewish. But Bogart's anger with Audrey and Wilder was far surpassed by his outright hatred of William Holden. Bogart never thought much of Holden as an actor, and became convinced that he was trying to steal the picture. Their feud was a carry-over from an earlier joint-venture on the 1940 film *Invisible Stripes*, and had only intensified with time. At one point, they exchanged blows on the set and had to be restrained.

Most critics applauded Bogart's casting against type, and to some extent his discomfort works in his favor, as it was entirely appropriate to the character. He was too old for the role and for Audrey (*Sabrina* is the first of several films in which Audrey is romantically paired with an actor twice her age), but he was also too good an actor not to make it work. We're never quite sure exactly when Linus allows himself to fall in love with Sabrina, and that is as it should be.

William Holden, then 36 (the same age as Gregory Peck in *Roman Holiday*) was better suited to play opposite Audrey, but as the irresponsible youngest son David, whose behavior is more suited to a teenager, his casting sometimes seemed as anomalous as Bogart's. Life imitated art when Holden fell in love with Audrey, though he was married at the time. The attraction was mutual, and at one point Holden was ready to leave his wife, but when Audrey learned that Holden was no longer able to have children her affection cooled. Decades later on a talk show, Holden revealed that Audrey was the one woman in his life that he truly loved.

With her two co-stars saddled with casting handicaps, a director who publicly stated that he "fell in love with Audrey within five seconds of seeing her on the set," and flattered her in every shot, and a wardrobe by

Hubert de Givenchy (their first collaboration), Audrey was given a chance to shine and made the most of it. But it is a testament to all three stars of *Sabrina* that none of their backstage melodramas are visible in watching the movie, which was one of 1954's most popular offerings.

In a 1987 interview, Audrey appeared to either have forgotten or forgiven Bogie's derision of her inexperience; "He knew what I was going through, and there wasn't anybody sweeter or more helpful," she said (see B002).

F10 WAR AND PEACE (Ponti-De Laurentiis/Paramount, 1956; 208 minutes; color)

Available on Videocassette and Laserdisc (Paramount)
Awards: Academy Award nominations for Best Director, Best Cinematography (color) and Best Costume Design (color)

Credits
Directed by King Vidor; Written by Bridget Boland, Robert Westerby, King Vidor, Mario Camerini, Ennio De Concini, Ivo Perilli and (uncredited) Irwin Shaw, based on the novel by Leo Tolstoy; Produced by Dino De Laurentiis; Photographed by Jack Cardiff and Aldo Tonti; Music by Nino Rota; Edited by Stuart Gilmore and Leo Cattozzo; Music Direction by Franco Ferrera. Art Direction by Mario Chiari, Franz Bachelin and Giani Polidori; Set Direction by Piero Cherardi; Costumes by Maria De Matteis

Cast
AUDREY HEPBURN (NATASHA ROSTOV), Henry Fonda (Pierre Bezukhov), Mel Ferrer (Prince Andrei Bolkonsky), Vittorio Gassmann (Anatole Kuragin), John Mills (Platon Karatsev), Herbert Lom (Napoleon), Oscar Homolka (Gen. Mikhail Kutuzov), Anita Ekberg (Helene), Helmut Dantine (Dolokhov), Barry Jones (Count Ilya Rostov), Anna Maria Ferrero (Mary Bolkonsky), Milly Vitale (Lise), Jeremy Brett (Nicholas Rostov), Lea Seidl (Countess Rostov), Wilfred Lawson (Prince Nicholas Bolkonsky), Sean Barrett (Petya Rostov), Tullio Carminati (Prince Vasili Kuragin), May Britt (Sonya Rostov), Patrick Crean (Vasili Denisov), Gertrude Flynn (Peronskaya), Teresa Pellati (Masa), Maria Zanoli (Mayra), Alberto Carlo Lolli (Rostov's Major-Domo), Mario Addobati (Young Mlle. Georges), Gianni Luda, Eschilo Tarquini, Alex D'Alessio, Alfredo Rizzo (Soldiers during the Rostovs' Exile), Mauro Lanciani (Young Prince Nicolai Bolkonsky), Ina Alexeiva (His Governess), Don Little (Young

Dancing Partner of Natasha), John Horne (Old Gentleman Dancing with Natasha), Sdenka Kirchen (Old Maid at Rostov's), Nando Gallai (Count Bezukhov's Servant), Michael Tor (Pope), Piero Pastore (Andrei Bolkonsky's Servant), Vincent Barbi (Balaga, Dolokhov's Coachman), John Douglas, Robert Stephens (Officers Talking with Natasha during Exile), Luciano Angelini (Young Soldier at Borodino), Charles Fawcett (Russian Artillery Captain), Piero Palermini (Russian Artillery Lieutenant), Angelo Galassi, David Crowley, Patrick Barrett, Michael Billingsley (Russian Soldiers), Aldo Saporetti, Dimitri Konstantinov, Robin White Cross, Lucio de Santis (Young Officers at Orgy), Robert Cunningham (Pierre's Second at Duel), Andrea Eszterhazy (Dolokhov's Second), Marianne Leibl (Servant at Bolkonsky's), Marisa Allasio (Matriosa, Dolokhov's Servant), Stephen Garrett (Coachman/Doctor), Micaela Giustiniani (Woman), Cesare Barbetti (Young Boy), Francis Foucaud (French Soldier), Savo Raskovitch (Czar Alexander I), George Brehat (French Officer at Execution), Gilberto Tofano (Young Dying Soldier), Umberto Sacripante (Old Man), Paole Quagliero (Young Girl Protected by Pierre), Christopher Hofer (French Officer During Retreat), Carlo Delmi (Young Guard), Enrico Olivieri (French Drummer), Eric Oulton, Archibald Lyall, John Stacey, Mino Doro (Russian Generals), Alan Furlan, Joop van Hulsen (Russian Officers), Giovanni Rossi-Loti (Young Russian Officer at Austerlitz), Giacomo Rossi-Stuart (Young Cossack), Guido Celano (Napoleon's Officer), Jerry Riggio, Geoffrey Copplestone, Mimmo Palmara, Giorgio Constantini (French Officers), Richard McNamara (De Beausset), Andrea Fantasia (Constand, Napoleon's Valet), Stephen Lang (Tichon), Carlo Dale, Paul Davis (Young French Officers)

Synopsis

At the beginning of the 19th century, Napoleon's forces controlled much of Europe. In Russia, one of the few countries still unconquered, the army prepared to face Napoleon's troops in Austria. Among the soldiers are Nicholas Rostov and Prince Andrei Bolkonsky. Pierre Bezukhov, a friend of Andrei's and self-styled intellectual who "knows what's right but still does wrong," is not interested in fighting. Pierre's life changes when his father dies, leaving him a vast inheritance. He is attracted to Natasha Rostov, Nicholas's brother, but gives in to baser desires and marries the shallow, materialistic Princess Helene. The marriage quickly ends when Pierre discovers his wife's true nature.

Andrei is captured and later released by the French, and returns home only to watch his wife die in childbirth. During a visit to the country months later, Pierre and Andrei meet again. Andrei sees Natasha and falls in love, but his father will only permit the marriage if they postpone it one year. While Andrei is away in Poland on a military mission, Natasha is drawn to Anatole Kuragin, a scoundrel and libertine. Pierre tells Natasha of Anatole's past before she can elope with him.

Napoleon invades Russia. Pierre visits Andrei on the eve of battle, and observes the battle that follows. Traumatized by the carnage, he vows to kill Napoleon himself. Andrei is mortally wounded and transported back to Moscow, a city in the midst of evacuation. He reconciles with Natasha before dying. Pierre is unable to assassinate Napoleon, and is thrown in jail. He later escapes when the French army, fatigued and ill after months in Russia's winter, are driven out of the country. Pierre and Natasha are reunited, and declare their love.

Reviews

"There are sequences and moments of fire and beauty, and certainly the mighty spectacles of clashing armies and Napoleon's retreat from Moscow are pictorially impressive and exciting beyond words. But alas, the human stories that Tolstoy told so significantly in the book are sketchy and inconsequential, despite the time devoted to them...Natasha, played by Miss Hepburn, is a charmingly girlish sort whose amorous infatuations with Prince Andrei and the leering Anatole are represented without warmth." (*New York Times*, August 22, 1956)

"Of the film's three stars, only Audrey Hepburn, with her precocious child's head set upon a swanlike neck, looks the part. In her playing, Audrey catches the gamine qualities of Natasha, and her softness. What is lacking is the steely courage that would let Natasha brand her flesh with a red-hot iron to prove her love...Fonda acts to the very limit of his considerable powers, and sometimes gives the impression of being the only man in the huge cast who has read the book." (*Time*, September 10, 1956)

"A visual epic that is assured of permanent stature in the annals of the motion picture industry. It is a rich contribution to the art form of the picture business in the best tradition. Audrey Hepburn is the epitome of wholesome young love under benevolent aristocratic rearing." (*Variety*, August 22, 1956)

Additional Reviews

America (September 1, 1956); *Commonweal* (September 14, 1956); *Film Comment* (September-October 1973); *Film Daily* (August 22, 1956); *Films and Filming* (March 1956); *Films in Review* (August-September 1956); *Hollywood Reporter* (August 22, 1956); *The New Yorker*

(September 1, 1956); *Newsweek* (July 30, 1956); *Saturday Review* (September 8, 1956); *Sight and Sound* (Winter 1956-1957)

Commentary

Leo Tolstoy wrote *War and Peace* over a period of six years. It took Dino De Laurentiis twelve years to make the movie. Tolstoy's 600,000 word novel was believed unfilmable, and probably is, but that hasn't stopped filmmakers from trying. A Russian silent film version was made in 1916, the De Laurentiis adaptation premiered in 1956, and in 1968 the Russians tried again with a 507-minute epic produced, directed and written by Sergei Bondarchuk. The latter version, backed by the Soviet government at a cost of over $100 million, is seldom seen due to its daunting length.

De Laurentiis, with a paltry $6 million by comparison at his disposal, still managed with director King Vidor to create the most viewer-friendly adaptation, though lovers of Tolstoy will certainly be disappointed at the inevitable omission of many episodes that appeared in the text. The budget allowed for the use of 8000 horses, 90 tailors to create the uniforms of the warring French and Russians, and the services of the Italian army as extras. It also paid for Audrey's salary of $350,000, a staggering jump from the $12,500 she received for *Roman Holiday*. By comparison, Audrey's husband Mel Ferrer was paid $100,000.

There was speculation at the time that Ferrer would not have even been cast were it not for Audrey's insistence. It was the type of rumor that persisted throughout the 1950's, as Audrey's star rose and Mel's stalled. "Actually, he was asked to play the part of Prince Andrei long before I was even approached," she told *Photoplay* . "As a matter a fact, before we were even married, while I was resting in Switzerland! So there was never any question of 'get him and you'll get her' as has been reported" (see B090).

But it was Audrey's casting that activated production. In 1955, while De Laurentiis and King Vidor were in pre-production, David O. Selznick was preparing to film *War and Peace* from a script by Ben Hecht. Producer Michael Todd was also readying a version, with a script by Robert Anderson. All three projects expressed a desire for Audrey to play Natasha--when she signed with De Laurentiis, Selznick and Todd gave up. Tolstoy's description of Natasha in the novel explains why she topped everyone's list; "a dark-eyed girl full of life, with a wide mouth, her childish bare shoulders, which shrugged and panted in her bodice from her rapid motion, her black hair brushed back, her slender bare arms...her shoulders thin, her bosom undefined. And such was Natasha with her wonder, her delight, her shyness." "One thing is certain," said Vidor, "Audrey *is* Natasha. She is fresh out of the book." Even Tolstoy's granddaughter commented that any other actress would have been 80 unthinkable in the role. It is probably not just coincidence that Ludmila Savelyeva, who played Natasha in Bondarchuk's version, bore a striking resemblance to Audrey.

But for all its superb technical credits, particularly production design, and the astonishing mass movement of troops in the battle scenes, a King Vidor specialty dating back to *The Big Parade* (1925), and even with Audrey as the only Natasha imaginable, *War and Peace* still turned out slow, stiff, episodic, confusing and melodramatic. The task would have been difficult under the best of circumstances, but Vidor had more than a few additional troubles to contend with, which contributed to the less-than-satisfying result. According to *Films in Review* magazine, Vidor was "coerced into premature filming in two countries (Italy and Yugoslavia) before he had a completely satisfactory script; the film he shot was processed in two other countries (England and the U.S.); his multi-national financing was not smoothly coordinated, and principal photography was completed in just four months" (see B186).

Although Audrey was happy to be back at Cinecitta Studios, where *Roman Holiday* was filmed, there were obvious disadvantages to filming winter scenes during a blazing Italian summer. "Audrey, all bundled up in heavy winter clothing, had to get along without the horse she had been sitting on; the horse collapsed from the heat," reported *Newsweek*, noting that "Audrey herself did a full day's work." *Newsweek* did not mention that Audrey had suffered a miscarriage before filming began, which certainly affected her performance (see B144). Shooting out of sequence was another handicap, one that Audrey vowed not to tolerate again. Though she looked exquisite as Natasha it was not her most assured performance, though Vidor did rank her as one of the three "supremely talented actresses" he had directed, along with Laurette Taylor and Lillian Gish. And contrary to the review in *Time*, Audrey had indeed read the book. Twice.

Other performances varied. Mel Ferrer was a dashing Prince Andrei, but Henry Fonda seemed uneasy as Pierre. Vittorio Gassmann cannot make Natasha's sudden, all-consuming passion for Anatole believable, though the way it's scripted didn't help. The frequent use of voiced-over thoughts as the actors stare silently is uncomfortably reminiscent of soap opera. It is appropriate that the film is best-remembered today for its louder and more spectacular sequences, rather than its quiet moments.

F11 FUNNY FACE (Paramount, 1957; 103 minutes; color)

Available on Videocassette (Paramount)
<u>Awards</u>: Academy Award nominations for Best Screenplay, Best Cinematography, Best Art Direction and Best Costume Design

Credits

Directed by Stanley Donen; Written by Leonard Gershe, based on his unproduced musical libretto "Wedding Bells"; Produced by Roger Edens; Photographed by Ray June (VistaVision, Technicolor); Music by George Gershwin, Ira Gershwin, Roger Edens and Leonard Gershe; Edited by Frank Bracht; Music Direction by Adolph Deutsch; Art Direction by George W. Davis and Hal Pereira; Set Decoration by Sam Comer and Ray Moyer; Costumes by Edith Head and Hubert de Givenchy; Special Effects by John P. Fulton; Choreography by Fred Astaire and Eugene Loring; Makeup by Wally Westmore

Cast

AUDREY HEPBURN (JO STOCKTON), Fred Astaire (Dick Avery), Kay Thompson (Maggie Prescott), Michel Auclair (Prof. Emile Flostre), Robert Flemyng (Paul Duval), Dovima (Marion), Virginia Gibson (Babs), Suzy Parker, Sunny Harnett, Don Powell, Carole Eastman (Specialty Dancers), Sue England (Laura), Ruta Lee (Lettie), Alex Gerry (Dovitch), Iphigenie Castiglioni (Armande), Jean Del Val (Hairdresser), Albert D'Arno (Beautician), Nina Borget (Assistant Hairdresser), Marilyn White, Dorothy Colbert (Receptionists), Louise Glenn, Heather Hopper, Cecile Rogers (Junior Editors), Nancy Kilgas (Melissa), Emile Stevens (Assistant Dance Director), Paul Smith (Steve), Diane Du Bois (Mimi), Karen Scott (Gigi), Gabriel Curtiz (Man Next to Hand Stand), Peter Camlin (Man Buyer), Elizabeth Slifer (Mme. La Farge), Donald Lawton (Airport Clerk), Karine Nordman (French Girl), Genevieve Aumont (French Actress), Nesdon Booth (Southern Man), George Dee, Marcel de la Brosse, Albert Godderis (Seedy Men), Jerry Lucas (Bruiser), Jack Chefe (Frenchman), Jan Bradley (Crying Girl), Jerry Chiat (Man on Head), Elsa Peterson (Woman Buyer), Fern Barry (Southern Wife)

Synopsis

Fashion photographer Dick Avery, in search of an intellectual backdrop for an airheaded model, expropriates a Greenwich Village bookstore. When the photo session is over the store is left in a shambles, much to salesgirl Jo Stockton's dismay. Avery stays behind to help her clean up. Later, he examines the photos taken there and sees Jo in the background of one shot. He is intrigued by her unique appearance, as is Maggie Prescott, the editor of a leading fashion magazine. They offer Jo a modeling contract, which she reluctantly accepts only because it includes a trip to Paris. Eventually, her snobbish attitude toward the job softens, and Jo begins to enjoy the work and the company of her handsome photographer.

Reviews

"It is reasonable to reckon that you won't see a prettier musical film--or one more extraordinarily stylish--during the balance of this year...Miss Hepburn has the meek charm of a wallflower turned into a rueful butterfly, and Mr. Astaire plays her lens-hound suitor softly, as if afraid to turn on too much steam. Even so they make very nice music." (*New York Times*, March 29, 1957)

"Hepburn not only looks her limpid best from first to last; she also does some snazzy dancing (she is better solo than Astaire), and even sings effectively in a sort of absinthetic *Sprechstimme* with a touch of wood alcohol in the low notes." (*Time*, April 1, 1957)

"[The] May-December pairing gives the Roger Edens production the benefits of Astaire's debonair style and terp accomplishments and the sensitive acting talents of Miss Hepburn, each adding to the plot's high style world of fashion and models." (*Variety*, Februaury 13, 1957)

Additional Reviews

America (April 20, 1957); *BFI/Monthly Film Bulletin* (April 1957); *Commonweal* (April 5, 1957); *Dance Magazine* (May 1957); *Film Daily* (February 13, 1957); *Films and Filming* (May 1957); *Films in Review* (April 1957); *Hollywood Reporter* (February 13, 1957); *Motion Picture Herald Product Digest* (February 16, 1957); *The New Republic* (June 10, 1957); The New Yorker (April 6, 1957); *Newsweek* (April 1, 1957); *Saturday Review* (April 13, 1957); *Sight and Sound* (Summer 1957)

Commentary

Fred Astaire starred in a Broadway musical called *Funny Face* in 1927, two years before Audrey was born. Beyond its title and star, however, the movie musical *Funny Face* had little in common with its Broadway counterpart. The film's origins lay in a libretto written by Leonard Gershe entitled "Wedding Bells," loosely based on the life of photographer Richard Avedon. Composer Vernon Duke and lyricist Ogden Nash added a score, and the musical was scheduled to open on Broadway in 1951.

When the project fell through the script found its way to MGM, where Stanley Donen was signed to direct a film version with Fred Astaire as star. Somewhere along the way the decision was made to scrap the original score in favor of old reliable standards. MGM wanted Gershwin tunes, which were owned by Warner Bros.. Warners agreed to trade out the songs in exchange for film rights to *The Pajama Game* (1957). But nothing could convince Paramount Pictures to loan Audrey Hepburn, who was Astaire's first choice for Jo Stockton. "This could be the last and only opportunity I'd have to work with the great and lovely Audrey and I was not going to miss it. Period." said Astaire (see B348).

Since Paramount had also recently signed a two-picture deal with Astaire, the project moved once again, and was retitled *Funny Face* after one of the songs used in the film. Astaire's praise for Audrey continued throughout the production; he called her a "show-biz phenomenon" and a "wonderful artist." For her part, Audrey was equally thrilled at the opportunity to dance with the already legendary Fred Astaire, and despite her dance background she attended a Paris ballet school for three months to prepare. Her dancing received excellent reviews, but Audrey was characteristically modest; "It isn't fair to judge me in that because you so often find Fred makes you look better than you are," she told *Dance* magazine (see B072). Audrey was thirty years younger than her co-star, in the second of her three fifties roles opposite much older men. Astaire was among the most ageless of performers, however, and moved with a grace that belied his 57 years. His wonderful dance outside Jo's balcony ranks with his best musical moments on screen.

If she had not played Eliza in *My Fair Lady* (1964), Audrey would have come close here in this *Pygmalion*-like story of a meek bookstore clerk who is transformed into a glamorous fashion model by a photographer, who first serves as mentor and later desires to be much more. Photographer Richard Avedon, whose marriage to one of his models provided the basis for the story, served as visual consultant on the film, and with Stanley Donen he created some truly memorable images.The sequence in which Audrey descends a staircase in the Louvre museum is well-known, but the Corot-inspired finale, in which Fred and Audrey dance through a country churchyard in Chantilly, is nothing short of magnificent. *Funny Face* is the film in which Audrey's collaboration with designer Givenchy reaches its apex.

The film broke no new ground musically, but when the Gershwin hit parade commences (see D1) it's hard to complain. In her rendition of "How Long Has This Been Going On?" and her duets with Astaire and co-star Kay Thompson, Audrey reveals a singing voice that is pleasant and expressive, ideal for gentle ballads such as her solo here and later on "Moon River" (see F17). She would star in only one more musical (see F21), but her songs would be performed by Marni Nixon.

Funny Face is the first of five Audrey Hepburn films set partly or completely in Paris. The cast dances on or through every major monument in the city, at times almost taking a backseat to the travelogue-like footage. When filming was completed, *Photoplay* reported that most of the male members of the company were "a little in love" with Audrey (see B091). "The French crew dug into their faded blue jeans and got a collection to buy her a magnificent bouquet of roses, then proudly went home with autographed pictures of her for each member of their families." 'La petite, elle est formidable,' was the summation ("The little one, she is terrific.").

F12 LOVE IN THE AFTERNOON (Allied Artists, 1957; 130 minutes; black and white)

Available on Videocassette and Laserdisc (CBS/Fox)

Credits
Directed and produced by Billy Wilder; Written by Billy Wilder and I.A.L. Diamond (based on the novel Ariane by Claude Anet); Photographed by William Mellor; Music by Franz Waxman; Edited by Leonid Azar; Art Direction by Alexander Trauner; Costumes by Hubert de Givenchy

Cast
Gary Cooper (Frank Flannagan), AUDREY HEPBURN (ARIANE CHAVASSE), Maurice Chevalier (Claude Chavasse), Van Doude (Michel), John McGiver (Mons. X), Lise Bourdin (Mme. X), Bonifas (Commissioner of Police), Audrey Wilder (Brunette), Gyula Kokas, Michel Kokas, George Cocos, Victor Gazzoli (Four Gypsies), Olga Valery (Lady With Dog), Leila Croft, Valerie Croft (Swedish Twins), Charles Bouillard (Valet at the Ritz), Minerva Pious (Maid at the Ritz), Filo (Flannagan's Chauffeur), Andre Priez (1st Porter at the Ritz), Gaidon (2nd Porter at the Ritz), Gregory Gromoff (Dooman at the Ritz), Janine Dard, Claude Ariel (Existentialists), Francois Moustache (Butcher), Gloria France (Client at Butcher's), Jean Sylvain (Baker), Annie Roudier (1st Client at Baker's), Jeanne Charblay (2nd Client at Baker's), Odette Charblay (3rd Client at Baker's), Gilbert Constant, Monique Saintey (Lovers on Left Bank), Jacques Preboist, Anne Laurent (Lovers Near the Seine), Jacques Ary, Simone Vanlancker (Lovers at Right Bank), Richard Flagy (Husband), Jeanne Papir (Wife), Marcelle Broc (1st Rich Woman), Marcelle Praince (2nd Rich Woman), Guy Delorme (Gigolo), Olivia Chevalier (Little Girl in the Gardens), Eve Marley, Jean Rieubon (Tandemists), Christian Lude, Charles Lemontier, Emile Mylos (Generals), Alexander Trauner (Artist), Betty Schneider, Georges Perrault, Vera Boccadoro, Marc Aurian (Couples Under Water

Wagon), Bernard Musson (Undertaker), Michele Selignac
(Widow), Diga Valley Gypsies

Synopsis

In Paris, detective Claude Chavasse is hired to follow a wife suspected of
infidelity with the notorious American libertine Frank Flannagan. When
the husband learns that his suspicions are accurate, he tells Claude of his
plan to kill Flannagan. Claude's daughter Ariane overhears the threat and
warns Frank of the coming trouble. She then plays the part of a worldly
socialite with a list of conquests as long as Flannagan's. The bemused
ladies' man returns to America the next day and Ariane, completely in
love, follows his romantic escapades in the news. She sees him again in
Paris the following year, and resumes her worldly guise, telling tales of
former lovers when they meet at his hotel in the afternoon. Frank,
amazed by the mystery girl and surprised to find himself jealous of her
past, hires Claude to uncover more information about her. When the
detective realizes what has happened, he asks Frank to not break his
daughter's heart. At the train station Frank and Ariane say goodbye, but
at the last moment he sweeps her off the platform and into his arms.

Reviews

"...this grandly sophisticated romance [is in] the great Lubitsch tradition,
right down to the froth on the champagne. And what delightful
performances Audrey Hepburn and Gary Cooper give as the cleverly
calculating couple who spar through the amorous afternoons!" (*New York
Times*, August 24, 1957)

"The allure of the movie depends almost entirely on the allure of these
three institutionalized film personalities. After a time, even the most loyal
fan is apt to wish for a change of face, of place, and particularly of pace."
(*Newsweek*, July 1, 1957)

"Under Billy Wilder's alternately sensitive, mirthful and loving-care
direction...the production holds enchantment and delight in substantial
quantity." (*Variety*, May 17, 1957)

Additional Reviews

America (September 7, 1957); *American Cinematographer* (August
1957); *BFI/Monthly Film Bulletin* (September 1957); *Commonweal*
(September 13, 1957); *Film Culture* (October 1957); *Film Daily* (June 3,
1957); *Films and Filming* (September 1957); *Films in Review* (August-
September 1957); *Hollywood Reporter* (June 3, 1957); *Motion Picture
Herald Product Digest* (June 8, 1957); *The New Yorker* (August 31,
1957); *Saturday Review* (August 10, 1957); *Sight and Sound* (Autumn

1957); *Time* (July 15, 1957)

Commentary

Claude Anet's story of a "hit and run lover" who "got run over himself," to quote Maurice Chavalier as Claude Chavasse, could have seemed scanadalous were it not for the light, deft touch of Billy Wilder. Unlike *Funny Face*, in which the age difference between Audrey and Fred Astaire is apparent but not intrusive, Gary Cooper looked every bit of his 56 years as the lothario Frank Flannagan, and though Audrey was closer to 30 than 20 she could still pass for a teenager. In her book *Big Bad Wolves: Masculinity in the American Film*, Joan Mellen singled out *Love in the Afternoon* as representative of many fifties films which are pervaded by a male sense of values. "Were the male lead Hepburn's age and the female that of Cooper, it would hardly be as romantic," she writes (see B316).

To combat the very real possibility that audiences would not cheer when Coop lifts Audrey into the train, Wilder shot his leading man in shadow and from a distance at every opportunity, and depicted what actually went on in those afternoon rendezvous with very subtle suggestions. Whatever disturbing, cynical elements remained were further cancelled out by the comical appearances of the gypsies, the gentle strains of "Fascination" and what *Films and Filming* called "the Hepburn sweetness." As a result, the train station finale would appear on most film lovers' short lists of favorite romantic endings.

Love in the Afternoon was actually the third film adaptation of the 1927 novel *Ariane*; Paul Czinner wrote and directed a German version in 1931 with Elisabeth Bergner in the title role, and one year later he filmed the story again, this time in French with Gaby Morlay as Ariane. Surprisingly, the film did not receive a single Academy Award nomination; at the very least Maurice Chevlaier's supporting performance deserved recognition. Audrey already had the scene-stealing reputation, but she almost loses this film to Chevalier's delightful work as Ariane's protective father. It was the first Hollywood performance in twenty years for the renowned French entertainer, and he was nervous about his English line-readings.When Audrey expressed her nervous excitement about working with two co-stars approaching legendary status, she and Chevalier helped each other overcome their butterflies. Before production ceased, Audrey received a telegram from her on-screen father which read "How proud I would be, and full of love I would be, if I really had a daughter like you."

The movie was filmed at the Studios de Boulogne and on location throughout Paris. The brunette with Gary Cooper in the Paris Opera sequence was Billy Wilder's wife, Audrey.

F13   MAYERLING (NBC-TV, February 4, 1957; 90 minutes; color)

Credits
Directed by Anatole Litvak; Produced by Anatole Litvak and Mort Abrahams; Settings by Otis Riggs; Costumes by Dorothy Jenkins; Musical direction by George Bassman

Cast
AUDREY HEPBURN (MARIA VETSERA), Mel Ferrer (Prince Rudolph), Diana Wynyard (The Empress), Basil Sydney (The Emperor), Raymond Massey (The Prime Minister), Judith Evelyn (The Countess Larische), Isobel Elsom, Nehemiah Persoff, Lorne Greene, Ian Wolfe, David Opatoshu, Nancy Marchand, John McGovern, Monique Van Vooren, Pippa Scott, Michael Evans

Synopsis
The true story of Rudolph, crown prince of Austria and son of the powerful Emperor Franz Joseph, and his beautiful seventeen-year-old mistress Maria Vetsera. Rudolph is forced into a marriage of blue-blood alliance, but continues to meet with Maria whenever possible. He pleads with his father for an annulment and the freedom to marry the only woman he loves, but Franz Joseph and later the pope both issue stern refusals. In the winter of 1889, the lovers vow never to be separated again. After a party in the palace in which they boldly dance together in front of outraged relatives, the couple flees to Mayerling, a remote hunting lodge in the Vienna Woods. That night, the prince shoots Maria while she sleeps, and then turns the gun on himself.

Reviews
"*Mayerling* proved that television needs only a good story and a good cast to provide entertainment equal to any other medium. TV never had a prettier performer than Audrey Hepburn." (*Los Angeles Times*, February 6, 1957)

"It was a spectacular on all counts except one, the drama. Mr. Ferrer, as the Archduke, and Miss Hepburn, as Maria, never really came close to the tragic content of the romance that could not be. Miss Hepburn is a piquant young lady, but she did not truly tear at the heartstrings." (*New York Times*, February 5, 1957)

"Sharing top honors with Litvak was Miss Hepburn, for her vibrant and controlled love scenes and her unsophisticated youth captured the charm and compassion of this Vienesse idyll. What could have been sentimental and maudlin was brought to life as a warm and feeling story. She was exquisite in her child-like beauty. Ferrer was the embodiment of soulful tragedy and if hardly the equal of Miss Hepburn in histrionics, this rates as one of his best performances to date." (*Variety*, December 6, 1957)

Commentary

Live ninety-minute productions were aired every fourth Monday on NBC under the title *Producers Showcase*. Among the classic programs the series produced during its four year run (1954-1957) were *Peter Pan* with Mary Martin, Paul Newman, Eva Marie Saint and Frank Sinatra in a musical version of *Our Town,* and Humphrey Bogart, Lauren Bacall and Henry Fonda in *The Petrified Forest. Mayerling,* with its $620,000 budget, thirty lavish sets, ten costume changes for Audrey and a cast of over one hundred, was one of the most ambitious television presentations of the1950's. Even critics who found the drama lacking praised the live production as a "technical tour de force" (*New York Times*).

This was director Anatole Litvak's second go at the story, which he filmed in 1937 with Charles Boyer and Danielle Darrieux as the doomed lovers. The film was an international hit, and it is difficult to figure out what more Litvak hoped to accomplish with a smaller-scale remake. The use of color film is the only enhancement evident. Audrey spent two weeks and four days preparing for the broadcast, which was her only professional commitment in 1957. She had told the press of her plan to take a year off to spend with her husband, and since he played opposite her she managed to add another credit to her resume` without breaking her word. The result received mixed reviews, but Audrey's presence and the impressive production design were enough to earn *Mayerling* a theatrical release in Europe.

In 1968, Terence Young wrote and directed yet another version of Austria's great tragic love story, starring Omar Sharif as Rudolph and Catherine Deneuve as Maria. Despite a fine cast that also includes James Mason and Ava Gardner, the '68 *Mayerling* received disappointing notices.

F14 THE NUN'S STORY (Warner Bros., 1959; 149 minutes; color)

> Available on Videocassette (Warner Bros.)
> Awards: Academy Award nominations for Best Picture, Best Actress (Audrey Hepburn), Best Director, Best Writing, Best Sound, Best Score

Credits

Directed by Fred Zinnemann; Written by Robert Anderson, based on the book by Kathryn C. Hulme; Produced by Henry Blanke; Photographed by Franz F. Planer (Technicolor), Music by Franz Waxman; Edited by Walter Thompson; Art Direction by Alexander Trauner; Set Direction by Maurice Barnathan; Costumes by Marjorie Best; Makeup by Alberto De Rossi

Cast

AUDREY HEPBURN (SISTER LUKE, GABRIELLE VAN DER MAL), Peter Finch, Dr. Fortunati), Edith Evans (Mother Emmanuel, Superior General), Peggy Ashcroft (Mother Mathilde), Dean Jagger (Dr. Van der Mal), Mildred Dunnock (Sister Margharita), Beatrice Straight (Mother Christophe), Patricia Collinge (Sister William), Eva Kotthaus (Sister Marie), Ruth White (Mother Marcella), Niall McGinnis (Father Vermeuhlen), Patricia Bosworth (Simone), Barbara O'Neil (Mother Katherine), Lionel Jeffries (Dr. Goovaerts), Margaret Phillips (Sister Pauline), Rosalie Crutchley (Sister Eleanor), Colleen Dewhurst (Archangel), Stephen Murray (Chaplain), Orlando Martins (Kalulu), Errol John (Illunga), Jeannette Sterke (Louise Van der Mal), Richard O'Sullivan (Pierre Van der Mal), Diana Lambert (Lisa), Marina Wolkonsky (Marie Van der Mal), Penelope Horner (Jeanette Milonet), Ave Ninchi (Sister Bernard), Charles Lamb (Pascin), Ludovice Bonhomme (Bishop), Dara Gavin (Sister Ellen), Elfrida Simbari (Sister Timothy), Dorothy Alison (Sister Aurelie), Molly Urquhart (Sister Augustine), Frank Singuineau, Juan Aymerich, Giovanna Galletti

Synopsis

In 1930, young Gabrielle Van der Mal enters a convent in her native Belgium to become a nun. Almost immediately she has difficulty adjusting to the cloistered life, and its vows of charity, humility and obedience. She doubts her own ability, even as she takes her final vows. Gabrielle, now called Sister Luke, excels in her medical studies and dreams of serving in the Belgian Congo. When she is asked by the Reverend Mother to fail her exams on purpose to show humility, she cannot bring herself to do so. However, despite her excellent score she is not sent to the Congo, but to a sanitarium in Brussels.

Her pride and intellectual curiosity, the qualities that make her an excellent nurse, continue to cause her problems as a nun. She finally receives her transfer to the Congo, where she serves as the surgical nurse to the rakish Dr. Fortunati. There she makes innovations in patient care but is chastised by the church for calling attention to herself. Fortunati comes to respect her nursing abilities, but tells her that she is too worldly to be a nun.

Sister Luke is ordered to escort a seriously ill patient back to Brussels, and then to begin work at a hospital in Holland. World War II begins, and as Europe falls the church urges its nuns to maintain neutrality. Sister Luke finds herself helping out the Resistance, and realizes that she cannot continue to be obedient without question. After informing her superiors, she leaves the church.

Reviews

"In a brilliant synthesis of idea and pictorial imagery, which includes stunning contrasts of color, the tempo of action and moods, Mr. Zinnemann has made this off-beat drama describe a parabola of spiritual afflatus and deflation that ends in a strange sort of defeat...In the role of the nun, Miss Hepburn is fluent and luminous. From her eyes and her eloquent expressions emerge a character that is warm and involved." (*New York Times*, June 19, 1959)

"This is a simple, serene account of a proud young woman's inner spiritual struggle, and it is a tribute to the moviemakers that they have not resorted to tears, hysterics or romance to liven things up." (*Newsweek*, June 29, 1959)

"Audrey Hepburn has her most demanding film role, and she gives her finest performance. Despite the seriousness of the underlying theme, *The Nun's Story* has the elements of absorbing drama, pathos, humor, and a gallery of memorable scenes and characters." (*Variety*, May 1, 1959)

Additional Reviews

America (May 23, 1959); *BFI/Monthly Film Bulletin* (September 1959); *Catholic World* (July 1959); *Commonweal* (July 17, 1959); *Film Daily* (May 6, 1959); *Filmfacts* (July 15, 1959); *Films in Review* (June-July 1959); *Good Housekeeping* (July 1959); *Hollywood Reporter* (May 6, 1959); *Library Journal* (June 15, 1959); *Life* (June 8, 1959); *The Nation* (July 4, 1959); *The New Republic* (June 29, 1959); *The New Yorker* (June 27, 1959); *Saturday Review* (June 27, 1959); *Time* (July 6, 1959)

Commentary

It could be argued that all of Audrey's lead film roles, beginning with *Roman Holiday*, were variations on the Cinderella theme; *Roman Holiday* is Cinderella-in-reverse, with Audrey playing a princess who dreams of life as a commoner. Her follow-up, *Sabrina*, is the story of a chauffeur's daughter who ends up marrying the son of her father's employer, and living in the huge mansion that as a child she gazed at longingly from afar. In *Funny Face* she plays a meek bookworm who is transformed into a glamorous fashion model; in *Love in the Afternoon* she transforms herself, from innocent schoolgirl to a jetset woman of the world. Only her performance as Natasha in *War and Peace* doesn't exactly fit the mold, but even here there are some similarities--Natasha, like Princess Anne, lives an almost fairy-tale like existence in the Moscow before Napoleon's invasion, but the naivete` of her childhood is replaced by sobering maturity as a young adult who must face the harsh reality of war.

It was *The Nun's Story* that broke the pattern, and brought Audrey the most recognition and awards of any role in her career save *Roman Holiday*. Having already proven herself in musicals and romantic comedy, she now tackled the arduous dramatic role of Sister Luke and satisfied any critics who may have thought she was coasting on her gamine image. There would be no help from Givenchy this time, and her beauty, though still unmistakable, was not a factor in her performance. The role was even more challenging because the nuns in Sister Luke's order were discouraged from speaking or gesturing with any animation. Audrey was thus forced to rely almost solely on facial expression to convey the inner turmoil that Sister Luke struggled with throughout her years of religious service.

"Miss Hepburn reveals the kind of acting talent that can project inner feelings, of both depth and complexity, so skillfully you must scrutinize her intently on second and third viewings of *The Nun's Story* to perceive how she does it." wrote *Films In Review* magazine. "Her portrayal of Sister Luke is one of the great performances of the screen." (see B186). It may have been the very quiet introspection of the performance that cost her the Academy Award, which tends to honor more overt acting expressions. In Europe, where drama that emerges from inner soul-searching is more commonplace, Audrey received several awards, including the British and Italian equivalents of the Oscar.

The Nun's Story was based on the 1956 novel by Kathryn C. Hulme, which was translated into twelve languages and sold three million copies in the United States alone. It was based on the actual experiences of a woman named Louise Habetts, and the scenes of the postulants' training and the day to day life inside the convent walls have a definite feel of authenticity. If anything, the film version softened the novel's chronicling of Habetts' life as a nun. Audrey met with both the author and Ms. Habetts prior to starting work on the film. During production she would not look in a mirror or play phonograph records, two activites that would have been forbidden to Sister Luke.

At first Audrey was apprehensive about filming in Africa, but she quickly fell in love with the country and its people. Far more difficult were the scenes in which Sister Luke reacts to the German invasion of Holland and Belgium, which brought back painful memories of her own experiences of growing up under Nazi occupation.

The Nun's Story may be one of the best films ever made to not receive even one Academy Award, despite six nominations. Coincidentally, it was another religious film, *Ben Hur*, that dominated the proceedings in 1959. Both films were in production at the same time at Rome's Cinecitta studios, and it has been rumored that Audrey joined one of *Ben Hur*'s crowd sequences as a gag (the film was produced by her old friend and colleague William Wyler).

Reviews were almost unanimously favorable, but the review that Audrey may have appreciated the most came from Louise Habetts, who saw the film three times. "I'm never going to see it again," she added, "because if I do I'm going to run right back to the convent."

F15 GREEN MANSIONS (MGM, 1959; 104 minutes; color)

Credits
Directed by Mel Ferrer; Written by Dorothy Kingsley, based on the novel by William Henry Hudson; Produced by Edmund Grainger; Photographed by Joseph Ruttenberg (CinemaScope, Metrocolor); Music by Hector Villa-Lobos and Bronislau Kaper; Edited by Ferris Webster; Art Direction by William A. Horning and Preston Ames; Set Decoration by Henry Grace and Jerry Wunderlich; Costumes by Dorothy Jeakins; Choreography by Katharine Dunham; Special Effects by A. Arnold Gillespie and Lee LeBlanc and Robert R. Hoag

Cast
AUDREY HEPBURN (RIMA), Anthony Perkins (Abel), Lee J. Cobb (Nuflo), Sessue Hayakawa (Runi), Henry Silva (Kua-Ko), Nehemiah Persoff (Don Panta), Michael Pate (Priest), Estelle Hemsley (Cla-Cla), Bill Saito, Yoneo Iguchi (Native Guides)

Synopsis
Abel, a political refugee, hides out in the Venezuelan jungles after his father is killed. He is taken in by a tribe of Indians, where he bides his time waiting for the opportunity to avenge his father's death. Rumors circulate of gold in the area, and while Abel searches for the mine he meets Rima, the bird-girl. They fall in love, but the Indians believe Rima to be an evil spirit and destroy her. Rima's foster grandfather Nuflo leads Abel to the hidden gold, and in a jungle clearing Abel sees a hint that Rima may have

survived in another form.

Reviews
"For without the ethereal Miss Hepburn vaporing lightly through the Venezuelan woods, floating out to charm a masculine intruder or pose wistfully with great tears in her eyes when she makes a sad discovery of man's deceptions, this could be a pretty foolish film...Miss Hepburn conducts herself all through it with grace and dignity, making Rima both poignant and idyllic, if not in the least logical." (*New York Times*, March 20, 1959)

"...this film version of the book, directed by actor Mel Ferrer, catches little of the leafy rustle of Hudson's woodland fantasy, comes out as just another Hollywood jungle bungle...Audrey Hepburn is spritely enough, but actor Perkins clumps through the greenery as gingerly and gracelessly as an oversized boy scout bound for a merit badge in campcraft." (*Newsweek*, April 6, 1959)

"This is one of those screen versions that is likely to confuse those who haven't read the book and irritate those who have...Miss Hepburn is pretty as the strange young woman, but with no particular depth. Perkins seems rather frail for his role." (*Variety*, March 13, 1959)

Additional Reviews
Commonweal (April 17, 1959); *Good Housekeeping* (May 1959); *Library Journal* (April 15, 1959); *New Yorker* (March 28, 1959); *Saturday Review* (April 11, 1959); *Time* (April 6, 1959)

Commentary
Green Mansions is the only one of Audrey's post-*Roman Holiday* films that has not been released on videocassette, and has remained virtually out of circulation for years. During this time it has acquired a reputation both as an undiscovered gem and a complete misfire.

According to *Films and Filming*, *Green Mansions* "was as near perfect as one could hope for in a film...made by a Hollywood company" (see B017). *Films in Review* offered an opposing view; responding to Audrey's comment that being directed by her husband Mel Ferrer was "as natural as brushing my teeth," the magazine suggested that "if Miss Hepburn won't change husbands, or directors, she at least owes it to the public to change her brand of toothpaste." The film was labeled "Ferrer's fiasco" and was lambasted for being filmed in "an appalling greenish patina that makes it look as if it had been filmed in a decaying parsley patch." Audrey herself is criticized for looking "as if she had been given an overdose of chlorophyll" (see B186).

Green Mansions, like War and Peace, was a unique challenge to bring to the screen, and had several false starts before finding a director and star to commit for the duration. W.H. Hudson's 1904 novel was purchased by RKO in 1931, and was slated to be a David O. Selznick production with King Vidor directing and Dolores Del Rio starring as Rima. When that fell through the studio tried again in 1935 with Dorothy Jordan as Rima, and then again in 1938 with Anne Shirley. Three strikes and out for RKO, who sold the rights to MGM in 1943. Three years later, a musical version was pitched with Peruvian singer Yma Sumac, but this was abandoned as was an Alan Lerner script written for Elizabeth Taylor. Producer Pandro S. Berman stepped in and at last the first Green Mansions film footage was shot, with Italian actress Pier Angeli as the bird-girl. But when Angeli became pregnant another contender hit the canvas.

Dorothy Kinglsey then wrote a script and gave it to Mel Ferrer, who was looking for a project that would star his wife and that he could direct. The studio consented, probably fed up with the material by then, and Ferrer left for Venezuela and Guyana to scout locations. The result was Audrey's first critical and box office disappointment, though for the most part Audrey escaped blame for its failure.

"If any film star could portray Rima, Audrey Hepburn is she," wrote Films in Review, "but Rima has an animal purity no actress could ever project." Audrey had a backlog of experience in screen purity, thus it was the "animal" side of the role that intrigued many filmgoers. One cannot help being struck by the contrast from her chaste, restrained performance in her previous film to the overt sexuality she exudes as the scantily-dressed Rima. Critics who had expressed a desire to see Audrey break away from ingenue roles now had their wish granted--from The Nun's Story to Green Mansions, it's hard to imagine a wider gamut.

If the film brought her no awards it did provide Audrey with an affectionate new pet. Ip, the fawn that was Rima's comrade in the film, was adopted by Audrey and became an unlikely companion for her terrier, Famous.

F16 THE UNFORGIVEN (Hecht-Hill-Lancaster/United Artists, 1960; 125 minutes; color)

Available on Videocassette (MGM/UA)

Credits
Directed by John Huston; Written by Ben Maddow, based on a novel by Alan LeMay; Produced by James Hill; Photographed by

Franz Planer (Panavision/Technicolor); Music by Dimitri Tiomkin; Edited by Hugh Russell Lloyd; Music Direction by Tiomkin; Art Direction by Stephen Grimes; Makeup by Frank McCoy

Cast

Burt Lancaster (Ben Zachary), AUDREY HEPBURN (RACHEL ZACHARY), Audie Murphy (Cash Zachary), John Saxon (Johnny Portugal), Charles Bickford (Zeb Rawlins), Lillian Gish (Mattilda Zachary), Albert Salmi (Charlie Rawlins), Joseph Wiseman (Abe Kelsey), June Walker (Hagar Rawlins), Kipp Hamilton (Georgia Rawlins), Arnold Merritt (Jude Rawlins), Carlos Rivas (Lost Bird), Doug McClure (Andy Zachary)

Synopsis

Texas in the 1850's; tension between settlers and the Kiowa Indians are running high. The Zachary family, Mattilda and her sons Ben, Cash, Andy and daughter Rachel, try to raise cattle and avoid the frequent outbursts of violence. Abe Kelsey, a shadowy figure from the family's past, begins spreading rumors that Rachel is actually a Kiowa, who was stolen from the tribe and adopted by the Zacharys. The Indians send a party to the Zachary ranch to purchase the girl. When their offer is vehemently rejected, they kill Rachel's boyfriend.

Ben and Cash track down Abe Kelsey, but he refuses to retract his allegation, even when a noose is tied around his neck. Mattilda, outraged at how Abe's arrival has torn apart her family and the community, makes certain that the troublemaker does not escape hanging, but she is then forced to admit that his claim is true. Cash storms out after learning the story, and the Kiowas come calling again, this time with plans to take Rachel by force. The family survives several attacks, but when Mattilda is killed and the ammunition begins to run out the situation looks bleak. At the last minute, Cash returns with fresh supplies and the reunited Zacharys drive the Kiowas away.

Reviews

"As the girl, Audrey Hepburn is a bit too polished, too fragile and civilized among such tough and stubborn types as Burt Lancaster." (*New York Times*, April 7, 1960)

"The film starts out as an absorbing drama of human passions and finishes with a long stretch of the wildest sort of melodrama. The large cast could hardly have been better chosen, while Huston's direction is fast and lusty." (*Newsweek*, April 18, 1960)

"There are many aspects of *The Unforgiven* that will elicit comparison with

Shane, particularly in regard to the composition of the scenes and the photography. Miss Hepburn...gives a shining performance as the foundling daughter of a frontier family.' (*Variety*, March 24, 1960)

Additional Reviews
America (April 30, 1960); *Commonweal* (April 22, 1960); *Film Daily* (March 30, 1960); *Film Quarterly* (Summer 1960); *Filmfacts* (1960); *Films and Filming* (July 1960); *Films in Review* (May 1960); *Life* (May 16, 1960); *McCall's* (May 1960); *The Nation* (April 9, 1960); *The New Republic* (April 25, 1960); *The New Yorker* (April 16, 1960); *Saturday Review* (April 16, 1960); *Time* (April 11, 1960)

Commentary
The Unforgiven has earned the dubious distinction of being the only one of John Huston's films that he fervently disliked. "Despite some good performances, the overall tone is bombastic and over-inflated," he said years later. "I watched it on TV one night recently, and after about half a reel I had to turn the damned thing off. I couldn't bear it."

Audiences were generally less critical, and the film was a minor hit despite mixed reviews. Its chief flaw was the result of backstage conflict between Huston, who had hoped to make a thinking man's western with an anti-racism message, and the studio, who argued for an old-fashioned cowboys and Indians shoot-'em-up. The film ended up somewhere down the middle, which didn't please either camp.

Audrey's reasons for portraying Rachel Zachary are unrecorded. It seems an odd choice, coming off her most poorly-received film, to tackle a genre for which she has never expressed any particular affection, and a role that was not worthy of her abilities, nor particularly suited to them. Rachel may be the fulcrum around which the plot revolves, but she is only allowed to react to the forces at work around her, rather than initiating the action. Few would argue that it was the worst miscasting in her career; she was never going to pass for an Indian, and her melodious voice did not mesh well with a prairie accent.

For the part, Audrey was required to ride a spirited stallion named Diabolo bareback. Although she had not ridden a horse since childhood, Audrey refused a stand-in and hopped aboard. The horse threw her, and she wound up in the hospital with four fractured vertebrae. She was flown from the Durango, Mexico location to Los Angeles for treatment, and was nursed back to health by Louise Habetts, the real-life Sister Luke. Though still in pain, she returned to the set three weeks later, saddled up and fulfilled her vow to ride the horse once more. Needless to say, Diabolo did not join Ip and Famous in Audrey's household menagerie. Audrey's fall was but one of the problems that plagued *The Unforgiven* throughout its production; co-star Audie Murphy almost drowned while duck hunting, and three technicians were killed in a plane crash.

Despite these and other less tragic mishaps, the film does have some provocative moments, such as when Mattilda, in response to the ominous sounds of the Kiowa Indian flutes, drags the family's upright piano outside and tries to soothe the savages with music. And of the otherwise unremarkable scene in which Lillian Gish combs out Audrey's hair, author Charles Affron in his book *Star Acting* observes that "two of the screen's most extraordinary faces are united" (see B240). Alan LeMay, who wrote the novel on which *The Unforgiven* was based, would later write *The Searchers*, which contained a similar theme and was transformed into one of the greatest westerns ever made.

F17 BREAKFAST AT TIFFANY'S (Paramount, 1961, 115 minutes; color)

Available on Videocassette and Laserdisc (Paramount)
<u>Awards</u>: Academy Awards for Best Song ("Moon River") and Best Score; nominations for Best Actress (Audrey Hepburn), Best Screenplay, Best Art Direction-Set Direction

Credits
Directed by Blake Edwards; Written by George Axelrod, based on the novella by Truman Capote; Produced by Martin Jurow and Richard Shepherd; Photographed by Franz E. Planer (Technicolor), Music by Henry Mancini; Music and Lyrics "Moon River" by Mancini and Johnny Mercer; Edited by Howard Smith; Costumes by Edith Head

Cast
AUDREY HEPBURN (HOLLY GOLIGHTLY), George Peppard (Paul Varjak), Patricia Neal (2-E), Buddy Ebsen (Doc Golightly), Martin Balsam (O.J. Berman), Mickey Rooney (Mr. Yunioshi), Vilallonga (Jose da Silva Perriera), John McGiver (Tiffany's Clerk), Dorothy Whitney (Mag Wildwood), Stanley Adams (Rusty Trawler), Elvia Allman (Librarian), Alan Reed, Sr. (Sally Tomato), Beverly Hills (Stripper), Claude Stroud (Sid Arbuck), Putney (Cat)

Synopsis
Struggling writer Paul Varjak moves into a New York apartment building and becomes intrigued by his pretty, quirky neighbor Holly Golightly. Holly's lifestyle confuses and fascinates Paul; in public she flits through parties with a sexy, sophisticated air, but when they're alone she changes into a sweetly vulnerable bundle of neuroses. Part of the mystery of Holly

is solved when Doc Golightly, her estranged and much older husband, arrives from the country to reclaim his wife. Paul learns that they were married when Holly was thirteen and still using her real name of Lulamae Barnes. Holly tells Doc she does love him, but refuses to return to the farm.

Paul and Holly grow closer, and he finds inspiration in the lady which helps him resume his writing career. He ditches his "sponsor," an older woman who has been paying the bills throughout his dry spell, and professes his love for Holly. In return, she announces her intention to marry a South American millionaire. She continues to flee from the real love offered by Paul, and plans to fly to Rio even after her millionaire breaks the engagement. Paul does not give up, however, and at last Holly stops running from her last chance at happiness.

Reviews
"*Breakfast at Tiffany's* is the gayest sophisticated comedy Hollywood has served up in years." (*Life*, September 8, 1961)

"It is a completely unbelievable but wholly captivating flight into fancy composed of unequal dollops of comedy, romance, poignancy, funny colloquialisms and Manhattan's swankiest East Side areas captured in the loveliest of colors. Above all, it has the overpowering attribute known as Audrey Hepburn, who, despite her normal, startled fawn exterior, now is displaying a fey, comic talent that should enchant Mr. Capote. In the person of Miss Hepburn, [Holly] is a genuinely charming, elfin waif who will be believed and adored when seen." (*New York Times*, October 6, 1961)

"Whitewashed and solidified for the screen, Truman Capote's *Breakfast at Tiffany's* emerges as unconventional but dynamic entertainment that will be talked about and, resultantly, commercially successful. What makes *Tiffany's* an appealing tale is its heroine, Holly Golightly, a charming, wild and amoral "free spirit" with a latent romantic streak. [In] the exciting person of Audrey Hepburn, she comes vividly to life on the screen." (*Variety*, October 5, 1961)

Additional Reviews
America (November 25, 1961); *BFI/Monthly Film Bulletin* (November 1961); *Commonweal* (October 20, 1961); *Esquire* (December 1961); *Film Daily* (October 5, 1961); *Filmfacts* (October 20, 1961); *Films in Review* (November 1961); *The New Republic* (September 18, 1961); *The New Yorker* (October 16, 1961); *Newsweek* (October 16, 1961); *Saturday Review* (September 30, 1961); *Time* (October 20, 1961)

Commentary

"Any moviegoer worthy of the label cherishes the memory of Audrey Hepburn's face as she rushes through the rain to rescue her cat in *Breakfast at Tiffany's*." wrote film critic Philip Wuntch, on the occasion of a USA Film Festival tribute to Audrey in 1991 (see B238). Along with Princess Anne and Eliza Doolittle, Holly Golightly remains one of her signature roles, and brought Audrey her fourth Oscar nomination in eight films.

The multi-faceted Holly--flighty, sexy, childlike, mercurial, sad--is arguably Audrey's best film performance. Repeat viewings expose different qualities in the character every time--her drunk scene alone is amazing. The role was an influential one in Hollywood as well; according the *Motion Picture Guide,* "Hepburn stands as a precursor to the liberated woman who would appear in the films of the late 1960's, one who, in spite of her independence, realizes that she is not as tough as she would have us believe (see B323). Martin Balsam, who plays Holly's agent in the film, puts it more succinctly; "She's a phony, all right, but a real phony."

The description of Holly in Truman Capote's 1958 novella would almost indicate that he had Audrey in mind at the typewriter; "a flat little bottom, chic thinness, her mouth was large, her nose upturned. It was a face beyond childhood, yet this side of belonging to a woman." And yet, when it came time to cast the film, Capote wanted Marilyn Monroe! "She would have been absolutely marvelous," said Capote according to his biographer Gerald Clarke. "Audrey is an old friend and one of my favorite people, but she was just wrong for that part" (see B254).

Capote had further cause for complaint when Hollywood tacked a happy ending on his downbeat novella, but watching the result, when Holly finds her man and her cat as the rain pours and the strains of "Moon River" swell on the soundtrack, it's hard to protest the alteration. The realities of Holly's "profession" were also softened, which suited Audrey just fine. "We couldn't have kept all the lines of the book, the censors wouldn't have allowed it." she said in a 1990 interview (see B200). "Besides, I don't think that Holly really has known as many men as she pretends. It's just a jazzy facade she creates, because basically she's a small-town girl who's out of her depth."

If the film has a flaw it is a lack of the timeless quality of *Roman Holiday*, *Sabrina* and *Love in the Afternoon*. *Breakfast at Tiffany's* is very much a document of its decade, and it would be hard to imagine the story being filmed today. The fashions and expressions and lifestyles portrayed seem dated now, as does the Japanese caricature essayed by Mickey Rooney.But there is nothing dated about Blake Edwards' skillful direction--the party scene in Holly's apartment is as expertly choreographed as any of the dances in *Funny Face*--or the superb Henry

Mancini score. After hearing Audrey perform "How Long Has This Been Going On?" in *Funny Face*, Mancini composed "Moon River" in the same "octave and one" range so she could handle it. In his autobiography (see B312), he regrets that a chorus was used for the song on the album version of the score. "There have been more than one thousand recordings of 'Moon River.' Mancini writes, "Of all of them, Audrey's performance was the definitive version."

A musical stage version of *Breakfast at Tiffany's* debuted in Philadelphia's Forrest Theatre on October 10, 1966, and closed while still in previews at New York's Majestic Theatre on December 14 of the same year. Music and lyrics were by Bob Merrill; the book was written by Abe Burrows, and later re-written by Edward Albee. The roles of Holly and Paul were played by Mary Tyler Moore and Richard Chamberlain. The supporting cast included Larry Kert, Art Lund and Sally Kellerman. One of its songs, "Ciao Compare," was recorded by both Vic Damone and Robert Goulet.

F18 THE CHILDREN'S HOUR (United Artists, 1961; 107 minutes; black and white)

Available on Videocassette (MGM/UA)
Awards: Academy Award nominations for Best Supporting Actress (Fay Bainter), Best Cinematography, Best Art Direction-Set Decoration, Best Costume Design and Best Sound.

Credits
Directed and produced by William Wyler; Written by John Michael Hayes, adaptation by Lillian Hellman from her play; Photographed by Franz Planer; Music by Alex North; Edited by Robert Swink; Art Direction by Fernando Carrere; Set Direction by Edward G. Boyle; Costumes by Dorothy Jeakins

Cast
AUDREY HEPBURN (KAREN WRIGHT), Shirley MacLaine (Martha Dobie), James Garner (Dr. Joe Cardin), Miriam Hopkins (Mrs. Lily Mortar), Fay Bainter (Mrs. Amelia Tilford), Karen Balkin (Mary Tilford), Veronica Cartwright (Rosalie), Jered Barclay (Grocery Boy), Mimi Gibson, William Mims, Hope Summers, Florence MacMichael

Synopsis
Best friends Karen Wright and Martha Dobie are headmistresses at a

successful private school for girls in New England. Mary Tilford, a spiteful, angry child, is caught in a lie and punished severely. In retaliation she tells her grandmother, a matriarch in the town, that Martha was "jealous" of Karen's relationhip with Dr. Joe Cardin, and that Martha's Aunt Lilly thought those feelings were "unnatural." Grandma believes her and pulls Mary out of school. The word quickly spreads and within days Karen and Martha are faced with empty classrooms. Joe is fired from the hospital for siding with the teachers.

Karen and Martha sue for slander in a case that makes national headlines, but lose when Lily refuses to retract her statement. The truth finally comes out when Mary's corroborating witness breaks down, but by then the lives of Karen, Martha and Joe are in ruin. They plan to leave town together, until Martha confesses that her feelings for Karen are indeed more than friendship. Overcome with shame and guilt, she hangs herself.

Reviews

"So this drama that was supposed to be so novel and daring because of its muted theme is really quite unrealistic and scandalous in a prim and priggish way. What's more, it is not too well acted, except by Audrey Hepburn in the role of the younger of the school teachers. She gives the impression of being sensitive and pure." (*New York Times*, March 15, 1962)

"Shirley MacLaine, all forlorn, gives the best performance of her career as the teacher who is sickened to find out she is partly homosexual. Audrey Hepburn, the other teacher, gives her standard, frail, indomitable characterization, which is to say that her eyes water constantly and her chin is forever cantilevered forward." (*Time*, February 9, 1962)

"The personalities of Audrey Hepburn and Shirley MacLaine, in the leading roles, beautifully complement each other. Miss Hepburn's soft sensitivity, marvelous projection and emotional understatement result in a memorable portrayal--one of potential Oscar nomination calibre. Wyler's direction is arresting, penetrating and sensitive." (*Variety*, December 6, 1961)

Additional Reviews

America (July 2, 1962); *Commonweal* (March 2, 1962); *Film Daily* (January 12, 1962); *Film Quarterly* (Spring 1963); *Filmfacts* (March 23, 1962); *Films and Filming* (September 1962); *Films in Review* (April 1962); *Hollywood Reporter* (December 8, 1961); *Motio n Picture Herald Product Digest* (December 20, 1961); *The New Republic* (April 16, 1962); *The New*

Yorker (March 17, 1962); *Newsweek* (March 12, 1962); *Saturday Review* (February 24, 1962); *The Village Voice* (March 1, 1962)

Commentary

Lillian Hellman's groundbreaking play *The Children's Hour* ran for over six hundred performances on Broadway in 1934. Katherine Emery and Anne Revere played the two school teachers accused of having an "unnatural" relationship. The play was first brought to the screen by William Wyler in 1936 under the title *These Three*. Hellman wrote the script, but the Film Production Code insisted on drastic changes, and the result is a well-acted (by Miriam Hopkins and Merle Oberon as the teachers) but sanitized version of the play.

Wyler wanted a second chance at the material, in which the relationship hinted at by Hellman is clearly spelled out. He paid $300,000 for the screen rights and thought of casting Katharine Hepburn and Doris Day (!), but was glad for the opportunity of working with Audrey again nearly ten years after *Roman Holiday*. Hopkins, who played Martha in the 1936 film, returned to play Aunt Lily.

The Children's Hour earned five Oscar nominations, but brought Audrey some of the worst notices in her career. They are not entirely undeserved, but no one else fares much better. Hopkins seems off her game, and Shirley MacLaine's shrill performance does not inspire compassion. Audrey's pairing with James Garner is her most unconvincing screen relationship. The climax, in which she goads Joe into asking her if she has been intimate with Martha, and then rejects him for doing so, does not ring true at all. Fay Bainter emerges best in her Oscar-nominated role as the gullible grandmother.

It's an unpleasant movie to watch, but Wyler does an admirable job of communicating the teachers' isolation and ostracism from the community. Scenes of people staring at their school from the side of the road as if it were a carnival attraction powerfully convey the film's themes of entrapment and intolerance. It is also notable as an early mainstream Hollywood treatment of homosexuality. Vito Russo's book *The Celluloid Closet* quotes MacLaine as wanting a more explicit development of Martha's growing awareness of her sexuality, but being rejected by Wyler because "middle America wasn't ready." (see B342). Audrey reportedly sided with MacLaine. The two actresses had become friends during production after a tentative first meeting. "I had plenty of qualms when I met Audrey for the first rehearsal. It took me quite a while to thaw her out-- about three hours. From then on, it was one big kick," said MacLaine, according to Ian Woodward in his Audrey Hepburn biography (see B366); "Audrey and I had a running gag all through the picture. She was supposed to be teaching me how to dress, and I was supposed to be teaching her how to cuss. Neither of us succeeded."

Several different endings actually were tried, including one that put the teachers in court where they are found guilty of "sinful sexual knowledge of one another." Bernard F. Dick, author of *Hellman in Hollywood*, credits the film with one intriguing twist on the original material--the possibility that Karen may also be a lesbian (see B260). Such an assessment is highly interpretive, and Dick admits that the implication doesn't entirely work because Audrey was "so completely feminine."

The *Children's Hour* was parodied in the 1993 play *Brave Smiles...another lesbian tragedy*. Dominique Dibbell played the Audrey Hepburn role.

F19 CHARADE (Universal, 1963; 113 minutes; color)

Available on Videocassette (MCA)
Awards: Academy Award nomination for Best Song ("Charade")

Credits
Directed and produced by Stanley Donen; Written by Peter Stone, based on the story "The Unsuspecting Wife" by Stone and Marc Behm); Photographed by Charles Lang, Jr. (Technicolor); Music by Henry Mancini, lyrics by Johnny Mercer; Edited by James Clark; Art Direction by Jean dEaubonne; Costumes by Givenchy

Cast
Cary Grant (Peter Joshua), AUDREY HEPBURN (Regina Lambert), Walter Matthau (Hamilton Bartholemew), James Coburn (Tex Panthollow), George Kennedy (Herman Scobie), Ned Glass (Leopold Gideon), Jacques Marin (Inspector Edouard Grandpierre), Paul Bonifas (Felix), Dominique Minot (Sylvie Gaudet), Thomas Chelimsky (Jean-Louis Gaudet)

Synopsis
Regina Lambert returns to Paris from a ski holiday in Switzerland to find that her husband has been murdered. She is later told by CIA agent Hamilton Bartholemew that Charles Lambert was one of five men who stole $250,000 in gold from the U.S. government during World War II, and the government wants it back. The money was not found among his possessions, and Regina can shed no light on its whereabouts.

Later that day she is visited by Peter Joshua, whom she had met briefly while on holiday. When her husband's former partners in crime, who were double-crossed by Charles, start calling her looking for the money, Peter offers to help find it. Thus begins an elaborate charade in which friends turn out to be enemies, and enemies are revealed to be friends. When the dust settles all the crooks end up dead, Peter Joshua's true identity is uncovered, and the lost fortune is found in the one place that had been thoroughly searched by every interested party.

Reviews

"The players have at it in a glib, polished, nonchalant way that clearly betrays their awareness of the film's howling implausibility. Miss Hepburn is cheerfully committed to a mood of how-nuts-can-you-be in an obviously comforting assortment of expensive Givenchy costumes." (*New York Times*, November 29, 1963)

"Not since John Huston's *Beat the Devil* has there been such a gay romp as *Charade*, [an] absolute delight in which Cary Grant and Audrey Hepburn schottische about with evident glee." (*Newsweek*, December 16, 1963)

"*Charade* has all the ingredients of success, some in spades, blended into a tasty dish that spells ticket-selling ambrosia. First time teaming of Cary Grant and Audrey Hepburn, a natural, gives the sophisticated romantic caper an international appeal, plus the selling points of adventure, suspense and superb comedy." (*Variety*, September 20, 1963)

Additional Reviews

America (December 21, 1963); *BFI/Monthly Film Bulletin* (April 1964); *Commonweal* (December 13, 1963); *Film Daily* (September 25, 1963); *Films and Filming* (March 1964); *Films in Review* (December 1963); *Hollywood Reporter* (September 24, 1963); *Motion Picture Herald Product Digest* (October 2, 1963); *The New Republic* (December 21, 1963); *The New Yorker* (December 14, 1963); *Saturday Review* (December 14, 1963); *Sight and Sound* (Spring 1964); *Time* (December 20, 1963); *Vogue* (January 1, 1964)

Commentary

Charade, my personal favorite among Audrey's films, ranks among the best comic thrillers ever made. Under Stanley Donen's superb direction, the film deftly manages to be equally effective as an Alfred Hitchcock-like thriller, and as a spoof of Hitchcock's stylish suspense tales. The teaming of Cary Grant and Audrey Hepburn should have been inevitable--at the time each set the Hollywood standard for their gender in aristocratic class. The film is set in Paris, the perfect backdrop for their escapades. The clothes were by Givenchy and the score was by Henry Mancini. If there is such thing as a foolproof formula for success, this was it.

An opening title sequence by Maurice Binder, who designed the memorable titles for the James Bond films, is followed by the shot of a gun, in close-up, pointed at the head of Regina Lambert. The trigger is pulled, and Regina is squirted with water. The movie continues to alternate between ominous and whimsical moments, with a new red herring planted almost every ten minutes. The solution to the mystery of the missing $250,000 is ingenious, and a satisfying payoff after ninety minutes of deception.

The dialogue absolutely sparkles throughout Peter Stone's script, and no two performers could deliver such lines as "I don't bite, of course--unless it's called for" more deftly then Cary Grant and Audrey Hepburn. Though Audrey was once again paired with a man 25 years her senior, this time the situation was acknowledged in the storyline and became a source of amusement. Grant insisted on a romance with a minimum of physical expression, but the chemistry between the two is so overpowering that nothing more overt is needed.

In a December, 1963 interview in *Look*, Cary Grant said "All I want for Christmas is another movie with Audrey Hepburn!" The two got along famously; "That girl mothered our entire company. The day she left we were bereft," said Cary of Audrey. "We had to stick around for our fight scenes without her, and we were absolutely lost." The stars almost worked together on three other occasions; Grant wanted Audrey for his co-star in *Father Goose* (1964), but when she was busy the role went to Leslie Caron. Grant was the studio's choice to play Professor Higgins in *My Fair Lady*, but he refused the role and practically demanded that it be given to Rex Harrison. Finally, MGM offered big money and a cut of the box office if Cary and Audrey would team up again for a remake of *Goodbye, Mr. Chips* in 1968, but by then Grant had retired. Nearly ten years before *Charade*, they almost co-starred in *Sabrina*, but when Grant proved unavailable Humphrey Bogart stepped in to play Linus Larrabee.

If they were only fated to co-star once, at least they found a property, a director and a supporting cast (Walter Matthau, James Coburn, George Kennedy) worthy of their magic. *Charade* was hailed by Pauline Kael as the best film of 1963 and was a hit with audiences, but only its music received Oscar recognition.

F20 PARIS WHEN IT SIZZLES (Quine-
Charleston/Paramount, 1964; 110 minutes; color)

Available on Videocassette (Paramount)

Credits
Directed by Richard Quine; Written by George Axelrod, based on

a story by Julien Duvivier and Henri Jeanson; Produced by George Axelrod and Richard Quine; Photographed by Charles Lang, Jr. (Technicolor); Music by Nelson Riddle; Edited by Archie Marshek; Art Direction by Jean d'Eaubonne; Set Direction by Gabriel Bechir; Costumes by Hubert de Givenchy and Christian Dior; Special Effects by Paul K. Lerpae; Makeup by Frank McCoy

Cast
William Holden (Richard Benson), AUDREY HEPBURN (GABRIELLE SIMPSON), Gregoire Aslan (Police Inspector), Raymond Bussieres (Gangster), Christian Duvallex (Maitre d'Hotel), Noel Coward (Alexander Mayerheimer) Tony Curtis (2nd Policeman), Marlene Dietrich, Mel Ferrer (Guest Stars), Fred Astaire, Frank Sinatra (Singing Voices), Thomas Michel, Dominique Boschero, Evi Marandi

Synopsis
Typist Gabrielle Simpson arrives at the Paris apartment of screenwriter Richard Benson, to transcribe the script he had allegedly been working on for months. But Richard confesses to Gabrielle that he hasn't even started on the project, and is now faced with writing an entire screenplay in two days. He pulls a title out of the air, The Girl Who Stole the Eiffel Tower," and inspired by his pretty typist he begins concocting a romance-espionage story on the spot. After visualizing himself and Gaby in the lead roles, he is compelled to change the original downbeat ending of his story, to reflect the love that has bloomed between them.

Reviews
"George Axelrod and Richard Quine attempt to spoof the cliches' of film writing and moviemaking and only succeed in creating a Technicolored cliche' themselves. Miss Hepburn, sylphlike as ever in pastel-covered Givenchy frocks and tailleurs, is a willing heroine, but she seems slightly bewildered by the trumped-up zaniness in which she is involved. Mr. Holden, who is just as willing and properly frenzied as the anxious scenarist, shows signs of strain and a decided lack of conviction." (*New York Times*, April 9, 1964)

"Besides Mr. Holden and Miss Hepburn, who appear to have had a marvelous time making this picture...I should also mention, as a sort of footnote to film history, that Givenchy is given credit not only for Miss Hepburn's wardrobe but for her perfume. Alas, it doesn't travel." (*The New Yorker*, April 11, 1964)

"Pretty soon one ceases to be concerned with the story and settles for watching the pretty images darting and dancing across the screen. Prettiest image by far is Miss Hepburn, a refreshingly individual creature in this era of the exaggerated curve." (*Variety*, March 9, 1964)

Additional Reviews
New Republic (April 25, 1964); *Newsweek* (April 20, 1964); *Saturday Review* (April 18, 1964); *Time* (April 17, 1964)

Commentary
Paris When it Sizzles was an American remake of the 1955 French film *Henriette's Holiday*, directed by Julien Duvivier and starring Michel Auclair and Hildegard Knef in the roles played by William Holden and Audrey Hepburn. The names of Holden and Hepburn are enough to assign the film to the "classics" section of the video store, but the classification is hardly accurate.

Near the beginning of the film, in Richard's first visualization of the "movie within a movie" that comprises most of *Paris When it Sizzles*, Frank Sinatra is heard singing the title song from "The Girl Who Stole the Eiffel Tower." Marlene Dietrich emerges from a white Bentley, and Tony Curtis pops up as the love interest of the female lead. Later, Audrey primps in a mirror while Fred Astaire is heard singing "That face, that face..." and at a party scene she runs into her off-screen husband Mel Ferrer. Had they continued to parade out the guest stars and guest voices, the film would have at least remained interesting as a curio. Stopping the cameos was a mistake, because the script didn't have much else to offer.

Holden and Hepburn play off each other well in the screenwriting scenes, but Holden had never fully recovered from his infatuation (some say affair) with Audrey while they filmed *Sabrina*, and was extremely apprehensive about seeing her again. Bob Thomas, author of the Holden biography *Golden Boy*, writes that his subject told Ryan O'Neal how he felt like "a condemned man" when he arrived in Paris to begin filming. "I realized I had to face Audrey Hepburn and I had to deal with my drinking. And I didn't think I could handle either situation." (see B354). Audrey's affection for and kindness toward Holden made him drink even more, and he ended up in the Chateau de Garche, a hospital for alcoholics, which shut down production. It's a miracle that his physical and emotional traumas did not show up on screen.

Gossip columnists played up the rumors of an affair between the stars, and Audrey did not emerge unscathed. "Everyone in the know had his fingers crossed that the romance between two big married stars is just a passing fancy that will be forgotten when the picture they're doing together is finished." wrote Hedda Hopper. "Meanwhile, it's proved to be such a juicy bit of gossip that the names Liz and Burton have almost been forgotten." Tabloid articles ran such headlines as "But is it Really True What They're Saying about Little Audrey and William Holden?" (see B178) and reported that Audrey was seeing a European psychiatrist to help her decide what to do in her romantic triangle.

Such stories were never verified, but they were certainly more interesting than the movie that prompted them. Critics buried the film but praised Audrey, though they also had some fun at her expense with the credit line for Givenchy's perfume, mentioned in the *New Yorker* review. One scene that is now more entertaining in retrospect is when Richard Benson explains how *Frankenstein* and *My Fair Lady* are actually the same story, and thus unintentionally foreshadows Audrey's next movie.

F21   MY FAIR LADY (Warner Bros., 1964; 170 minutes; color)

Available on Videocassette and Laserdisc (CBS/Fox)
Awards: Academy Awards for Best Picture, Best Actor (Rex Harrision), Best Director, Best Cinematography, Best Art Direction, Best Costume Design, Best Sound, Best Score; nominations for Best Supporting Actor (Stanley Holloway), Best Supporting Actress (Gladys Cooper), Best Screenplay and Best Editing

Credits
Directed by George Cukor; Written by Alan Jay Lerner, based on a musical play by Lerner, Frederick Loewe and the play *Pygmalion* by George Bernard Shaw; Produced by Jack L. Warner; Photographed by Harry Stading (Super Panavision, Technicolor); Music by Frederick Loewe; Edited by William Ziegler; Production Designed by Cecil Beaton; Music Direction by Andre Previn; Art Direction by Gene Allen; Set Direction by George James Hopkins; Costumes by Cecil Beaton; Choreography by Hermes Pan; Makeup by Gordon Bau

Cast
AUDREY HEPBURN (ELIZA DOOLITTLE), Rex Harrison (Prof. Henry Higgins), Stanley Holloway (Alfred P. Doolittle), Wilfrid Hyde-White (Col. Hugh Pickering), Gladys Cooper (Mrs. Higgins), Jeremy Brett (Freddy Eynsford-Hill), Theodore Bikel (Zoltan Karpathy), Isobel Elsom (Mrs. Eynsford-Hill), Mona Washbourne Maids), Jacqueline Squire (Parlor Maid), Gwen Watts (Cook), Eugene Hoffman, Kai Farrelli (Jugglers), Raymond Foster, Joe Evans, Marie Busch, Mary Alexander, William Linkie, Henry

Sweetman, Andrew Brown, Samuel Holmes, Thomas Dick, William Taylor, James Wood, Goldie Kleban, Elizabeth Aimers, Joy Tierney, Lenore Miller, Donna Day, Corinne Ross, Phyllis Kennedy, Davie Robel (Cockneys), Iris Briston, Alma Lawton (Flower Girls), Gigi Michel, Sandy Steffens, Sandy Edmundson, Marlene Marrow, Carol Merrill, Sue Bronson, Lea Genovese (Toffs), Jack Greening (George), Ron Whelan (Algernon/Bartender), John Holland (Butler), Roy Dean (Footman), Charles Fredericks (King), Lily Kemble-Cooper (Lady Ambassador), Barbara Pepper (Doolittle's Dance Partner), Ayllene Gibbons (Fat Woman at Pub), Baroness Rothschild (Queen of Transylvania), Ben Wright (Footman at Ball), Oscar Beregi (Greek Ambassador), Buddy Bryan (Prince), Grady Sutton, Orville Sherman, Harvey Dunn, Barbara Morrison, Natalie Core, Helen Albrecht, Diana Bourbon (Ascot Types), Moyna MacGill (Lady Boxington), Colin Campbell (Ascot Gavotte), Marjory Hawtrey, Paulie Clark, Allison Daniell (Ad Libs at Ascot), Betty Blythe (Ad Lib at Ball), Nick Navarro (Dancer), Tom Cound, William Beckley (Footmen), Alan Napier (Ambassador), Geoffrey Steele (Taxi Driver), Jennifer Crier (Mrs. Higgins' Maid), Henry Daniell (Prince Gregor of Transylvania), Pat O'Moore (Man), Victor Rogers (Policeman), Michael St. Clair (Bartender), Brendon Dillon (Leaning Man), Olive Reeves-Smith (Mrs. Hopkins), Miriam Schiller (Landlady), Elzada Wilson, Jeanne Carson, Buddy Shea, Jack Goldie, Sid Marion, Stanley Fraser, George Pelling, Colin Kenny, Phyllis Kennedy, LaWana Backer, Monika Henried, Anne Dore, Pauline Drake, Shirley Melline, Wendy Russell, Meg Brown, Clyde Howdy, Nicholas Wolcuff, Martin Eric, John Mitchum (Ad Libs at Church), Maj. Sam Harris (Guest at Ball)

Synopsis

A chance meeting between two noted British linguists, Prof. Henry Higgins and Col. Hugh Pickering, leads to a wager that will test Higgins' skills. After they hear a cockney flower girl caterwaul in the street, Higgins proposes to transform the girl, Eliza Doolittle, into a refined Victorian lady with an aristocratic accent. After some hesitation Eliza agrees to become their test case. Arduous training sessions in diction and manners follow, until her tutors agree that she is ready to try out her lessons in public. She charms the professor's mother at Ascot, but at one point the excitement of the race causes a brief relapse. Later, they squire her to a grand ball, and are amazed themselves to gaze upon the genteel lady they have molded. In fact, they are so taken with themselves that they forget all about Eliza, who storms out, angry and embarrassed. Higgins soon feels her absence, and realizes as he listens to early recordings of her untrained voice that he has fallen in love. Eliza returns, and begins to speak the phrases on the record. The professor, inwardly overjoyed, can only manage to order Eliza to bring his slippers.

Reviews
"*My Fair Lady* [is] a film that enchantingly conveys the rich endowments of the famous stage production in a fresh and flowing cinematic form. The happiest single thing about it is that Audrey Hepburn superbly justifies the decision of the producer, Jack L. Warner, to get her to play the title role that Julie Andrews so charmingly and popularly originated on the stage. All things considered, it is the brilliance of Miss Hepburn as the cockney waif ...that gives an extra touch of subtle magic and individuality to the film." (*New York Times*, October 22, 1964)

"I approached the movie version of *My Fair Lady* with considerable skepticism--how could Audrey Hepburn possibly make as charming an Eliza Doolittle as Julie Andrews? [The] mavelous fact of the matter is that *My Fair Lady* has survived very nearly intact. Miss Hepburn wisely makes no pretense of not owing much to her illustrious predecessor in the role, but her qualities as an actress and as a personality soon turn her Eliza into an utterly different, though no less captivating, creature than that of Miss Andrews." (*New Yorker*, October 31, 1964)

"It has riches of story, humor, acting and production values far beyond the average big picture. It is Hollywood at its best. Only incurably disputatious persons will consider it a defect of *Lady* on screen that Julie Andrews has been replaced by the better known Miss H. She is thoroughly beguiling as Eliza." (*Variety*, October 28, 1964)

Additional Reviews
America (November 7, 1964); *BFI/Monthly Film Bulletin* (March 1965); *Commonweal* (November 13, 1964); *Dance Magazine* (December 1964); *Esquire* (February 1965); *Film Daily* (October 22, 1964); *Films in Review* (November 1964); *Hollywood Reporter* (October 22, 1964); *Life* (November 20, 1964); *Motion Picture Herald Product Digest* (October 28, 1964); *National Review* (January 12, 1965); *The New Republic* (November 14, 1964); *Newsweek* (November 2, 1964); *Saturday Review* (November 14, 1964); *Sight and Sound* (Spring 1965); *Time* (October 30, 1964)

Commentary
When Audrey Hepburn died in 1993, many of the remembrances in the press ran a variation on *Entertainment Weekly's* headline--"Farewell, Fair Lady." The role of Eliza Doolittle is now considered one of her greatest

triumphs, but when filming began both audiences and the motion picture industry questioned her casting.

Throughout her career Audrey received overwhelmingly favorable press coverage--columnist Liz Smith wrote "I don't recall one unkind or bitchy word about Audrey Hepburn. In life, that is rare. In this business, a miracle!" *My Fair Lady* is the closest brush she had with an unflattering controversy, and there were indeed unkind words uttered and written. When the film was released critics and audiences cheered, but Hollywood was not as quick to forgive.

My Fair Lady came to the screen via Broadway, but the actual roots of the story date back to antiquity, and the Greek myth of Pygmalion and Galatea. George Bernard Shaw updated the story for his play *Pygmalion*, which was filmed in 1938 with Leslie Howard as the patronizing professor determined to make a lady out of cockney Wendy Hiller. Alan Jay Lerner and Frederick Loewe added music to the story, and *My Fair Lady* opened on Broadway in 1956. Rex Harrison played Professor Higgins opposite newcomer Julie Andrews as Eliza. The musical was a Tony Award-winning triumph that ran for six years at the Mark Hellinger Theater.

Jack L. Warner paid $5 million for the movie rights, and planned to spend $20 million on the production. At those prices he didn't want to take any chances with the material. He approached Cary Grant to play Higgins and Audrey Hepburn to play Eliza, two names that practically guaranteed big box office. But Grant refused the role, and told Warner that if Rex Harrison wasn't cast he wouldn't even see the movie! Audrey also said no at first, but later accepted the role of Eliza. She explained her reasons in a 1991 interview; "I understood the dismay of people who had seen Julie on Broadway. Julie made that role her own, and for that reason I didn't want to do the film when it was first offered. But Jack Warner never wanted to put Julie in the film. He was totally opposed to it, for whatever reason. Then I learned that if I turned it down, they would offer it to still another movie actress. So I felt I should have the same opportunity to play it as any other film actress."

But it was Audrey who bore the brunt of the public outcry caused by Warner's refusal to gamble with an unknown stage performer in a high-budget, high-profile feature film. Audrey's one million dollar salary also raised some eyebrows, and the rumble grew even louder when it was announced that Audrey would not do her own singing in the part, though this was not the plan from the beginning. Before production commenced Audrey began taking vocal lessons eight hours a day for five weeks with singing coach Susan Seton, and when rehersals began she was prepared to tackle the Lerner-Loewe score. She recorded every one of Eliza's songs, but the decision was later made to replace her vocals with those of Marni Nixon, a veteran vocal understudy who also dubbed the songs for Deborah Kerr in *The King and I* (1956) and for Natalie Wood in *West Side Story* (1961). "With Marni Nixon doing the singing," chided Hedda Hopper, Audrey Hepburn gives only half a performance."

According to George Cukor's biographer Patrick McGilligan, (see B315), Audrey was "devastated" when she heard the news, "yet the actress carried on with her dignity intact, her chin up." Weeks later, the entire cast and crew were devastated by the news of President John F. Kennedy's assassination. Cukor found out first, but was incapable of making the announcement. It was Audrey who borrowed a loudspeaker and said in a calm voice, "The President of the United States is dead." She paused. "Shall we have two minutes of silence, to pray or do whatever you feel is appropriate?" At the end of the two minutes, she said simply, "May he rest in peace." Said Cukor later, "I don't know how she did it."

Julie Andrews would not remain unknown in Hollywood for long. After losing *My Fair Lady* she accepted an offer from Disney to star in *Mary Poppins*, which became the other blockbuster film musical of 1964. When the Academy Award nominations were announced, the headline on the *Los Angeles Times* front page read "Julie Andrews Chosen, Audrey Hepburn Omitted." *My Fair Lady* was selected in twelve categories, but Audrey did not receive a nomination as Best Actress. *Mary Poppins* received thirteen nominations, including one for Julie Andrews.

The story snowballed. Audrey accepted a last-minute invitation to present the Best Actor award after Patricia Neal suffered a series of strokes. Her sportsmanship was lauded in the trade newspapers, and she took the stage to the longest ovation of the evening. She opened the envelope and exclaimed "And the winner is Rex Harrison for *My Fair Lady*!" The moment could not have been scripted any better. Harrison took the stage, hugged Audrey five times, and diplomatically ended his remarks with "Deep love to--uh, well, two fair ladies."

Julie Andrews won the Oscar for Best Actress, and received a bouquet of flowers the following day from Audrey. "I think Audrey should have been nominated," said Julie at the time. Robert Windeler's Andrews biography (see B366) records that she was disappointed at losing the role of Eliza, and "if it had been anyone but Audrey, she would have been blazing mad." Both praised the other's performance, and the feud that certain scribes tried so desperately to fuel never came to pass.

Rex Harrison saved his thoughts on the subject for his book *A Damned Serious Business* (1991--see B283). He referred to Audrey's stepping in for Julie as "an unenviable task," but "in the end she gave an enchanting performance, and contributed greatly to the film's success and lasting popularity." He called Julie Andrews' Oscar win "a kind of rough justice, Hollywood style." Stanley Holloway, who also worked in both the stage and film productions, wrote in his autobiography *Wiv A Little Bit O'Luck* (see B290) that he is frequently asked to compare his "daughters." "I just think I was lucky to have appeared with them both," he writes. "I once told Rex that he should regard himself as lucky too...'Rex,' I said, 'you can't put a cigarette paper's width between them for quality.' He looked at me, smiled, and nodded. He knew."

If she was offended by the Academy snub, Audrey never said so for the record. Her only comment on the matter regarded a telegram she received from Katharine Hepburn after the nominations were announced. "She said not to worry, that one day I would be nominated for a role that wasn't nearly so demanding. Three years later I was nominated for *Wait Until Dark*, when I liked myself better in *Two For the Road* that same year" (see B237). She would later select *My Fair Lady* as her personal favorite of her movies (though *Roman Holiday* gets the nod in other articles). Julie Andrews would later be aced out of her other Broadway triumph by Hollywood as well when Vanessa Redgrave played Guinevere in the film version of *Camelot* (1967).

F22 HOW TO STEAL A MILLION (20th Century-Fox, 1966; 127 minutes; color)

Available on Videocassette (Magnetic Video)

Credits
Directed by William Wyler; Written by Harry Kurnitz, based on the story "Venus Rising" by George Bradshaw; Produced by Fred Kohlmar; Photographed by Charles Lang (Panavision, DeLuxe Color); Music by Johnny Williams; Edited by Robert Swink; Production Designed by Alexander Trauner; Costumes by Hubert de Givenchy; Makeup by Alberto De Rossi and Freddie Williamson

Cast
AUDREY HEPBURN (NICOLE BONNET), Peter O'Toole (Simon Dermott), Eli Wallach (David Leland), Hugh Griffith (Charles Bonnet), Charles Boyer (De Solnay), Fernand Gravey (Grammont), Marcel Dalio (Senor Paravideo), Jacques Marin (Chief Guard), Moustache (Guard), Roger Treville (Auctioneer), Eddie Malin (Insurance Clerk), Bert Bertram (Marcel), Louise Chevalier (Cleaning Woman in Museum), Remy Longa (Young Man), Gil Delamare (Stunt Double for Audrey Hepburn)

Synopsis
Charles Bonnet, the latest in a long line of master art forgers, donates

one of his father's best works, a faux Cellini Venus, to a Paris museum despite his daughter Nicole's objections. Later, Nicole surprises a tuxedo-clad burglar in her father's workshop. She can't call the police because her father's hobby might be discovered, so she ends up driving the man--Simon Dermott--back to his hotel. Dermott is actually an inspector who is gathering evidence against Bonnet, but his attraction to Nicole complicates the assignment.

Charles learns that the museum plans to conduct a test on the Venus for insurance purposes, which he knows will expose the statue as a fake. To save her father from jail, Nicole asks Simon to steal it, unaware of his true identity. Simon, intrigued by the challenge and now smitten with Miss Bonnet, agrees to try. During the heist, which is successful, Simon reveals his real motivation for taking the job. He agrees to keep Charles's secret safe if he promises never to forge another masterpiece.

Reviews
"Absolute, unabashed deception, not only as a plot element but as a method of wooing the audience into charmed and uncontentious belief, is beautifully and cheerfully practiced in this wholly ingratiating film...cheers all around for everybody." (*New York Times*, July 15, 1966)

"How strangely derivative the whole thing is. At casual first glance it looks like another of those lovely figures for gamine and guy, played breezily in Paris or Rome: *Love in the Afternoon, Gigi, Sabrina, Roman Holiday*. Casting accounts for much of the sense of deja vu. Audrey Hepburn is at it again, dressed to the nines by Givenchy, bejeweled by Cartier, terribly chic and terribly anxious to protect that irrepressible old forger of a father." (*Newsweek*, July 2, 1966)

"An entertainment treat which should captivate every type audience and fits patly into the class category." (*Variety*, July 13, 1966)

Additional Reviews
Christian Science Monitor (July 22, 1966); *Commonweal* (August 19, 1966), *Film Daily* (June 30, 1966); *Film Quarterly* (Winter 1966-1967); *Filmfacts* (September 1, 1966); *Films and Filming* (October 1966); *Films in Review* (August-September 1966); *Hollywood Reporter* (June 30, 1966); *Illustrated London News* (August 20, 1966); *Life* (August 5, 1966); *The London Times* (August 4, 1966); *Motion Picture Herald Product Digest* (July 13, 1966); *New Statesman* (August 5, 1966); *The New Yorker* (July 16, 1966); *Playboy* (October 1966); *Time* (July 22, 1966); *The Village Voice* (August 11, 1966)

Commentary

The film's original title was "How to Steal a Million Dollars and Live Happily Ever After", but it was abbreviated before release much to the relief of movie marquee letterers everywhere. The title wasn't all that was too long--130 minutes is a bit much to stretch a lightweight caper movie, but the material is expertly played and still remains one of Audrey's (and Peter O'Toole's) most underrated films.

Though she has played a nun and a prostitute, an Indian and a sprite, it is roles like Nicole Bonnet, as the *Newsweek* review observed, that will forever be identified with Audrey Hepburn. There is Paris, once again, and there is Audrey in some very chic Givenchy outfits, a woman desired by experienced men of the world, but still an innocent young girl at heart whose closest male relationship is dear old dad. The mood is breezy and light, no one gets hurt, and Audrey's character is in love and plans to live happily ever after as the closing credits roll.

The most memorable and well-executed sequence in *How to Steal a Million* is the museum break-in, which merits comparison to *Rififi* (1954) and *Topkapi* (1964), the standard-bearers of the genre. The burglary is meticulously devised and superbly directed by William Wyler, who returns to romantic comedy for the first time since *Roman Holiday*. The aim was clearly to blend comedy and suspense as masterfully as *Charade*; *How To Steal a Million* is too prolonged and a bit too coy, but with Audrey, Peter O'Toole and Charles Boyer at their best and Wyler behind the camera the result is a beguiling film that rises above its flaws.

After spending eleven days together in a tiny closet for one of the film's key scenes, Audrey and Peter O'Toole could not help but get to know each other well. O'Toole would often tell Audrey jokes just before Wyler yelled "Action!" and then wait for her to break up during the scene. Countless takes were ruined, and there were moments when Audrey had to hold in her giggles until her stomach hurt. "They react on each other like laughing gas," said Wyler, "and the trouble is they're in almost every scene together."

There's a marvelous inside joke in the scene preceding the robbery, when Simon dresses Nicole as a cleaning woman so she will have access to the museum after hours. He looks at her in the drab uniform and drolly observes "That does it." "Does what?" she answers. "Well, it gives Givenchy the night off." Many Hepburn fans may have also taken special note of the scene in which Audrey drops Peter O'Toole off at the Ritz in Paris, the same place where she met Gary Cooper in *Love in the Afternoon* (1957).

F23 TWO FOR THE ROAD (20th Century-Fox, 1967; 112 minutes; color)

Available on Videocassette and Laserdisc (CBS/Fox)
Awards: Academy Award nomination for Best Screenplay

Credits

Directed and produced by Stanley Donen; Written by Frederic Raphael; Photographed by Christopher Challis (Panavision, DeLuxe Color); Music by Henry Mancini; Edited by Richard Marden and Madeleine Gug; Art Direction by Willy Holt and Marc Frederic; Set Direction by Roger Volper; Costumes by Hardy Amies, Ken Scott, Michele Posier, Paco Rabanne, Mary Quant, Foale and Tuffin; Special Effects by Gilbert Manzon; Makeup by Alberto De Rossi and Georges Bouban

Cast

AUDREY HEPBURN (JOANNA WALLACE), Albert Finney (Mark Wallace), Eleanor Bron (Cathy Manchester), William Daniels (Howard Manchester), Claude Dauphin (Maurice Dalbret), Nadia Gray (Francoise Dalbret), Georges Descrieres (David), Gabrielle Middleton (Ruth Manchester), Jacqueline Bisset (Jackie), Judy Cornwell (Pat), Irene Hilda (Yvonne de Florac), Dominique Joos (Sylvia), Kathy Chelimsky (Caroline), Carol Van Dyke (Michelle), Karyn Balm (Simone), Mario Verdon (Palamos), Roger Dann (Gilbert, "Comte de Florac"), Libby Morris (American Lady), Yves Barsacq (Police Inspector), Helene Tossy (Mme. Solange), Jean-Francois Lalet (Boat Officer), Albert Michel (Customs' Officer), Joanna Jones, Sophia Torkeli, Patricia Viterbo, Olga George Picot, Clarissa Hillel (Joanna's Touring Friends), Cathy Jones

Synopsis

The ten-year marriage of Mark and Joanna Wallace is on the rocks. In flashback they recall their first meeting, memorable moments in their courtship and early wedded life, their travels through Europe, their broken vow never to have children, and the increasing tensions that led to both of them having extra-marital affairs. They discuss divorce, but choose instead to stay together and concentrate on the love that still exists between them.

Reviews

"*Two For the Road* doesn't tell us very much about marriage and life...However, there are some precious moments of romantic charm in the bitter account of domestic discord amid surroundings that should inspire nothing but delight." (*New York Times*, April 28, 1967)

"The trip's real point is the slick Hollywood surface, which apparently dazzled the filmmakers out of deciding on a core for their work. Hepburn, whose limitless sophistication could have made those lovers' quarrels into monuments of wit, and Finney, who lacks couth but has ample energy and acting talent, are both abused in this epic of wanderlust." (*Newsweek*, May 15, 1967)

"Miss Hepburn is amazing in her ability to portray a very young girl, a just-pregnant wife of two years, and a beginning-to-be-bored wife of five years. Helped partially by variations in her hairdos but mostly by her facial expressions, she's completely believable, lovable and totally delightful." (*Variety*, May 3, 1967)

Additional Reviews
America (May 27, 1967); *BFI/Monthly Film Bulletin* (September 1967); *Christian Century* (July 19, 1967); *Commonweal* (May 12, 1967); *Film Daily* (April 28, 1967); *Film Quarterly* (Summer 1967); *Films and Filming* (September 1967); *Films in Review* (May 1967); *Hollywood Reporter* (May 18, 1967); *Life* (May 12, 1967); *Motion Picture Herald Product Digest* (May 10, 1967); *The New Republic* (May 27, 1967); *Saturday Review* (May 6, 1967); *Sight and Sound* (Autumn 1967); *The Village Voice* (May 11, 1967)

Commentary
"Audrey Hepburn Swings? You're Kidding" was the headline of a 1967 *Ladies Home Journal* article about *Two for the Road*, which expressed bemused shock at Audrey's donning of blue jeans, miniskirts and swimsuits for her portrayal of Joanna Wallace. "We knew she had legs, but we'd never seen so much of them." (see B097)

Much of the hoopla about this role, which was hailed as a drastic departure from her screen image, centered on Audrey's use of profanity, and her consent to do a nude scene. One of the trade papers even ran an editorial on it, and Audrey herself said it was "inconceivable" that it could have been offered to her ten years ago, or even five. Watching the film today, one could not be blamed for wondering what the fuss was about; the profanity amounted to the word "bastard," uttered twice. The nude scene would not even be labeled as such now, and could be shown during the family hour on television unedited.

However, there are also scenes, such as when Audrey starts clucking like a chicken in one of the film's funniest moments, that seem hard to connect with the girl who was once Princess Anne. Another more interesting departure is her being cast opposite a younger man. Albert Finney was seven years her junior, and according to *Ladies Home Journal* they carried on "like a pair of kids with a perfect understanding

Audrey as Jo Stockton in *Funny Face* (1957).

and a shorthand of jokes and references that closed out everybody else." "Albie's just plain wonderful, and that's all there is to it," raved Audrey. The article reported that when Mel Ferrer visited the set, "Audrey and Albie got rather formal and a little awkward, as if now they had to behave like grown-ups." Such articles led to the usual rumors of an off-screen affair.

Director Stanley Donen does his best Jean-Luc Godard imitation in filming *Two for the Road* in the style of the French New Wave. The narrative is developed in a non-linear format, with jump cuts back and forth in time between scenes connected only by the film's central metaphor--the road. Every episode in the lives of Mark and Joanna occurs during or just after a road trip. The technique is not as murky as in European films from the same genre--the audience can easily keep track of the point at which the Wallaces' relationship has developed by the kind of car Mark drives, and by the fashions and hairstyles worn by Joanna. Nothing by Givenchy this time, but the metallic dress worn by Audrey at a party scene late in the film is as memorable as any in her haute couture history, and emphasized the fact that at age 38 she was still one of the most beautiful women in film.

In 1976 producer Richard Zanuck called Audrey's performance in *Two for the Road* the best by an American actress in the 1960's. Albert Finney's notices were not as positive, but to be fair his character did not have the same opportunity to grow as Audrey's. Today the film has a devoted cult following, but has also acquired a reputation as being dated--the *Motion Picture Guide* compared it to "an inexpensive wine that has not aged well." (see B323) Henry Mancini contributed his third outstanding score to an Audrey Hepburn film, after being asked to do so by Audrey herself.

F24 WAIT UNTIL DARK (Warner Bros., 1967; 107 minutes; color)

Available on Videocassette and Laserdisc (Warner Home Video)
Awards: Academy Award nomination for Best Actress (Audrey Hepburn)

Credits
Directed by Terence Young; Written by Robert Carrington and Jane-Howard Carrington, based on the play by Frederick Knott; Produced by Mel Ferrer;Photographed by Charles Lang (Technicolor); Music by Henry Mancini; Edited by Gene Milford; Art Direction by George Jenkins; Set Direction by George James Hopkins; "Wait Until Dark" music and lyrics by Henry Mancini, Jay Livingston and Ray Evans (sung by Bobby Darin); Makeup by

Gordon Bau

Cast
AUDREY HEPBURN (SUSY HENDRIX), Alan Arkin (Roat),
Richard Crenna (Mike Talman), Efrem Zimbalist, Jr. (Sam
Hendrix), Jack Weston (Carlino), Samantha Jones (Lisa), Julie
Herrod (Gloria), Frank O'Brien (Shatner), Gary Morgan (Boy), Jean
Del Val (The Old Man)

Synopsis
Commercial artist Sam Hendrix returns to New York from a business trip
and at the airport is given a child's doll by a mysterious woman. After the
woman disappears, Sam takes the doll home to his wife Susy, unaware
that it contains a fortune in heroin. Mr. Roat, the intended recipient of the
drug, tracks the doll to Sam's apartment and enlists two associates to
retrieve it. Because Susy is blind, the crooks don't anticipate much
trouble. After luring Sam away, Roat and his cohorts show up at the
apartment posing as police officers. They convince Susy that the doll is
important evidence in a murder investigation, but when she tries to find it
for them she discovers that Gloria, a little girl who lives upstairs, has stolen
it.

Susy learns that the phone number given to her by one of the
bogus cops is actually that of a phone booth across the street, and
realizes that something is amiss. The psychotic Roat kills his partners and
returns to the apartment prepared to murder Susy. When he attacks she
tries to even the odds by smashing all the lights. By the time Sam and the
real police arrive Susy has earned the title she jokingly bestowed upon
herself earlier--"World's Champion Blind Lady."

Reviews
"It is just [a] barefaced melodrama, without character revelation of any
sort, outside of the demonstration of a person with the fortitude to
overcome an infirmity. But the sweetness with which Miss Hepburn plays
the poignant role, the quickness with which she changes and the skill
with which she manifests terror attract sympathy and anxiety to her, and
give her genuine solidity in the final scenes." (*New York Times*, October
27, 1967)

"Valiant is the name of Audrey through all this. Miss Hepburn's
performance is appealing and expert, with as much humor and grace as
anyone could bring to bear on the barely sufferable dialogue."
(*Newsweek*, November 6, 1967)

"*Wait Until Dark* emerges as an exciting suspense drama, effective in casting, scripting, direction and genuine emotional impact. Audrey Hepburn stars [in] a superior performance." (*Variety*, October 17, 1967)

Additional Reviews
America (December 9, 1967); *BFI/Monthly Film Bulletin* (August 1968); *Film Daily* (October 24, 1967); *Film Quarterly* (Spring 1968); *Films and Filming* (August 1968); *Films in Review* (December 1967); *Hollywood Reporter* (October 20, 1967); *Motion Picture Herald Product Digest* (October 25, 1967); *Senior Scholastic* (October 19, 1967); *The Village Voice* (November 2, 1967)

Commentary
Wait Until Dark was based on the 1966 hit Broadway play that starred Lee Remick as Susy. Writer Frederick Knott also wrote the Alfred Hitchcock film *Dial M for Murder* (1954), and *Wait Until Dark* also has a strong Hitchcock feel; the doll becomes the "McGuffin," or the generic object that launches the plot. Susy is the innocent party caught in a web of intrigue and danger, and the film builds to a thrilling climax reminiscent of the Master's best works. The events preceding and following Alan Arkin's lunge from darkness at Audrey comprise a superb set piece that is one of the most frightening scenes in film history. Some movie theaters further accentuated the suspense by shutting off all the house lights for the final 15 minutes.

The theatrical roots of the material are apparent in its concentration of the action into one set. But director Terence Young moves fluidly through the rooms of Susy's apartment and diminishes the impression of watching a play on film.

To prepare for the role of Susy Hendrix, Audrey studied with students from the Lighthouse For the Blind School in New York City. Reviews of her performance, even among critics who disliked the film, were overwhelmingly favorable. During filming, director Young felt that the famous Hepburn eyes were too expressive to suggest blindness, and fitted her with special contact lenses. Audrey detested the irritating lenses, but carried on despite the pain. When she learned that Givenchy would not be allowed to provide her costumes this time, she bought the clothes she wore in the film off the rack during a Paris shopping spree.

Most of Audrey's previous films were made in Europe, which was her preference. She was reluctant about shooting *Wait Until Dark* in New York, and conceded only after demanding and receiving a concession of her own; every day at 4 p.m. production would cease so the company could enjoy a traditional British teatime. Terence Young, a fellow Brit, was in favor of the idea, but the studio was not amused.

A "tea garden" was built on the soundstage, and soon the cast and crew began looking forward to the convivial breaks. Friendships quickly developed and the set was alive with practical jokes and high spirits. The only friction that pervaded the happy workplace was between Audrey and Mel Ferrer, who was also the film's producer. Their marriage was now in serious trouble, and they divorced soon after the film was completed.

Wait Until Dark was a huge box office success, and brought Audrey her fifth and final Academy Award nomination. She lost to the "other" Hepburn in Guess Who's Coming to Dinner. This would be Audrey's last movie appearance for almost ten years.

F25 ROBIN AND MARIAN (Columbia, 1976; 106 minutes; color)

Available on Videocassette (Columbia)

Credits
Directed by Richard Lester; Written by James Goldman; Produced by Denis O'Dell; Photographed by David Watkin (Technicolor); Music by John Barry; Edited by John Victor Smith; Production Designed by Michael Stringer; Art Direction by Gil Parrondo; Costumes by Yvonne Blake; Special Effects by Eddie Fowlie; Makeup by Jose Antonio Sanchez; Stunts by Joaquin Parra and Miguel Pedregosa (fights by Ian McKay and William Hobbs)

Cast
Sean Connery (Robin Hood), AUDREY HEPBURN (MAID MARIAN), Robert Shaw (Sheriff of Nottingham), Richard Harris (King Richard), Nicol Williamson (Little John), Denholm Elliot (Will Scarlett), Kenneth Haigh (Sir Ranulf de Pudsey), Ronnie Barker (Friar Tuck), Ian Holm (King John), Bill Maynard (Mercadier), Esmond Knight (Old Defender), Veronica Quilligan (Sister Mary), Peter Butterworth (Surgeon), John Barrett (Jack), Kenneth Cranhan (Jack's Apprentice), Victoria Merida Roja (Queen Isabella), Montserrat Julio (1st Sister), Victoria Hernandez Sanguino (2nd Sister), Margarita Minguillon (3rd Sister)

Synopsis
It has been twenty years since Robin Hood and Little John left England to join King Richard at the Crusades. After the king loses his sanity and his life in short order, the legendary heroes are free to leave Europe and head home. They find Sherwood Forest little changed, and are greeted by original Merry Men Will Scarlett and Friar Tuck. Alan-A-Dale has passed

away, but his folk tunes of Robin's exploits have made the outlaw famous throughout England.

Robin Hood is eager to be reunited with Maid Marian, but is surprised to learn that she is now running a nunnery! She is both thrilled and outraged to see him again, but refuses to leave the other nuns. King John and the Sheriff of Nottingham are still in charge, and have ordered all those still loyal to Rome to be exiled. Though she claims to neither want nor need his help, Robin and Little John slip into Nottingham castle and release the nuns who have already been captured, and take Marian back to Sherwood Forest.

The nobleman Sir Ranulf de Pudsey hears of Robin's return and decides to boost his reputation by bringing the aging bandit to justice. He is unsuccessful. Pudsey then joins forces with the Sheriff, who has never forgotten the indignities he suffered in Sherwood. Both sides prepare for war, until Robin proposes to the Sheriff that they fight one on one, to cut down on bloodshed. The sheriff agrees. Robin kills his opponent but is mortally wounded, and is taken by Marian to the abbey. Sir Ranulf orders his army to attack, and the war both leaders hoped to avoid is waged anyway. Marian pours a glass of wine laced with poison, which she gives to Robin and then drinks from herself, knowing she could not bear to go on without him again. Robin's last act is to shoot an arrow through the window, and to instruct Little John to bury them where the arrow lands.

Reviews

"The return of Audrey Hepburn to movies is a genuine event, something to shout about, and mean it." (*Los Angeles Herald-Examiner*, March 12, 1976)

"The film depends almost entirely on the presences of Mr. Connery and Miss Hepburn, to generate responses that are not otherwise supported...the intensity of the images they project are such that we are convinced that their late-August love is important and final." (*New York Times*, March 12, 1976)

"*Robin and Marian* is a film that must stand or fall on the strength of its stars...Audrey Hepburn has not made a movie in seven years. The moment she appears on screen is startling, not for her thorough, gentle command, not even for her beauty, which seems heightened, renewed. It is rather that we are reminded of how long it has been since an actress has so beguiled us and captured our imagination. Hepburn is unique and, now, almost alone." (*Time*, March 22, 1976)

Additional Reviews

America (March 20, 1976); *BFI Monthly Film Bulletin* (May 1976); *Christian Century* (June 23, 1976); *Film Bulletin* (March 1976); *Film Heritage* (1976); *Film Illustrated* (June 1976); *Films and Filming* (June1976); *Films in Review* (May 1976); *Hollywood Reporter* (March 11, 1976); *Independent Film Journal* (March 17, 1976); *The Los Angeles Times* (March 28, 1976); *Millimeter* (May 1976); *Motion Picture Herald Product Digest* (March 24, 1976); *Movietone News* (June 1976); *The New Republic* (March 27, 1976); *New Statesman* (May 28, 1976); *New York* (March 29, 1976); *The New Yorker* (March 22, 1976); *Newsweek* (March 22, 1976); *Saturday Review* (April 17, 1976); *Social Policy* (November - December 1976); *Variety* (March 10, 1976); *The Village Voice* (March 29, 1976)

Commentary

"How can it be a comeback when I never really left?" insisted Audrey as interview after interview heralded her return to the movies after a nine-year absence. "I had no intention of staying away so long," she told columnist Liz Smith. "It happened mainly because I felt my family needed me, and I, them, more than I needed to make movies. My life today is basically guided by my husband's free time."

Audrey, then 46, was married to Dr. Andrea Dotti, an Italian psychiatrist, and quite content to remain in their Roman villa and cook pasta for her family and friends. She rejected countless scripts between 1968 and 1975, but was lured back for *Robin and Marian* because of the convenient shooting location and schedule, the imaginative script by James Goldman, and the opportunity to work with Sean Connery. The film ended up receiving mixed to favorable reviews, but Audrey's return was greeted as a cause for celebration. "It couldn't come at a more welcome time, when the film industry is suffering from a lack of both women's roles and charismatic actresses to play them." wrote the *Dallas Morning News* (see B236). *The Washington Star* simply stated, "After all these years, Audrey Hepburn still has the biggest eyes and the loveliest cheekbones in the business" (see B134).

Writer Goldman utilized the same "history with a twist" approach he brought to *The Lion in Winter* (1968), maintaining the dignity of the characters but deflating their larger-than-life image. The scene in which Robin and Little John rescue the nuns, for instance, shows them to be true heroes, but as they struggle to hurl their old bones over a castle wall they are revealed as all too human as well. When the world didn't end after Audrey uttered the word "bastard" in *Two For the Road*, she was then free to unleash a few more choice epithets as Maid Marian, without causing headlines. But the most memorable dialogue may be Robin's classic response when Marian asks why he never wrote in twenty years--"I don't know how."

The film was shot in 36 days, which Audrey at first thought would be an advantage. However, the frenetic pace set by director Richard Lester was quite different from her previous experience, what *Time* called "the more leisurely tempo of old-style Hollywood filmmakers." The director refused to slacken speed for retakes when she wanted, and insisted on shooting a scene when Audrey was suffering from a sore throat and laryngitis. She extolled his style in print--"he is unencumbered by ego or dramatics, and a whiz-bang with his many cameras and single takes."--but her actual opinion may not have been as complimentary, especially after she was dumped into the river on a horsecart that was not supposed to turn over, an occurrence viewed by Lester as a stroke of luck that he used in the final print. Said one studio executive in *Time*: "Audrey could get along with Hitler, but Lester is not in her scrapbook of unforgettable characters" (see B211).

F26 BLOODLINE (Paramount, 1979; 116 minutes; color)

Available on Videocassette (Paramount)

Credits
Directed by Terence Young; Written by Laird Koenig, based on the novel by Sidney Sheldon; Produced by David V. Picker and Sidney Beckerman; Photographed by Freddie Young (Movielab Color); Music by Ennio Morricone; Edited by Bud Molin; Production Designed by Ted Haworth; Costumes by Enrico Sabbatini, Hubert de Givenchy

Cast
AUDREY HEPBURN (ELIZABETH ROFFE), Ben Gazzara (Rhys Williams), James Mason (Sir Alec Nichols), Claudia Mori (Donatella), Irene Papas (Simonetta Palazza (Michelle Phillips (Vivian Nichols), Maurice Ronet (Charles Martin), Romy Schneider (Helene Martin), Omar Sharif (Ivo Palazzi), Beatrice Straight (Kate Erling), Gert Frobe (Inspector Max Hornung), Wolfgang Preiss (Julius Prager), Marcel Bozzuffi (Man in Black), Pinkas Braun (Dr. Wal), Wulf Kessler (Young Sam Roffe)

Synopsis
Sam Roffe, president of a multi-national pharmaceutical corporation, is killed while mountain-climbing. It is first determined to be an accident, but Inspector Max Hornung later deduces that Roffe was murdered. Sam's daughter Elizabeth assumes control of the company, and while traveling through Europe she immediately becomes a target as well. Suspicion

falls on the Roffe cousins, all of whom want to go public with the company and sell their stock at a huge profit. Since this would be against her father's wishes, Elizabeth rejects their advice and decides to keep the company within the family.

As Inspector Hormung investigates the background of the cousins, more attempts are made on Elizabeth's life. Hormung is able to connect these attempts to a series of murders on prostitutes, which are recorded on snuff films, and reveal the guilty party for both crimes as deranged cousin Alec.

Reviews

"Terence Young is a director of some comic style, but though *Bloodline* is often laughable, it has no sense of humor. It's the kind of fiction that is glumly disapproving of its own sordid details. *Bloodline* takes Miss Hepburn's Givenchy clothes more seriously than it does the actress who wears them, not always becomingly." (*New York Times*, June 29, 1979)

"If I were Sidney Sheldon, I'd demand to have my name removed from the title of this torpid turkey." (*Newsweek*, July 9, 1979)

"Freddie Young's camera mostly stays at a respectful distance from Audrey Hepburn, whose prim, unflamboyant character sets exceedingly narrow emotional parameters for the story. Though it would take several pictures on the level of *Bloodline* to seriously damage her stature, it's a shame she picks something like this now that she works so seldom." (*Variety*, July 2, 1979)

Additional Reviews
New Leader (July 30, 1979); *New Yorker* (July 16, 1979), *Time* (July 16, 1979)

Commentary
"The book was fun, didn't you think? It should give people a good time as a movie too. Plenty happens in it anyway, and the director (Terence Young) is a master at this kind of thing." (see B133) Thus Audrey explained her reasons for starring in the most poorly-received film of her career. She was certainly correct about Young, who directed her in the superb thriller *Wait Until Dark*, and also helmed the first three James Bond films. But considering that neither Audrey nor Young needed the money or the work at the time, and that both had previously shown exceptional taste in selecting material, their involvement in this very seedy business is difficult to understand.

At first Audrey turned the part of Elizabeth down, but Young was persistent. "I spent two weeks persuading her to accept the principle that she might make another movie. The next step was persuading her to read the script. Then persuading her that it was a good script. Then persuading her that she wouldn't wreck her child's life by working again." he told the *Los Angeles Times*. Her acceptance was welcomed not only by Young but also by writer Sidney Sheldon. Elizabeth Roffe was 23 in Sheldon's book, but after he learned Audrey would play the role on screen he changed her age to 35 in the paperback edition of the book. Audrey was actually nearing 50 at the time, but this discrepancy is hardly the film's worst, and has nothing to do with its failure.

The globe-hopping story (London, Paris, New York, Switzerland) of intrigue among the rich and famous is typical Sidney Sheldon, and the cast of beautiful, aristocratic types certainly fit the mold--Michelle Phillips, James Mason, Romy Schneider, Omar Sharif and others turn up, each in their own subplot. Problem is, only some of the side stories are wrapped up, while others, such as the company's creation of an anti-aging drug and Sharif's adultery, are never resolved. The flashback to Elizabeth's father and his creation of the company seems to belong to another movie, as do the very explicit scenes in which the prostitutes are murdered. The paychecks must have been pretty good to attract such a roster. Gert Frobe emerges best as the intrepid inspector, but no one gets out of *Bloodline* with their dignity intact. Audrey picked up her now-standard $1 million plus a percentage of the gross, but very few kind words from critics.

F27 THEY ALL LAUGHED (Time-Life Films-Moon/20th Century-Fox/United Artists Classics, 1981; 115 minutes; color)

Available on Videocassette and Laserdisc (Vestron)

Credits
Directed and written by Peter Bogdanovich; Produced by Geroge Morfogen and Blaine Novak; Photographed by Robby Muller (DeLuxe Color); Music by Douglas Dilge; Edited by Scott Vickrey; Art Direction by Kert Lundell; Set Direction by Joe "Peppy" Bird

Cast
AUDREY HEPBURN (ANGELA NIOTES), Ben Gazzara (John Russo), John Ritter (Charles Rutledge), Colleen Camp (Christy Miller), Patti Hansen (Deborah "Sam" Wilson), Dorothy Stratten (Dolores Martin), George Morfogen (Leon Leondopolous), Blaine Novak (Arthur Brodsky), Sean Ferrer (Jose), Linda

MacEwen (Amy Lester), Glenn Scarpelli (Michael Niotes), Vassily Lambrinos (Stavros Niotes), Antonia Bogdanovich (Stefania Russo), Alexandra Bogdanovich (Georgina Russo), Sheila Stodden (Barbara Jo), Lisa Dunsheath (Tulips), Joyce Hyser (Sylvia), Elizabeth Pena (Rita), Riccardo Bertoni (Martin), Shawn Casey (Laura), Earl Poole Ball, Jo-El Sonnier, Eric Kaz, Ken Kosek, Larry Campbell, Lincoln Schleifer, John Sholle, Brigitte Catapano, Parris Bruckner, Vivien Landau, Lillian Silverstone, Steve Cole, Steven Fromewick, Tzi Ma, William Craft, William DeNIro, Kelly Donnally, Linda Ray, Andrea Weber, Spike Spigener, Nick Micskey, Robert Hawes, Michael McGifford, V Vittorio Tiburz, Alex MacArthur, George Cardini, Robert Skilling, Kennely Noble, Anthony Paige, Violetta Landek, Brandy Roven, Joan Lauren, Debora Lass, Noel King, Don Marino, John Murray, Sharon Spits, Marty Greene, Harry Matson, Brett Smrz, Brian Smrz, Alex Stevens, Victoria Van Der Kloot

Synopsis
New York's Odyssey Detective Agency is hired by two different clients to follow two women suspected of infidelity. Ladies' man John Russo trails Angela Niotes, the elegant wife of a wealthy Italian industrialist, while Charles Rutledge and Arthur Brodsky follow Dolores Martin, the beautiful young wife of a jealous husband. Their respective cases are complicated when John falls for Angela, and Charles falls for Dolores. After a brief fling Angela returns to her husband, but Charles and Dolores remain together.

Reviews
"The title is *They All Laughed*. Would that anybody could laugh...Any way you look at it--as a comedy, as moviemaking, as a financial investment, *They All Laughed* is an immodest disaster. Audrey Hepburn, whom Mr. Bogdanovich treats so shabbily that if this were a marriage instead of a movie, she'd have grounds for immediate divorce." (*New York Times*, November 20, 1981)

"Bogdanovich's insouciant script is not so much plot as poetry, a lyrical farce that restores friendliness to desire. Always good with actors, Bogdanovich gets adorable performances from everyone." (*Newsweek*, November 30, 1981)

"At 52 [Hepburn], the eternal gamine has become a figure of icy chic; the lilt in her voice now has the gravity of years; But she is still a radiant presence, and she blesses the end of *They All Laughed* with a display of poignant maturity. One would gladly pay to hear her read the Bel Air phone book. One would not be surprised to know that was Bogdanovich's next project." (*Time*, November 23, 1981)

Additional Reviews
Hollywood Reporter (November 30, 1981); *The Los Angeles Times* (December 17, 1981); *Variety* (August 21, 1981); *The Village Voice* (November 25, 1981)

Commentary
They All Laughed is best remembered now--by those who remember it at all--as Dorothy Stratten's last film. The former Playboy Playmate of the Year, and the mistress of the film's director Peter Bogdanovich, was murdered by her husband Paul Snider soon after *They All Laughed* was completed. The fact that her role as Dolores, a woman suspected of infidelity by a jealous husband, contained many parallels to her own tragically brief life, cast a shadow over what was intended as a lighthearted comedy.

The film's unique narrative structure was praised as stylish by some critics of the time, but most just found it irritating. There is no beginning-middle-end to the story; the audience just drifts in with the action already underway and is expected to catch up. It takes awhile to fall into sync with the non-linear script, which seems to unfold with little direction and meanders lazily toward a roundabout resolution. Twentieth Century-Fox was not enthused about the finished product, and refused to release the film. Bogdanovich was forced to buy it back from the studio and distribute it himself. It was during the interim that Stratten was killed, but even this did not provoke enough lurid interest to pick up the box office.

Audrey was top-billed though the role is a supporting one at best--her character doesn't speak until one hour into the film. The most enjoyable scenes are those Audrey shares with Ben Gazzara. Their impossible romance strikes a poignant chord, but buying Gazzara's seemingly limitless charm is a stretch. Audrey's son Sean has a few brief scenes as Dolores's paramour, and has one scene with his mother.

The film has little else to recommend; Bogdanovich makes good use of the New York City locations, John Ritter is given ample opportunity to indulge in the broad physical comedy that he peddled for years on *Three's Company*, and there are some competent country songs on the soundtrack performed by Colleen Camp.

F28 DIRECTED BY WILLIAM WYLER (Documentary, 1986; 58 minutes; color and black and white)

Credits

Directed and edited by Aviva Slesin; Produced by Catherine Tatge; Narration and interviews by A. Scott Berg

Cast (interviews with)

Bette Davis, Samantha Eggar, Greer Garson, Lillian Hellman, AUDREY HEPBURN, Charlton Heston, John Huston, Laurence Olivier, Gregory Peck, Ralph Richardson, Terence Stamp, Barbra Streisand, Billy Wilder, Talli Wyler and William Wyler

Synopsis

A tribute to director William Wyler consisting of interviews and excerpts from his many classic films.

Reviews

"*Directed by William Wyler* is full of informed admiration." (*New York Times*, September 20, 1986)

Commentary

William Wyler directed Audrey Hepburn in *Roman Holiday*, *The Children's Hour* and *How To Steal a Million*. He was also had the helm of numerous other timeless films, including *Wuthering Heights* (1939), *Mrs. Miniver* (1942), *The Best Years of Our Lives* (1946), and *Funny Girl* (1968). The director's daughter Catherine initiated this salute to his career, which was released in a New York theater to follow a new print of Wyler's 1936 film *Dodsworth*.

The Wyler reputation was not in need of rehabilitation, writes the *New York Times*, but it had suffered in the sixties and seventies when he was unfavorably compared to "auteurs," a term defined by the *Times* as "those directors whose work could be more easily identified as idiosyncratic." Wyler's ability to submerge instead of amplify his contribution is praised in the documentary, which includes an interview with the director himself conducted just one week before his death in 1981. Audrey recalls how Wyler "scared her into tears" on the set of *Roman Holiday*, but testifies to the director's talent of coaxing the best performances out of his actors.

F 29 LOVE AMONG THIEVES (ABC-TV, February 23, 1987; 100 minutes; color)

Credits

Directed by Roger Young; Written by Stephen Black,Sally Robinson and Henry Stern; Produced by Robert A. Papazian and Karen Mack; Photographed by Gayne Rescher; Music by Arthur B Rubinstein; Edited by James Mitchell; Production designed by Peter M. Wooley; Set Decorated by Donald Remacle; Costumes by Ann Lambert and Alexander D'Alessio; Miss Hepburn's gowns by Givenchy; Makeup by Del Acevado

Cast
AUDREY HEPBURN (CAROLINE DULAC), Robert Wagner (Mike Chambers), Jerry Orbach (Spicer), Patrick Bachau (Alan Channing), Brion James (Andre), Christopher Neame (Ian), Ismael Carlo (Mazo), Samantha Eggar (Solange DuLac), Alma Beltran (Airline Clerk), John Chandler (Hotel Clerk), Bob Cota (Waiter in Cafe), Dante D'Andre (Doctor), Joy Garrett (Hooker), Tonyo Melendez (Airport Official), Maurice Orozco (Goat Herder), Maria Rubell (Flight Attendant), Cynthia Steele (Theresa)

Synopsis
Caroline DuLac, a baroness and concert pianist, steals three jewel-incrusted Faberge` eggs from a San Francisco museum. The eggs were demanded as ransom for her kidnapped fiance`. She boards a plane for the Latin American city of Ladera, as per instructions, and is met by Mike Chambers. Caroline first believes that Mike is one of the kidnappers, until a mysterious man in a trenchcoat tries to kill her, and Mike comes to the rescue. They are then both captured by a band of Mexican banditos, who also may or may not be part of the scheme.

Reviews
"A romantic escapade without romance." (*Los Angeles Times,* February 23, 1987)

"Audrey Hepburn can do no wrong. She can, however, be done wrong. She is done so in *Love Among Thieves.* Hepburn, who deserves a Tiffany setting, is a sickly fragile Faberge` egg among this paste." (*New York*, February 23, 1987)

"Miss Hepburn, who has plodded through the rest of the picture in a single print dress with broad shoulders, does finally get to make an elegant exit in a red version of what appears to be her favorite Givenchy gown. She deserves several more in a range of colors for having to trudge through this turkey." (*New York Times*, February 23, 1987)

Additional Reviews
People (February 23, 1987), *Variety* (March 11, 1987)

Commentary

Critics, too young perhaps to remember *Mayerling*, called this Hitchcock-inspired thriller Audrey's TV-movie debut. The production is very similar to *Charade* in its blend of comedy and suspense, and its romance between an innocent woman caught up in dangerous circumstances, and a debonair man whose true identity is not revealed until the climax. However, the similarities ended there, as *Love Among Thieves* did not even approximate *Charade*'s sophisticated style and technical proficiency. There is, however, some novelty value in watching Audrey, now in the icon stage of her career, participating in silly sight gags, car chases and other assorted hijinks that are the antithesis of her screen image. As was often the case with her less successful feature films, she received more pity than blame in the scathing reviews.

F30 ALWAYS (Universal, 1989; 121 minutes; color)

Available on Videocassette and Laserdisc (MCA/Universal)

Credits

Directed by Steven Spielberg; Written by Jerry Belson, based on the screenplay "A Guy Named Joe" by Dalton Trumbo, from a story by Frederick Hazlitt Brennan, Chandler Sprague and David Boehm; Produced by Steven Spielberg, Frank Marshall and Kathleen Kennedy; Photographed by Mikael Salomon (Deluxe Color); Edited by Michael Kahn; Music by John Williams; Production Designed by James Bissell; Art Direction by Chris Burian-Mohr; Set Direction by Carl Stensel; Special Effects by Mike Wood and Industrial Light & Magic; Costumes by Ellen Mirojnick; Choreography by Bob Banas; Stunts by Steve Lambert; Makeup by James McCoy

Cast

Richard Dreyfuss (Pete Sandich), Holly Hunter (Dorinda Durston), Brad Johnson (Ted Baker), John Goodman (Al Yackey), AUDREY HEPBURN (HAP), Roberts Blossom (Dave), Keith David (Powerhouse), Ed Van Nuys (Nails), Marg Helgenberger (Rachel), Dale Dye (Fire Boss), Brian Haley (Alex), James Lashly (Charlie), Michael Steve Jones (Grey), Kim Robillard (Air Traffic Controller), Jim Sparkman (Dispatcher), Doug McGrath (Bus Driver), Joseph McCrossin (Mechanic), J.D. Souther (Singer), Gerry Rothschild (Carl the Barkeep), Loren Smothers (Bartender), Taleena Ottwell (Bar Girl)

Synopsis
Aerial firefighter Pete Sandrich's daredevil tactics are a constant source of worry for his long-time girlfriend, Dorinda. After his most recent brush with death, Dorinda gives him an ultimatum--either take a teaching job and retire from flying, or lose her for good. Pete agrees to stay on the ground and teach, but a serious fire forces him to fly one last mission. While saving the life of his friend and fellow pilot Al Yackey, Pete is killed in a crash. He wakes up in a bucolic setting and is greeted by Hap, a spirit who explains to Pete the meaning of life; as he had received inspiration to become a great pilot from spirits during his time on earth, so must he now provide the same inspiration to another. His earthly protege` is Ted Baker, a handsome but shy and awkward flyer who is in love with Dorinda!

Pete helps Ted become an ace flyer, but he is reluctant to help him find happiness with Dorinda. When Pete sees his former love fly into a life-threatening situation to rescue Ted, however, he realizes that her life must go on. He guides Dorinda through her dangerous mission, and then lets her go.

Reviews
"Although *Always* is filled with big, sentimental moments, it lacks the intimacy to make any of this very moving...The film's occasional moments of sweetness--Audrey Hepburn appearing briefly as an angel gently alerting Pete to his new status--are too easily upstaged by clutter and silly, implausible gags." (*New York Times*, December 22, 1989)

"...in a cameo as the heavenly sage who sends Dreyfuss back to earth, Audrey Hepburn is incandescent. Her dialogue is treacle, but she sells it with an effortless grace that shows why she is still a legend at sixty. Hepburn's brief appearance can't fill the void in *Always*, but her movie-star magic demonstrates precisely what the rest of the film is missing." (*Rolling Stone*, January 25, 1990)

"*Always* is a relatively small-scale, engagingly casual, somewhat silly, but always entertaining fantasy...Audrey Hepburn [is] alluring as always, but corny as a live-action fairy godmother." (*Variety*, December 20, 1989)

Additional Reviews
America (January 20, 1990); *New York* (January 8, 1990); *The New Yorker* (January 8, 1990); *Newsweek* (January 1, 1990); *People* (January 15, 1990); *Video* (August 1990)

Commentary
Always is a remake of the 1943 MGM tearjerker *A Guy Named Joe*, which

starred Spencer Tracy as Pete, the fallen pilot played in *Always* by Richard Dreyfuss, Holly Hunter in the Irene Dunne role, Van Johnson as the pilot who receives divine guidance (played in *Always* by Brad Johnson) and Ward Bond as Pete's best buddy, essayed in the remake by John Goodman.

Audrey received a "Special Appearance By" credit for her two brief scenes. She's been called an angel by admirers for decades, and was finally given the chance to become one--or did she? "Nobody knows what I am, even Steven Spielberg," she said in a 1989 interview. "I would say I'm a spirit more than anything. But not an extraterrestrial. No, it's just plain old me with a sweater on" (see B037). The character is supposedly called "Hap" according to the credits, but Dreyfuss seems to pronounce it "Hep" to accentuate the connection between actress and role.

In *A Guy Named Joe*, the spirit was played by Lionel Barrymore as a deceased military man referred to as "The General." Aside from the World War II backdrop, the casting in *Always* of the Heavenly adviser is the most notable departure from its parent. Barrymore sits behind a desk in a nondescript office, who apprises Spencer Tracy of his assignment the same way any commanding officer would give orders to an enlisted man. Hepburn, in keeping with the kinder, gentler time in which *Always* is set, eschews the spit and polish and gently eases Dreyfuss through his confusing transition. There are no offices in Spielberg's Heaven--Dreyfuss learns the afterlife routine in a lush, pastoral setting.

Always is an old-fashioned, uplifting story that was criticized for being just that. It's a lovely homage to the type of film, like *A Guy Named Joe*, that was made to entertain and comfort the nation during World War II. Except for updating the time and place the film adds nothing new to the mix, but who says it has to? Surprisingly, the song "Always" is not used in the film's soundtrack, which combines contemporary music with vintage songs from the 1940's and '50's. Instead, "Smoke Gets in Your Eyes" serves as the love theme.

This is Audrey's last film appearance, and after the missteps of *Bloodline* and *They All Laughed* it is both fitting and gratifying that she capped her career with a performance of beauty, simplicity and class.

5

Radio

R1   **The U.N. Story** (CBS) 1954; 30 minutes

Produced by the United Nations Children's Fund, this
program consisted of stories sent in from different nations
by U.N. workers. Bing Crosby served as narrator, and Audrey was
among the prestigious list of guest performers that also included
Kirk Douglas, Shirley Booth and Deborah Kerr.

R2   **Stagestruck** (CBS) May 2, 1954; 60 minutes

Mike Wallace hosted this review of the 1953-54 theatrical
season. Guests: Robert Sylvester, Claude Rains, Joan
Greenwood, Katharine Cornell, Rodgers and Hammerstein,
Mary Martin, Ezio Pinza, Alfred Drake, Yul Brynner, Noel Coward,
Hermione Gingold, Harry Belafonte, AUDREY HEPBURN, Mel
Ferrer, Shirley Booth, Eddie Cantor, Phil Silvers, Jack Benny,
Danny Kaye, Victor Borge, Carol Channing, Kaye Ballard, Ben
Gazzara and Basil Rathbone.

R3   **Friars Club Annual Testimonial Dinner**
(CBS) January 8, 1961; 30 minutes

Broadcast live from the Beverly Hilton Hotel. Hosted by Barry
Merkin, with George Jessel as toastmaster. Audrey is joined by
Jack Benny and George Burns in paying tribute to honoree Gary
Cooper, her leading man in *Love in the Afternoon* (1957--see
F12). A recording of the dinner that includes Audrey's recitation
of the poem "What is a Gary Cooper?" was released by the Friars

136 Audrey Hepburn

Club (see D2).

R4   This Is New York (WCBS) August 19, 1957; 30 minutes

Interview.

6

Television

T1   We, the People (NBC-TV) December 21, 1951; 30
minutes; black and white

This early talk show, a staple on radio for the previous twelve years,
invited both celebrities and ordinary citizens to discuss pivotal
experiences in their lives. Audrey recalls the Christmas of 1944 that she
spent in war-torn Arnhem, when her favorite gift was ten potatoes.

T2   Leave It To the Girls (NBC-TV) December 30, 1951; 30
minutes; black and white

Audrey was a guest on this light-hearted discussion show in which an all-
female panel squares off against one lone male for a debate about love
and relationships.

T3   Toast of the Town (CBS-TV) February 10, 1952; 60
minutes; black and white

Toast was a Sunday night staple from 1948 to 1971, and was responsible
for the television debuts of more performers than any other series in
history. Introduced by host Ed Sullivan as the star of Broadway's *Gigi*
(1951--see S4), Audrey is featured in a dramatic sketch entitled "Nine
Days A Queen."

T4   The Kate Smith Hour (NBC-TV) February 26, 1952; 60
minutes; black and white

A live weekly variety show hosted by Kate Smith, one of radio's favorite and most familiar personalities. The program features Broadway and Hollywood stars in excerpts from famous plays, as well as musical numbers and comedy sketches. Audrey plays a young lady who is impervious to the charms of the great lover Casanova in the dramatic sketch "The Girl From Venice."

T 5 CBS Television Workshop (CBS-TV), April 13, 1952; 30 minutes; black and white

 Audrey stars along with Carmen Matthews and Paul Langton in the drama "Rainy Day In Paradise Junction."

T 6 Toast of the Town (CBS) May 25, 1952; 60 minutes; black and white

Twelve years before they would co-star in *My Fair Lady* (1964), Audrey and Rex Harrison play Anne Boleyn and King Henry VIII in a scene from the Broadway play *Anne of a Thousand Days.*

T 7 The Today Show (NBC-TV) August 27, 1953; 60 minutes; black and white

Audrey is interviewed about *Roman Holiday* (1953--see F8)

T 8 Colgate Comedy Hour (NBC-TV) March 7, 1954; 60 minutes; black and white

This big-budget comedy series was the first successful counterprogramming to the mighty *Ed Sullivan Show*. Among its principal hosts were Eddie Cantor, Dean Martin and Jerry Lewis, Fred Allen, Abbott and Costello, Bob Hope and Jimmy Durante. In Hollywood, Eddie Cantor talks to Audrey on split-screen from New York, and presents her with the Look Movie Award for Best Actress of 1953 (see A6).

T 9 The 26th Annual Academy Awards (NBC-TV) March 25, 1954; 120 minutes; black and white

Audrey receives the Best Actress Oscar for her performance in *Roman*

Holiday. The award is presented by Jean Hersholt.

T10   The 27th Annual Academy Awards (NBC-TV)
March 30, 1955; 120 minutes; black and white

Audrey presents the Best Story and Best Screenplay awards to the writers of *Broken Lance* (story) and *The Country Girl* (screenplay).

T11   The Today Show (NBC-TV) November 9, 1955; 60
minutes; black and white

Audrey is interviewed with Mel Ferrer in Rome on the set of *War and Peace* (1956--see F10).

T12   The 28th Annual Academy Awards (NBC-TV)
March 21, 1956; 120 minutes; black and white

Appearing on film from London, Audrey presents the Best Picture Oscar to *Marty*.

T13   Mayerling (NBC-TV) February 4, 1957; 90 minutes; color

A made-for-television movie, broadcast live, in which Audrey plays Maria Vetsera opposite husband Mel Ferrer as Prince Rudolph (see F13).

T14   The 33rd Annual Academy Awards (NBC-TV) April
17, 1961; 120 minutes; black and white

Audrey presents the Best Picture Oscar to Billy Wilder, her director in *Sabrina* (1954--see F9), for his production of *The Apartment*.

T15   The 35th Annual Academy Awards (ABC-TV) April
8, 1963; 120 minutes; black and white

From Paris, Audrey presents the Oscar for Best Costume Design to the films *Whatever Happened To Baby Jane* (black and white) and *The Wonderful World of the Brothers Grimm* (color).

T16   The 37th Annual Academy Awards (ABC-TV) April

Audrey as Maria Vetsera opposite Mel Ferrer as Prince Rudolph in the 1957 television production of *Mayerling*.

5, 1965; 120 minutes; color

Despite being denied an Oscar nomination for her performance in *My Fair Lady*, (1964--see F21) Audrey agreed to replace an ailing Patricia Neal and present the Best Actor award, which went to her *Lady* co-star Rex Harrison.

T17 The 39th Annual Academy Awards (ABC-TV) April 10, 1967; 120 minutes; color

Audrey presents the Best Picture Oscar to Fred Zinnemann for *A Man For All Seasons.*

T18 The 40th Annual Academy Awards (ABC-TV) April 10, 1968; 120 minutes; color

Rod Steiger receives the Best Actor Oscar from Audrey for his work in *In the Heat of the Night.*

T19 The 1968 Tony Awards (NBC-TV) April 21, 1968;120 minutes; color

Audrey receives a special Tony Award, although she appeared in only two Broadway plays.

T20 A World of Love (CBS-TV) December 22, 1970; 90 minutes; color

The United Nations General Assembly Hall was filled with children for this UNICEF documentary film hosted by Bill Cosby and Shirley MacLaine. Celebrities including Barbra Streisand, Harry Belafonte, Richard Burton, Julie Andrews and Florence Henderson appeared to describe Christmas traditions in their native or adopted homelands. In Rome, Audrey explains the legend of "La Befana," which plays a prominent role in Italian Christmas festivities. The program was produced by Alexander H. Cohen, directed by Clark Jones and written by Hildy Parks.

T21 Commericals (1971).

Audrey filmed four one-minute commercials in Italy for a Tokyo wig manufacturer, who hoped to capitalize on her popularity in Japan, undiminished since the release of *Roman Holiday.*

T22   The American Film Institute Salute to William Wyler (CBS-TV) March 14, 1976; 90 minutes; color

Audrey introduces clips from her breakthrough film *Roman Holiday*, and pays tribute to its director--"If it weren't for Willy Wyler, I wouldn't have learned how to act." Later in the show she presents AFI scholarship awards to winning students.

T23   The 48th Annual Academy Awards (ABC-TV) March 29, 1976; 150 minutes; color

Presents Best Picture Oscar to *One Flew Over the Cuckoo's Nest*.

T24   The Tonight Show (NBC-TV) March 30, 1976; 90 minutes; color

Audrey's one and only appearance with Johnny Carson. The other guests were Charlie Callas, Dr. Keith Sehnert, Roz Clark and Buddy Hackett.

T25   The 51st Annual Academy Awards (ABC-TV) April 9, 1979; 150 minutes; color

Audrey presents an honorary award to King Vidor, her director on *War and Peace*.

T26   The American Film Institute Salute to Fred Astaire (CBS-TV) April 18, 1981; 90 minutes; color

Audrey recalls her excitement and apprehension at the thought of dancing with Fred Astaire in *Funny Face* (1957--see F11).

T27   The Kennedy Center Honors: A Celebration of the Performing Arts (CBS-TV) December 26, 1981; 120 minutes; color

Audrey reads a poem to her *Charade* leading man Cary Grant (1963--see F19), who was among the recipients of this annual tribute.

T28   The 58th Annual Academy Awards (ABC-TV)

March 24, 1986; 180 minutes; color

Audrey presents the award for Best Costume Design to *Ran*.

T29 The American Film Institute Salute to Billy Wilder (CBS-TV) April 26, 1986; 90 minutes; color

"I've been given a lot of advice as to what not to say to Billy tonight, as praise and sentiment might make him leave the room," said Audrey as she salutes her director on *Sabrina* and *Love In the Afternoon* (1957--see F12)

T30 Life: 50 Years (ABC-TV) November 15, 1986; 120 minutes; color

Hosted by Barbara Walters. Audrey is one of twelve recipients of the "Life Legend Award" which is given to the performers who appeared most frequently in *Life* Magazine (see A25). Audrey's nine *Life* covers are second only to Elizabeth Taylor's twelve.

T31 Love Among Thieves (ABC-TV) February 23, 1987; 100 minutes; color)

Audrey's first made-for-TV movie since *Mayerling* (see F29)

T32 The 60th Annual Academy Awards (ABC-TV) April 11, 1988; 180 minutes; color

Audrey and her *Roman Holiday* co-star Gregory Peck present the Best Screenplay Oscars to *Moonstruck* (screenplay written directly for the screen) and *The Last Emperor* (screenplay based on material from another medium).

T33 The American Film Institute Salute to Gregory Peck (NBC-TV) March 21, 1989; 60 minutes; color

Audrey serves as co-host of this tribute to one of her closest Hollywood friends. Entering to a standing ovation, she recounts Peck's early experiences in show business, and thanks him for his guidance and support during the production of *Roman Holiday.*

T34 The Barbara Walters Special (ABC-TV) March

29,1989; 60 minutes; color

During a relaxed, friendly twenty minute chat with Miss Walters, Audrey reflects on several prominent events in her life and career, such as dancing with Fred Astaire, the *My Fair Lady* controversy, her semi-retirement after *Wait Until Dark* (1967--see F24) and the fulfillment she had found with UNICEF.

T35   Larry King Live (CNN-Cable) April 19, 1989; 60 minutes; color

An informal interview with no major revelations.

T36   Good Morning America (ABC-TV) May 17, 1989; 90 minutes; color

Audrey is interviewed about her work for UNICEF.

T37   The 47th Annual Golden Globe Awards (TBS-Cable) January 20, 1990; 120 minutes; color

Audrey receives the Cecil B. DeMille Prize for lifetime achievement in film. Former co-stars Gregory Peck, George Peppard and Richard Crenna take part in the tribute.

T38   Donahue (syndicated-TV) January 23, 1990; 60 minutes; color

Audrey somewhat nervously greets a very enthusiastic audience and answers questions from host Phil Donahue about her life and work.

T39   Larry King Live (CNN-Cable) January 25, 1990; 60 minutes; color

Audrey's second Larry King appearance (see T33) proceeds along much the same format as her first.

T40   Reflections on the Silver Screen (American Movie Classics-Cable) February 1990; 30 minutes; color

An interview with Audrey conducted by Professor Richard Brown. Although awkwardly edited together,   it is one of the rare video records of Audrey discussing her achievements in film. Dressed in a white turtleneck similar to her wardrobe in *Always* (1989--see F 30), she reflected on being discovered by William Wyler for *Roman Holiday*, dancing with Fred Astaire in *Funny Face* (1957--see F11), and how the clothing she wore in character helped define her performance. Audrey claims that she "never really became an actress" because she never performed Shakespeare or any part in the classical repertoire. Brown calls her on this, revealing himself as a fan as well as an interviewer; "No one can do what you can do," he tells her.

T41   CBS This Morning (CBS-TV) October 1, 1990; 120 minutes; color

 Discussion of Audrey's most recent UNICEF-related travels.

T42   The Fred Astaire Songbook (PBS-TV) March 8, 1991; 90 minutes; color

Film clips and interviews with Astaire's many co-stars and dancing partners comprise this "Great Performances" presentation, hosted by Audrey. "Hepburn does her best," observed *Variety*, "but she's asked to articulate emotions and thoughts that almost defy description." Other reviews were lukewarm.

T43   Gardens of the World (PBS-TV) April-June, 1991; 60 minutes; color

This ongoing series, originally presented in eight parts but expanded since, grew from the book *Gardens of the World* by Penelope Hobhouse and Elvin McDonald (MacMillan, New York 1991--see B289). Audrey contributed the book's foreward, and hosts the series from the world's most famous gardens in the United States, Japan, Santo Domingo, Italy, Holland, France and England. The *Los Angeles Times* called Audrey "the perfect host...never intrusive, always appreciative of the natural and man-made beauty around her." The series was produced by Stuart Crowner, directed by Bruce Franchini and written by Glen Berenbeim. After Audrey's illness in 1992, Michael York stepped in as host.

T44   Larry King TNT Extra (TNT-Cable) October 21, 1991; 60 minutes; color

Audrey discusses her rejection of the title role of *The Diary of Anne Frank* (see W13)

T45 The Kennedy Center Honors: A Celebration of the Performing Arts (CBS-TV) December 26, 1991; 120 minutes; color

Audrey participates in the salute to honoree Gregory Peck. She tells the audience that is was Peck who insisted she receive co-star billing in her first Hollywood film, *Roman Holiday*.

T46 The 64th Annual Academy Awards (ABC-TV) March 30, 1992; 180 minutes; color

Audrey presents an honorary award for career achievement to filmmaker Satyajit Ray.

T47 Good Morning America (ABC-TV) September 29, 1992; 120 minutes; color

Coverage of Audrey's visit to Somalia as UNICEF ambassador.

T48 Entertainment Tonight (syndicated-TV) September 29, 1992; 30 minutes; color

Similar to T47, with footage of Audrey's visit to a U.S. Navy vessel stationed near Somalia.

T49 Danny Kaye International Children's Awards (Arts and Entertainment-Cable) May 18, 1993; 120 minutes; color

In one of her final public appearances, taped months before the date of broadcast, Audrey co-hosts this special from the Netherlands Congress Center in the Hague, which presents children from around the world in a performance competition. Also appearing are co-host Roger Moore, Julio Iglesias and Al Jarreau. Along with the performances, the show features short film clips highlighting UNICEF's field work in areas such as Somalia, other parts of Africa and Central America.

T50 Audrey Hepburn Remembered (Syndicated-TV) August 11, 1993; 60 minutes; color and black and white

A documentary about Audrey's life and career, hosted by Roger Moore and produced by Gene Feldman and Suzette Winter. Clips from many of her films is interspersed with interview footage of Audrey, her ex-husband Mel Ferrer, her son Sean and several former co-stars and friends. Among those who contributed loving remembrances are Hubert de Givenchy, Stanley Donen, Elizabeth Taylor, Gregory Peck, Henry Mancini and George Peppard. In the August 2, 1993 issue of the *Hollywood Reporter*, columnist Robert Osborne praised the tribute for its ability to "capture and capsulize both the real and the reel Hepburn in a way no one else has so briefly but expertly done before." Executive producer: Stephen Janson; Camera: Phil Gries, Robert Jaye, Rick Robertson, Jeremy Stavenhagen; Sound: David Jaunai; Music: Michael Bacon.

7

Discography

D 1 Funny Face

(1957, Verve 15001). Soundtrack of the motion picture (see F11).

Audrey performs "How Long Has This Been Going On," "Funny Face" (with Fred Astaire), "S'Wonderful " (with Astaire), "Bonjour Paris" (with Astaire and Kay Thompson), "On How To Be Lovely" (with Thompson). Other songs: "Let's Kiss and Make Up," "He Loves and She Loves" (danced by Astaire), "Clap Yo' Hands" (Astaire and Thompson), "Think Pink" (Thompson and chorus), "Marche Funebre."

Until the posthumous release of *Music from the films of Audrey Hepburn* (see D6), the *Funny Face* soundtrack provided the only example of Audrey's singing available to the record buyer. Marni Nixon dubbed all of Audrey's songs in *My Fair Lady* (1964) and although Audrey sings "La Vie En Rose" in *Sabrina* (1954) and "Moon River" in *Breakfast at Tiffany's* (1961), her versions do not appear on the respective motion picture soundtracks. Entries D2 through D5 are spoken word recordings.

Reviews

"...some tempting samples of Audrey Hepburn's fey vocal style, but a great deal of space is taken up by hectic Hollywooden attacks on a fine Gershwin score." (*New York Times*, July 21, 1957)

"Audrey Hepburn comes across in fine style with a sort of

'Sprechstimme' voice suggesting Marlene Dietrich with an English accent." (*Saturday Review of Literature*, April 27, 1957)

D 2 Gary Cooper Testimonial Dinner--Friars Club, January 8,1961
(Friars 2507)

Audrey reads a poem entitled "What is a Gary Cooper?" to her leading man in *Love in the Afternoon* (1957).

D 3 Fifty Years of Film
(1973, Warner Bros. 3XX2737)

Three discs of dialog excerpts from Warner Bros. motion picture soundtracks, from 1923 to 1973. Audrey is heard with Rex Harrison in the "Rain in Spain" scene from *My Fair Lady*.

Reviews
"A Treasure Trove" (*High Fidelity and Musical America*, April, 1974)

"The sound montages are in each case such expertly edited manipulations of memorable highlights that they easily manage to capture the flavor of the entire film." (*Stereo Review*, April,1974)

D 4 Carnival of the Animals
(1992, Dove Audio 30560. Also available on compact disc [Dove Audio 30700])

 A new recording of the famous Camille Saint-Saens composition, complete with the Ogden Nash lyrics, conducted by Lalo Schifrin. Celebrity narrators (Arte Johnson, Charleton Heston, James Earl Jones, Betty White, Lynn Redgrave, William Shatner, Joan Rivers, Ted Danson, Lily Tomlin, Deborah Raffin, Dudley Moore, Walter Matthau, Jaclyn Smith) perform each section. Audrey reads "The Birds." Proceeds from sales of the tape are donated to various animal rights organizations.

Reviews
"Fun, nutty, a four-star suggestion." (*USA Today*, December 24, 1992)

D 5   Audrey Hepburn's Enchanted Tales
(1993, Dove Audio 30790. Also available on compact disc [Dove Audio 30790])

Audrey received a posthumous Grammy Award for narrating this collection of familiar and obscure fairy tales, including "Sleeping Beauty", "Tom Thumb", "Beauty and the Beast" and "Laidronette, Empress of the Pagodes." The selections, adapted by Mary Sheldon, are woven together by the fictional commentary of an elderly French woman, who reminisces about hearing the stories told during her childhood by Maurice Ravel. Ravel's "Mother Goose Suite" accompanies the tales. The project was recorded just days prior to Audrey's last hospitalization, and was her last professional endeavor before her death. As with *Carnival of the Animals*, a portion of the proceeds from the recording are donated to the ASPCA.

Reviews
"Hepburn shapes the rich language with delicate clarity and her unique, captivating charm. The result is pure magic." (*Los Angeles Times*, April 10, 1993)

D 6   Music From the Films of Audrey Hepburn
(1993, Big Screen Records 9-24053-2. Available on compact disc)

A compilation of soundtrack excerpts from Audrey Hepburn films, including Audrey's vocal rendition of "Moon River" from *Breakfast at Tiffany's*. Other selections: "Moon River" (instrumental), the main title themes from *Charade*, *The Nun's Story*, *How to Steal a Million*, *Wait Until Dark* and *Two for the Road*, the overture to *My Fair Lady*, "John Bursts In" and "The End" from *Robin and Marian* and "Gabrielle" from *Paris When it Sizzles*. A curious choice is the inclusion of "He Loves and She Loves," performed by Fred Astaire, from the soundtrack of *Funny Face* . Audrey herself performed four songs on the soundtrack, but none of these selections are included (see D1).

Reviews
"This is a fine compilation which does what the best compilations do--include the standards as well as some new treats, presented with care and attention." (*Film Score Monthly*, July 1993)

OTHER SOUNDTRACKS TO AUDREY HEPBURN FILMS

The Lavender Hill Mob (Rank FM-117, [1951])
Roman Holiday (Seven Seas 118, [1953])
Sabrina (RCA 1-0422, [1954])
War and Peace (Columbia CL-930, Columbia Special Products ACL-930, [1956])
Love in the Afternoon (Verve V-5055, [1957])
The Nun's Story (Warner Bros. W-1306, [1959])
Green Mansions (United Artists UAL-7007, [1959])
The Unforgiven (United Artists UAL-4068, UAS-5068, [1960])
Breakfast at Tiffany's (RCA 2362, [1961], CD available)
Charade (RCA LPM-2755, LSP 2755, [1964])
Paris When it Sizzles (Reprise R-6113, RS-6113, [1964])
My Fair Lady (Columbia JST-20002, KOL-8000/KOS 2600, [1964])
How to Steal a Million (20th Century Fox 4183/S4183, [1966])
Two For the Road (RCA LPM 3802, [1966])
Wait Until Dark (RCA 4022, [1967])
Robin and Marian (Sherwood SH-1500, [1967])
Bloodline (Varese STV-81131, [1979])
They All Laughed (Moon Pictures 0001, [1980])
Always (MCA 8036, [1989], CD available)

8

Bibliography

Audrey Hepburn was never comfortable being interviewed, and submitted herself to the ordeal as infrequently as possible. In the early 1950's, as the new toast of Broadway and Hollywood, a great deal of publicity was inevitable, and with the encouragement of studios and agents Audrey talked often to magazines and newspapers. As soon as her status allowed her to decline such requests, she did not hesitate to do so. The number of interviews dwindled rapidly from the mid-1960's on, with only *Life* and *Photoplay* receiving substantial access. When she did speak to the press, however, it was with her trademark grace and candor, and from the 1980's on it was a price she was willing to pay again to promote the work of UNICEF. The list of magazine and newspaper articles that follows is as comprehensive as possible, but with few exceptions is limited to articles that first appeared in English. There is an abundance of additional material that exists in European and Asian publications.

Following the magazine listing are reviews of the four Audrey Hepburn biographies currently available, and a selection of books that mention Audrey in a significant or colorful way. Her death in 1993 has prompted a new abundance of material and remembrances, which began to appear as this book was being written.

ARTICLES

B001 Abramson, Martin. "Audrey Hepburn." *Cosmopolitan*. October 1955, pp 26-32.

Comprehensive, well-researched coverage of Audrey's youth and career. More objective than most pieces of the time, though interviews with everyone from her previous co-stars to her hairdresser supply ample acclaim. Several wonderful anecdotes, including Audrey convincing the manager of a New York hotel to lower the room rate; "I can't say just how she got me to change my mind. She didn't bargain with me-- Good Lord, you couldn't conceive of this elegant young woman lowering herself to haggle about money! She just talked and smiled and laughed and somehow I found myself bewitched into the notion that I had no right in the world to charge her fifteen dollars, even if it *was* our regular rate."

B002 Alexander, Ron. "A Glittering Tribute to Audrey Hepburn." *The New York Times*. October 22, 1987.

Audrey is the honoree at a $1000 a plate dinner hosted by the Museum of Modern Art. Proceeds went to the museum's Film Preservation Fund.

B003 Allen, Anita. "Please God, Help Me to Walk Again!" *Photoplay*. May 1959, pp 58, 99-100.

A soap opera-like account of Audrey's fall from a horse during production of *The Unforgiven*. Not up to the standard of previous *Photoplay* articles.

B004 *American Movie Classics*. "Audrey Hepburn."July 1990, pp 4-5.

A cover story of not much depth, but there's a nice color photo of Audrey and William Holden from *Sabrina*. "He certainly never wanted to marry me! My God, he was married!" she said, addressing old rumors about Holden.

B005 Archer, Eugene. "Audrey the Fair Scales the Summit." *New York Times*. November 1, 1964.

Audrey's negative press after accepting the role of Eliza in *My Fair Lady* is the subject of this telling interview, in which she appears "baffled" at "coming up against the weight of public opinion for the first time."

B006 *Architectural Digest*. "Academy Awards Collector's Edition."April 1992.

One photo, circa mid-1950's, of Audrey and Mel Ferrer playing table tennis.

B007 Barber, Rowland. "The Delightful Riddle of Audrey Hepburn." *Good Housekeeping*. August 1962, pp 61-62, 112-117, 124.

Inaccurate coverage of Audrey's wartime experiences, but otherwise an interesting, praise-loaded article which ventures to answer the question

"*Can* anybody really be so noble, so thoughtful, so perennially "good"? Anecdotes from the sets of *The Nun's Story* and *The Children's Hour* are repeated, along with complimentary comments from Shirley MacLaine, James Garner and director Fred Zinnemann.

B008 Beaton, Cecil. "Audrey Hepburn." *Vogue.* December 1, 1954, p.129.

Cecil Beaton, who would later design the sets and costumes for *My Fair Lady* , describes Audrey as "the public embodiment of our new feminine ideal."

B009 Beaton, Cecil. "Looks in Fashion." *Vogue.* January 1, 1963, p. 141.

Another love letter, accompanied by photos of Audrey on the set of *Paris When It Sizzles* . Audrey's physical features are dissected and praised, from her "gazelle eyes" and "exalted neck" to her "Modigliani dancer's body."

B010 Benson, Sheila. "A Second Look At Hepburn." *Los Angeles Times.* November 14, 1982.

Times film critic Sheila Benson re-examines Audrey's best-known films from an eighties perspective to see how well they "hold up." She quotes Nora Sayre's scathing indictment of Audrey's fifties screen image (see B344), and pans *Breakfast at Tiffany's*, but concludes that Audrey was popular then and now becuase she "filled a deep need." "She represented the princess side of our fantasies."

B011 Berg, Louis. "The Solid-Gold Audrey." *Los Angeles Times Magazine.* August 12, 1956.

Italian sculptor Renato Signorini asked Audrey to pose after being "captivated" by her in *War and Peace*. He produced two sculptures, a figurine in silver and a bust in 14-karat gold.

B012 Bernstein, Richard. "When Everyone's in Love With Audrey Hepburn." *New York Times*, April 24, 1991.

Coverage of the Hepburn tribute at the Film Society of Lincoln Center, attended by Gregory Peck, Harry Belafonte, Stanley Donen, Anthony Perkins, Alan Arkin, and Hubert Givenchy.

B013 Blume, Mary. "A Maid Marian for All Seasons." *Los Angeles Times*. July 20, 1975.

One of the first articles to announce Audrey's return to the screen in *Robin and Marian*.

B014 *Boston Herald*. "Hepburn went looking for fun & found 'Love'." February 21, 1987.

Love Among Thieves promotion. Interviews with Audrey and Robert Wagner.

B015 *Box Office*. "Welcome Audrey Hepburn Back After 8-year Absence." April 5, 1976.

Coverage of a black-tie champagne reception and screening of *Robin and Marian*. Among the one thousand film industry dignitaries and celebrities there to celebrate Audrey's return are William Wyler and Stanley Donen.

B016 Brady, James. "In Step With: Audrey Hepburn." *Parade*. March 3, 1991.

A brief, impromptu conversation between Audrey and James Brady on the ski slopes in Switzerland.

B017 Brett, Simon. "Audrey Hepburn." *Films and Filming*. March 1964, pp 9-12.

Excellent reviews of Audrey's films from *Roman Holiday* to *The Children's Hour*, along with insightful commentary about her film persona that manages to be affectionate without losing objectivity.

B018 Britten, R. "Audrey's Happiest Moment." *Photoplay*. April 1961, pp 59-64.

More Avedon photos of Audrey and son Sean, as is B062.

B019 Canby, Vincent. "Mr. Chips Stars to Share Gross." *New York Times*. January 13, 1966.

According to the *Times* article Richard Burton had been signed at a cost of $1 million plus points to star in the MGM remake of *Goodbye Mr. Chips* (1969). Audrey received the same offer. Burton backed out later and was replaced by Peter O'Toole.

B020 Carter, Charla. "Audrey Hepburn." *Harper's Bazaar*. December 1991.

An examination of Audrey's 40-year relationship with Givenchy, their enduring friendship and how each advanced the other's career. "Even today," said Givenchy, "I style with her in mind."

B021 *Celebrity*. "Audrey Hepburn: Trouble For Cinderella." August 1954, pp 46-49.

The "trouble" referred to is the choice Audrey will be "forced" to make between the stage and the movies. "So far she has been a smash hit in both mediums. How long she can continue to keep everyone happy, however, is hard to say."

B022 Ceruzzi, Aldo. "Why Mel Ferrer Flipped Over Fonda and Little Audrey." *Uncensored*. January 1957, pp 12-15.

According to this dubious account of turmoil on the set of *War and Peace*, Audrey and Henry Fonda did not get along, but they were still attracted to each other. Meanwhile jealous Mel Ferrer did his best to keep the couple apart. Not even fun to read as a guilty pleasure.

B023 Champlin, Charles. "Audrey Hepburn Sparkles With Aura of Stardom." *Los Angeles Times*. February 8, 1967.

Critic Charles Champlin interviews Audrey as she is about to start shooting *Wait Until Dark*; "This is a challenging picture...and I'm not terribly ambitious for challenge', she said, grinning."

B024 *Cine Revue*. July 24, 1975.

A feature story in a French publication.

B025 *Cine Revue*. November 29, 1979.

An article on the production of *Bloodline*.

B026 *Cine Revue*. January 8, 1987.

Feature article, in French.

B027 Clement, Carl. "Look Where You're Going, Audrey!" *Photoplay.* June 1957, pp 47, 82-83.

A strange article, which poses the question "Has this definite and determined girl who certainly has a blessing upon her *really* succeeded?" and then fails to provide an answer. The now familiar stories of Audrey's wartime experiences are retold, using excerpts from previous *Photoplay* interviews. A flimsy excuse to get her picture back in the magazine.

B028 Clurman, Harold. "Letter to Audrey Hepburn." *Nation.* March 6, 1954, p. 206

Much of Audrey's press coverage resembles love letters, but this is one of the few pieces that does not even attempt to disguise it. "You are enchanting (how tired you will soon be of hearing this!)" writes Harold Clurman. "You must forgive me if I begin this way because, though apparently self-evident, it is a statement that cannot be addressed to many actresses of our day...but young as you are, dear Audrey, you must guess that that is not the whole story, for it is clear that you are as bright as you are sensitive."

B029 Connolly, Mike. "Who Needs Beauty!" *Photoplay.* January 1954, pp 48-49, 72-73.

A superlative-laden story heralding Audrey's arrival in Hollywood as "the most phenomenal thing that's happened to the film capital since Marilyn Monroe!" For some reason Audrey always seemed to grant *Photoplay*'s interview requests, and as a result this is but the first of many articles chronicling her career. Here she addresses the rumors of a romance with *Roman Holiday* co-star Gregory Peck ("Who starts them?") and how she handles "New York and London wolves"--"I've never yet had to fight off a man!"

B030 Cook, Peggy. "A Photographer and His Model Make a Pretty Movie." *Cosmopolitan.* February 1957, pp 50-53.

Audrey is pictured on the cover of the magazine and in several photos inside taken by Richard Avedon. The brief article previews *Funny Face*.

B031 *Coronet.* "On Stardom's Stairway." January 1954, p. 35.

Audrey was chosen as one of the young actresses "on stardom's stairway," along with Debbie Reynolds, Terry Moore and a few others who didn't keep climbing.

B032 *Cue.* "Girl Hard To Find." November 17, 1951, p. 46.

B033 *Cue.* "Hollywood's New Hepburn." July 18, 1953, p. 22.

B034 *Cue.* "No Mermaid more Magical." March 27, 1954, p. 13.

One-page *Ondine*-related story with two photos from the play; "The Hepburn career is almost as magical as her impersonation of the sea-nymph she personifies in *Ondine*."

B035 Donen, Stanley. "Remembering Audrey." *Vogue.* April 1993, pp 391, 465-467.

Director Stanley Donen wrote this touching tribute to his friend, whom he directed in *Funny Face, Charade and Two for the Road*; "I didn't have to describe all the things she was--there she was being them: elegant, quiet, beautiful, with a grace unequaled by any other actress."

B036 Dowty, L. "Audrey Hepburn Makes the Scene." *Good Housekeeping.* August 1967, p.84.

Promotion for *Wait Until Dark*, with several photos and a brief interview in which Audrey recalled her son Sean's reaction after watching *My Fair Lady*--"Mommy, why did you *hate* to take a bath?"

B037 Dunn, Angela Fox. "Audrey Hepburn is a class act." *New York Democrat and Chronicle.* December 21, 1989.

Basic interview. Audrey talks about UNICEF, and her role in *Always* .

B038 Dunne, Dominick. "Audrey Hepburn." *Vanity Fair.* May 1991.

An excellent interview and career review, focusing mainly on Audrey's work for UNICEF. Lovely photos.

B039 Emerson, Gloria. "Co-Stars Again: Audrey Hepburn and Givenchy." *New York Times.* September 8, 1965.

Audrey's reunion with Givenchy during the production of *How to Steal a Million* is the subject of this interview. Audrey discusses her long relationship with the designer, her personal fashion preferences, and "the intense interest people show in her way of dressing."

B040 *Family Circle.* "Audrey Hepburn at 50." June 26, 1979, pp 21,

22, 106.

Fashion, makeup, skin care and perfume advice from Audrey, who again wonders why anyone would wish to look like she does.

B041 Feinstein, Herbert. "My Gorgeous Darling Sweetheart Angels: Brigitte Bardot and Audrey Hepburn." *Film Quarterly.* Spring 1962, pp 65-68.

Condescending, smug reviews of Audrey in *Breakfast at Tiffany's* and Brigitte Bardot in *The Truth.* The reviewer, Herbert Feinstein, sees much in common between the two actresses, commenting that "neither can act," but "they are beguiling personalities." He calls *Tiffany's* "the worst picture ever made after *El Cid*," but adds that "every time Miss Hepburn strolls past her store at 727 Fifth Avenue, it is like watching a whole Easter Parade."

B042 Ferguson, Gwen. "The Night Audrey Hepburn Can't Forget!" *Inside Story.* August 1957, pp 8-12.

"I don't know if you'll want to marry me when I tell you the terrible thing I MUST tell you," said Audrey to Mel according to this highly dubious tabloid tale. The story states that Audrey "was brutally kidnapped and subjected to terrible indignities when she was 13 years old." Half-truths at best.

B043 Fields, S. "Audrey Hepburn." *McCall's.* July 1954, pp 51,62-63.

Engaging interview in which Audrey still insists she hasn't learned how to act after winning an Oscar and a Tony. The story includes an amusing anecdote of Audrey watching her name go up in lights on the marquee for *Gigi.* "When the last letter of her name was being formed she dashed across the street impulsively, climbed the ladder and screwed the final bulb in--'just for luck.'"

B044 *Film.* "The Great Musical Performers." Summer 1964.

Audrey is included in the title group; "sheer personality and talent have often triumphed in the musical cinema to make a song-and-dance routine memorable. Audrey Hepburn barely sings, but her version of Gershwin's 'How Long Has This Been Going On?' surpasses the recordings of the great singers."

B045 *Film Dope.* "Audrey Hepburn." March 1982.

Filmography through *Bloodline*.

B046 *Film Review*. "My Favorite Role." 1955-1956, p.26.

Audrey selected *Roman Holiday* as her favorite film role, though at this point she didn't have many to choose from; "the role of a fairy-tale princess seemed a childhood dream come true."

B047 *Films Illustrated*. June 1976.

B048 Flynn, Margaret. "Audrey Hepburn's Raw Deal Marriage." *Inside*. May 1955, pp 18-23.

Mel Ferrer received a great deal of negative press in the early days of his marriage to Audrey; "Svengali was a rank amateur compared to the lean actor who mesmerized the pert wide-eyed water sprite." Cold, but colorfully written.

B049 *Fund Raising Management*. September 1989, p.47.

A story on UNICEF's 40th anniversary, accompanied by a picture of Audrey on one of her goodwill visits to Africa. The caption credits Audrey with helping to bring the problem of starving children before the American people.

B050 Gardella, Kay. "She's Still Our Fair Lady." *New York Daily News*. January 21, 1987.

Interview promoting the television movie *Love Among Thieves* (see F29). She also discusses the recent death of Cary Grant, the current state of movies and her contentment away from the limelight.

B051 Gilbert, Norma. "Did Sentiment Freeze Out Warners' Loverly Eliza?" *Film Bulletin*. March 1, 1965.

An amusing but sincerely angry response to Audrey's *My Fair Lady* snub by the Motion Picture Academy; "They must be kidding. They can't forget Audrey. It would be unpardonable. It's sinful. It's un-American. It's...Aiooo! They did it."

B052 Gittelson, Natalie. "Personalities." *McCalls*. August 1989, pp 36-39.

Audrey's role as UNICEF ambassador was the focus of this

interview/article, which includes reactions to her philanthropic work from such former co-stars and directors as Robert Wagner, Rex Harrison and Stanley Donen.

B053 *Glamour.* "Superstar Interviews." October 1968, pp 192-193.

Audrey's beauty regimen is chronicled, along with that of Jane Fonda, Julie Christie, Jacqueline Bisset and others. Her advice on keeping a slim figure--"Push your plate away."

B054 *Good Housekeeping.* "Who Says It's A Dog's LIfe?" March 1964, pp158-159.

.A two-page photo spread of Audrey and her new terrier, Assam.

B055 *Good Housekeeping.* "Audrey Hepburn." October 1984.

Excerpts from Charles Higham's biography of Audrey (see B286).

B056 Gordon, S. "My Fair Lady's Dream Come True." *Look.* February 25, 1964, pp 64-65.

Photos from *My Fair Lady.* When the article was written Audrey still believed that her singing voice would be heard in the film. "I took singing lessons from a New York vocal coach and pre-recorded all of Eliza's songs, but the final result will be a blend. It's wonderful what sound men can do with dials." For the final cut, they dialed her out completely.

B057 Graham, Roy. "Why Audrey Hepburn is wasting away!" *Exposed.* August 1956, pp 2-5.

Hilariously overdramatic account of Audrey's allegedly troubled marriage, in which Audrey's mother is depicted scouring the headlines for news of her daughter's separation. Audrey is again portrayed as a victim of her Svengali-like husband.

B058 Green, Tom. Obituary. *USA Today.* January 20, 1993.

B059 Haddad, M. George. "Staring a New Cycle?" *Coronet.* April 1976, pp 124-131.

More welcomes back to Hollywood for *Robin and Marian.*

B060 Haddad, M. George. "My Side." *Working Woman.* July 1979, p.80.

Brief, pedestrian interivew, though it does shed some light upon why Audrey chose to appear in a film like *Bloodline*.

B061 Haddad-Garcia, George. "Hepburn's Back." *The San Antonio Light*. January 10, 1982, p.4.

Audrey discusses her broken marriage to Dr. Dotti, her relationship with Robert Wolders, and her appearance in *They All Laughed*.

B062 Hamilton, J. "Audrey Hepburn and her strong son." *Look*. November 8, 1960. pp 89-90.

Audrey and newborn son Sean pose in their Givenchy-designed christening outfits. The American ambassador to Switzerland attended the christening and brought the baby two presents--an American passport and an American flag. The lovely photo of mother and son by Richard Avedon is more memorable than any he shot for B018.

B063 *Harper's Bazaar*. "The Fifties--A Random Symposium." July 1959.

In this special pull-out section reflecting upon the decade about to close, Audrey and Marilyn Monroe are cited as the two "film queens" of the fifties.

B064 *Harper's Bazaar*. "Paris Pursuit." August 1959.

A Richard Avedon photo essay starring Audrey, Mel Ferrer and Buster Keaton, set in Paris.

B065 *Harper's Bazaar*. "Over 40 and Sensational." September 1981.

Audrey, Sophia Loren, Natalie Wood and others are celebrated in gorgeous photos. Audrey, wearing Givenchy, discusses hair and makeup tips, and how she assesses her own appearance; "Oh, I'd like not to be so flat-chested, not to have such angular shoulders, such big feet, such a big nose." But adds, "I'm grateful for what God's given me. I've done pretty well."

B066 *Harper's Bazaar*. "Christmas Wishes." December 1990.

Asked with others for a Christmas wish, Audrey responded; "My one wish for children would be <u>peace</u>. Only then will the water we provide quench their thirst, the food nourish their bodies, the medicine make them well, and they will live to play and learn and their parents live to love them."

B067 Harris, Eleanor. "Audrey Hepburn." *Good Housekeeping*. August 1959. pp 61, 117-118, 120-121.

The first of three *Good Housekeeping* interview/articles with Audrey that would qualify her for sainthood. Her pre-stardom life is reviewed, and there are some interesting backstage stories about her then-current film, *The Unforgiven*.

B068 Harris, Radie. "Audrey Hepburn--the Girl, the Gamin and the Star." *Photoplay*. March 1955, pp 61, 99-102.

Hollywood Reporter columnist Radie Harris first met Audrey in 1951, and they remained close friends for many years. Harris recounts their first meeting, her first meeting and later marriage to Mel Ferrer, and how Harris incurred Ferrer's wrath after criticizing him in print for taking all of Audrey's *Ondine* curtain calls at her side. Harris's affection for Audrey is obvious, but this interview and career review is no more subjective than that of other scribes.

B069 Harris, Scott. Obituary. *Los Angeles Times*. January 20, 1993.

B070 Hartung, Philip T. "A Star Is Born." *Commonweal*. September 18, 1953, pp 58-59.

Critic Philip T. Hartung praises *Roman Holiday*, and found himself falling in love with Audrey; "this attractive girl who is such a curious mixture of innocence, naivete`, good breeding and sophistication."

B071 Haskell, Molly . "Our Fair Lady." *Film Comment*. March-April 1991, pp 9-17.

Cover story written by critic Molly Haskell that examines Audrey's career. The criticism is both scholarly and popular, with a generous helping of entertaining anecdotes complimenting Haskell's erudite observations about Audrey's arrival in Hollywood "at an historical moment, just before feminism, easy divorce, and the sexual revolution drove out a code of love based on delayed gratification and repression."

B072 Hawkins, William. "Interview With Audrey Hepburn." *Dance* Magazine. October 1956, pp 17,19,61

An interview focusing on Audrey's lifelong interest in dance, from her living-room recitals in war-torn Arnhem to her then-forthcoming performance in *Funny Face*. Excellent coverage of her youth and stagework in London.

B073 Hepburn, Audrey. "Audrey Hepburn's Fashion Formula." *Los Angeles Times Magazine*. November 11, 1962, pp 14, 16.

"It seems to me that it is within the reach of every woman to develop a similar individuality of style by learning to know herself" writes Audrey, who goes on to discuss how she selects her wardrobe for movies, and away from the camera.

B074 Hepburn, Audrey. "My Fair Lady." *Memories*. April/May 1989, pp 9-11.

Brief quotes, possibly lifted from other articles, on most of Audrey's films, with photos accompanying each blurb.

B075 Hepburn, Audrey. "Unforgettable Silence." *Newsweek*. October 26, 1992, p. 10

Audrey describes in agonizing detail the dead and dying children she saw during her trip to Somalia. "You really wonder whether God hasn't forgotten Somalia" she writes, but she praises the efforts of relief workers for trying to make a difference.

B076 Herrmann, Helen Markel. "Half Nymph, Half Wunderkind." *New York Times Magazine*. February 14, 1954, pp 15, 24-26.

Audrey provides amusing, self-deprecating retorts to the affectionate coverage she has received. To articles that referred to her as "coltish, gazelle-like and other-worldly," she said "I guess they mean I'm tall and skinny." When her eyes are described as "lake-haunted," she replied "Maybe I need sleep."

B077 Hewes, H. "Broadway Postscript." *Saturday Review*. November 15, 1952, pp 28-29.

Subtitled "Stars Who Danced," Audrey is interviewed along with dancer Robert Helpmann on how their ballet training was "responsible for the quick success they enjoyed when they made the jump into the legitimate theatre." Audrey credits her training with giving her the discipline to "learn in three weeks how to play a leading role in my first real acting job."

B078 *Holland Herald.* "Cover Story." November-December 1966. pp1, 13.

Audrey returned to Holland for the European premiere of Mel Ferrer's film *El Greco* (1966).

B079 *Hollywood Reporter.* Obituary. January 21, 1993

B080 *Hollywood Studio Magazine.* "Audrey Hepburn." October 1987.

Very basic, but friendly cover story and filmography, containing few details or revelations. However, the article suggests half-seriously that Audrey was responsible for John F. Kennedy being elected president; "It seems that Jacqueline Bouvier Kennedy was a fan since *Roman Holiday* and modeled her look after Audrey. The Audrey look became the Jackie look and aided JFK in the election." Right. There are no direct quotes in the story, but there are second-hand reports that Audrey "hated" the way she looked in *Robin and Marian, Bloodline* and *They All Laughed*, but was pleased with her appearance in the TV movie *Love Among Thieves*.

B081 Hopper, Hedda. "Hollywood's Newest Hepburn is Sensational." *Chicago Tribune Magazine.* December 6, 1953.

Raves from Hedda Hopper, who also quotes another Audrey fan, Joan Crawford; "She has that magic spark that pictures need."

B082 Hopper, Hedda. "Don't call him Mr. Hepburn." *Chicago Sunday Times Magazine.* August 7, 1957, p.23.

"Mel Ferrer is proud of his talented Audrey, but his own film career is important, too" writes Hedda Hopper in another interview with the happy couple.

B083 Hopper, Hedda. "They Go Happy-Go-Lucky." *Chicago Tribune Magazine.* February 1, 1959, p.19.

"Hollywood's light-hearted lovers," Audrey and Mel, are profiled by Hedda Hopper.

B084 *House and Garden.* January 1991, pp 42-44.

Coverage of the PBS series *Gardens of the World* (see T43) which Audrey hosted. The article mentions an excursion made by Audrey that was not aired in the series to her grandmother's house in the Netherlands for the official christening of the white 'Audrey Hepburn' tulip.

B085 *Houston Post.* "Hepburn is back!" March 21, 1976.

More glad tidings at Audrey's return to the movies.

B086 *The Independent.* "Fair Lady in Somalia." October 4, 1992.

Coverage of Audrey's press conference that followed her visit to Somalia; "When a child cannot smile any more, it doesn't bear description."

B087 *The Independent.* "You Dream-maker, you heartbreaker." January 24, 1993.

"When Audrey Hepburn walked into the movies, all Heaven broke loose," according to this London newspaper.

B088 *The Independent on Sunday.* "Audrey Hepburn." February 14, 1993.

Another moving tribute, focusing on Audrey's relationship with Givenchy.

B089 *Interview.* "Audrey Hepburn." August 1990.

In its trademark avant-garde style, this *Interview* article collects fond tributes and recollections of Audrey from Christian Lacroix, Hubert de Givenchy, Richard Avendon and others, primarily focusing on her look and fashion sense. Avedon's contribution is particularly moving; "She is impossible to photograph. I cannot lift her to greater heights-- she is already there."

B090 Jones, Mary Worthington. "My Husband Doesn't Run Me." *Photoplay.* April 1956, pp 53, 104-107.

"She's known dictators in her early war-shadowed life. And you can take it from Audrey Hepburn--she didn't marry one!" After being played out in the tabloids, the controversy over Mel Ferrer's alleged control over Audrey's career is addressed in a more responsible forum. In a candid interview, she disputes the rumors; "I've been fending for myself since I was 13 and thinking very carefully about a lot of important problems, and I don't think I've made many bad decisions. I'm very proud of that, about my ability to think for myself, and no one, not even my husband, whom I adore, can persuade me to do something against my own judgment."

Audrey is described as "infuriated"--a rare circumstance.

B091 Jones, Mary Worthington. "The Small, Private World of Audrey
Hepburn." *Photoplay*. February 1957, p. 67.

Another lengthy discussion in *Photoplay*, tied in to the release of *Funny Face*. Both Mel and Audrey are interviewed, and respond to ongoing gossip about their marriage.

B092 Judge, Phillip. "Audrey: Why She's Back." *Sunday Woman*. July
8, 1979, pp 2,3, 23.

"This very private star talks about youth, beauty--and her much-gossiped-about marriage" in this *Bloodline*-related article.

B093 Kalb, Bernard. "Closeup of a Pretty Performer on a Pinnacle."
New York Times. August 30, 1953.

Article praises Audrey's work in *Gigi* and speculates on her career to come. Audrey outlines her own career plans in an interview.

B094 Klein, Edward. "You Can't Love Without the Fear of Losing."
Parade. March 5, 1989, pp 4-6.

A cover story that contains several fascinating revelations, chief among which is Audrey's renewed relationship with her father, the facts of which she discusses in print for the first time. She calls the divorce of her parents "the most traumatic event in my life."

B095 Knight, Arthur. "Choreography for Camera; Funny Face." *Dance
Magazine*. May 1957, pp 16-21.

An extended review of *Funny Face*, with particular attention paid to the photographic affects and lighting used by Richard Avedon to create various moods and moments.

B096 *Ladies Home Journal*. "Audrey Hepburn." September 1963,.

Audrey is pictured on the cover, but inside there is just one paragraph about her appearance in *Charade* .

B097 *Ladies Home Journal*. "Look At Audrey Hepburn Now!" January
1967, pp 59-60, 110-111.

"Audrey Hepburn swings? You're kidding." So begins this very enjoyable piece, in which the writer expresses bemused astonishment at Audrey wearing mini-skirts, vinyl shorts and swimsuits in *Two For the Road* . Lively interviews with Audrey and director Stanley Donen about updating the Hepburn image.

B098 *Las Vegas Review-Journal.* "Mourners pay tribute to Hepburn." January 25, 1993.

Coverage of Audrey's funeral.

B099 Leduc, Violette. "Steal-scening With Hepburn and O'Toole." *Vogue.* April 1, 1966, pp 173-176, 203-207.

Audrey, described as "overpoweringly pretty," is briefly interviewed on the set of *How To Steal A Million* along with co-stars Peter O'Toole and Eli Wallach. Only new factoid worth mentioning is Audrey's praise of Garbo, with whom she was so frequently compared over a decade earlier; "She's the greatest personality in the film world. She's great because she's unique."

B100 Leighton, Jean. "Welcome Home, Audrey!" *Silver Screen.* July 1976, pp 47-49.

Run-of-the-mill interview with the usual denials from Audrey about her premature retirement.

B101 *Life.* "Audrey Is a Hit." December 10, 1951, pp 103, 104.

Audrey, described as "demure, but hinting of mischief," is hailed as the first new star of the Broadway season. The article covers her discovery by Colette and mentions her ability to dance and sing as well as act. "Broadway hopes to see her sooner or later in a triple-threat role in the style of Gertrude Lawrence."

B102 *Life.* June 29, 1953.

Photos of popular young actresses taken by photographer Eliot Elisofon are tinted into various colors. The photo of Audrey is given a blue tint.

B103 *Life.* "What Makes Audrey Charm." December 7, 1953, pp 35-38.

Audrey's first *Life* cover is certainly her most memorable; she is reclined seductively, clad only in a man's shirt. Over a dozen photos embellish a brief story and interview.

B104 *LIfe*. "Another Triumph for Audrey." March 8, 1954, pp 36-37.

Coverage of Audrey's return to Broadway in *Ondine* . "The sight of Audrey, with her hair dyed blond...sent the drama critics scurrying to find new ways of saying 'enchanting' and 'magical.'"

B105 *Life*. "Audrey Waits For Academy Decision." April 5, 1954, p.36.

A more straightforward account of Audrey's Academy Award victory than B142, and not as much fun to read.

B106 *Life*. "An Idyl for Audrey." July 18, 1955, p. 39.

A picture-laden cover story of Audrey and Mel on their farm in Italy.

B107 *Life*. "Celebrities On a Stylish Spree." September 7, 1959, pp 47-50

The same Avedon photo essay as B106.

B108 *Life*. "Audrey Stars in Givenchy Styles." May 11, 1962, pp 41-42.

More photos than text as Audrey models her favorites from the then-current Givenchy collection; "His are the only clothes in which I am myself."

B109 *Life*. "Scandal in Rehearsal: Mayerling." February 4, 1957, p. 56.

A preview of *Mayerling* (see F13), described as "one of the year's most elaborate TV productions." Several backstage photos of Audrey and Mel.

B110 *Life*. "Together Again: Hepburn and Givenchy." May 1979.

A very sweet photo of the designer and his most famous client, on the set of *Bloodline*.

B111 *London Times*. "Audrey Hepburn." January 22, 1993.

Obituary.

B112 *London Times.* "Followers of Fashion pay homage to eternal icon." January 22, 1993.

Article notes that throughout Audrey's career, "designers would repeatedly recreate the Hepburn look on catwalks and in the pages of glossy fashion journals."

B113 *Look.* "Audrey...the New Hepburn." October 21, 1952, pp 45-48.

A photo essay of Audrey that includes the famous *Roman Holiday* screen test .

B114 *Look.* "Chi-chi Cinderella." May 14, 1957, p. 116.

A favorable review of *Funny Face.*

B115 *Look.* "Cary Grant, Audrey Hepburn." December 17, 1963, pp 27-28.

Coverage of *Charade*, and Cary Grant exclaiming "All I want for Christmas is another movie with Audrey Hepburn!"

B116 Loos, Anita. "Everything Happens to Audrey Hepburn." *The American Weekly.* September 12, 1954. pp 11, 13.

Gigi author Anita Loos retells the Audrey Hepburn story from her birth in Belgium to her triumph in *Roman Holiday.*

B117 *Los Angeles Examiner.* "A Very Sick Girl." April 7, 1954.

An alarming story of Audrey's suffering from anemia, a drastic loss of weight and severe emotional exhaustion. "She will continue to perform in *Ondine*, but all other engagements are cancelled."

B118 *Los Angeles Times Magazine.* "Sweet and Saucy." August 30, 1953.

Brief cover story notes that Audrey's *Roman Holiday* screen test "began with a wink and ended with a giggle," neither of which were in the script.

B119 *Los Angeles Times.* "Audrey Hepburn Sleepy After Victory and Happy." March 27, 1954.

A post-Academy Award winning phone interview.

B120 *Los Angeles Times.* "Audrey Hepburn, Ferrer Marry in Swiss Chapel."September 26, 1954.

Coverage of Audrey's wedding to Mel Ferrer in Burgenstock, Switzerland.

B121 *Los Angeles Times Magazine.* "There's Only One Audrey--But Which One?" May 20, 1956, pp 18,44.

Photos of three remarkable Audrey lookalikes are run alongside the genuine article. Figuring out who's who is tougher than you might think.

B122 *Los Angeles Times.* "Hepburn gets a surprise $4000 to aid Somalis." September 22, 1992.

When U.S. sailors and marines heard that Audrey was making a surprise visit to the the Marine assault ship Tarawa, they decided to surprise her by raising $4000 for UNICEF in 90 minutes.

B123 *Los Angeles Times.* "Audrey Hepburn's Tumor found to be Cancerous." November 4, 1992.

A regrettably specious story in which doctors predicted that a tumor they removed from her abdomen was "not likely to cause any lasting damage."

B124 *Mademoiselle.*"The Mademoiselle Merit Awards." January 1954, p.38.

Audrey is lauded for "her incomparable technique, her mobile face and her combination of wistfulness and hauteur."

B125 *Mademoiselle.* "Young Beauties." June 1954.

Audrey's dress receives more coverage than she does in this one-paragraph, one-photo piece.

B126 Malin, Harry. "That's Our Fair Audrey." *New York Daily News.* April 21, 1991.

Enthusiastic praise on the eve of Audrey's Lincoln Center tribute; "Filmland salutes the girl who lived at the head of the class."

B127 Mansfield, Stephanie. "Audrey Hepburn, Eternal Waif." *New York Post*. August 31, 1985.

Interview with the "elusive, untouchable, terminally waiflike" Hepburn, with nothing new to offer.

B128 Maslin, Janet. "Audrey Hepburn: Farewell to the Swan." *New York Times*. January 21, 1993.

Critic Janet Maslin pays tribute.

B129 Maynard, J. "Audrey's Harvest of The Heart." *Photoplay*. September 1956, pp 42, 113-115.

A rare positive account of Audrey and Mel's marriage. In a heartfelt interview, she talks about her profound happiness and how being married has changed her for the better; "I've been restless, but that's over. I didn't know exactly where or what I wanted to be. Now I do. Wherever Mel is, I'm home." The article also contains more interesting details about Audrey's childhood, including her lack of regard for dolls ("They never seemed real to me.").

B130 *McCalls*. "McCalls Visits." June 1957, p.84.

A report from the set of *Love in the Afternoon*, including interviews with Audrey and Gary Cooper. "I've wanted to act with Miss Hepburn ever since seeing her in *Gigi*," Cooper said.

B131 McWilliams, Michael. "Audrey Hepburn: Still the fairest of them all." *Detroit News*. April 25, 1991.

More coverage of the Lincoln Center tribute (see B012).

B132 Miller, Gilbert. "The Search for Gigi." *Theatre Arts*. July, 1952, pp 49-51.

Gigi producer Gilbert Miller recounts the path taken by the play from conception to opening night. Of Audrey, he writes that neither he nor playwright Anita Loos have had cause to regret choosing her for the lead role, and he is pleased that "*Gigi* was the play and the role which introduced her to America and to stardom."

B133 Mills, Bart. "Hepburn The Homebody In Bloodline." *Los Angeles Times*. November 19, 1978, p.5.

Interviews about the production of *Bloodline* with Audrey, director Terence Young and co-stars James Mason and Michelle Phillips.

B134 Mills, Donia. "They Came to Hail Hepburn and Her Yorkshire Trifle." *Washington (D.C.) Star*. March 21, 1976.

Audrey appears at the *Robin and Marian* premiere.

B135 Morgan, Kelcy L. "The Little Audrey Story Nobody Knows." *Uncensored*. November 1955, pp 8-9, 72.

A less-than-sympathetic examination of Mel Ferrer's marriages prior to meeting Audrey.

B136 Morley, Sheridan. "Hepburn bows out as the last and only true princess." *London Sunday Times*. January 24, 1993.

Another moving tribute from Fleet Street, written by Sheridan Morley. "I have met most female members of the House of Windsor," writes Morley, "but the only true princess I ever met was Audrey Hepburn."

B137 *Movie Stars*. "Audrey's Problem: How Many Men Does it Take to Make a Woman Forget her First Love?" May 1964.

Tabloid stuff, but not as hyperbolic.

B138 *National Enquirer*. "Audrey Hepburn's last moments." February 9, 1993

An intimate chronicle of Audrey's last days, related by "an insider." Quite possibly fiction, but well-written.

B139 *New York Times*. "Chronicle." February 2, 1991.

Announcements of two New York Audrey Hepburn appearances--a dinner honoring her as UNICEF Goodwill Ambassador, and as the honoree of a tribute by the Film Society of Lincoln Center.

B140 *New York Times*. Obituary. January 20, 1993.

B141 *New Yorker*. Obituary. February 1, 1993.

Remembering the actress who "incarnated her era's feeling of optimism and entitlement."

B142 *New Yorker.* "Winner; New York portion of Hollywood's Academy Awards." April 3, 1954, pp 30-31.

Cleverly written, often hilarious account of the backstage goings-on in New York on Oscar night; "Desperately wanted to congratulate Hepburn. Felt it least I could do. Would justify whole evening, cumberbund, etc. Elbowed out of way by photographer. Hepburn, visibly shaken, posed again. 'Audrey, where's the Oscar?' photographer asked. 'I've lost it.' she said. Vision of loveliness. Eight beaters dispatched upstairs to find Oscar- -any Oscar."

B143 *New Yorker.* "Gigi." December 8, 1951, p.32.

The first American interview with Audrey, conducted after a ballet class. Credited with helping "to relieve the gloom of a generally overcast theatrical season" through her performance in *Gigi* . Audrey talked about her dreams of a career in ballet and the nightmare of Germany's wartime occupation of Holland--"any stories you've heard about that, no matter how awful, are probably true."

B144 *Newsweek.* "Big Screen 'War And Peace.'" July 30, 1956, pp 53-56.

An informative report from the set of *War and Peace* , plus brief biographies of Audrey and Mel and interviews about their plans for the future.

B145 *Newsweek.* "Flower Power." March 18, 1991.

A blurb on the "Newsmakers" page on Audrey's appearing as host of *Gardens of the World.*

B146 *Newsweek.* "A Princess in Disguise." February 1, 1993, p. 74.

Another obituary, more personal and affectionate than most; "It's hard to overestimate the effect Audrey Hepburn had upon the world when she breezed into prominence in the 1950's...She changed the way men looked at women--and, more important, the way women looked at themselves."

B147 Nichols, M. "Audrey Hepburn Goes Back to the Bar." *Coronet.* November 1956, pp 44-51.

A photo essay of Audrey studying ballet in preparation for her role in *Funny Face*. The article lists her measurements at age 27 at 32-21-35.

B148 *The Observer*. "A Life of Films and Famine." October 4, 1992.

A brief biographical article that concentrates on Audrey's UNICEF work.

B149 Oppenheimer, Peer J. ."Audrey Hepburn: Everybody's Fair Lady." *Family Weekly*. March 8, 1964, pp 4-6.

"She sounds too good to be true; but the truth is--she is that good." begins this complimentary article which features quotes from George Cukor and Billy Wilder.

B150 Osborne, Robert. "Remembering Legacy of Audrey Hepburn." *Hollywood Reporter*. January 22, 1993

"Two days later and the devastating loss of Audrey Hepburn still stings," writes columnist and longtime friend Robert Osborne. A very moving remembrance.

B151 Ostreich, James R.."Audrey Hepburn in Debut of Work on Anne Frank." *New York Times*. March 29, 1990.

A mixed review of the New York performance of the Concert for Life (see S6).

B152 O'Toole, Lawrence. "Farewell, Fair Lady." *Entertainment Weekly*. February 5, 1993, pp 26-27.

A brief but touching remembrance, plus a list of the best Audrey Hepburn films available on videocassette.

B153 *Parade*. "Remembering Audrey." February 28, 1993, p. 24.

Parade remembered Audrey "not only for her luminous screen presence but also for her tenderness and sensitivity toward others." The article quoted a condolence letter Audrey wrote to Cary Grant's widow Barbara, after Grant died in 1986.

B154 *Paris Match*. February 4, 1993.

Beautiful color cover photo and story.

B155 Parsons, Louella. "Audrey Hepburn--Greatest since Garbo?" *Cosmopolitan*. September, 1953, pp 10-11

Famed Hollywood columnist Louella Parsons compares Audrey to Garbo and the young Ingrid Bergman, calling her performance in *Roman Holiday* "truly magnificent." Her career to date is reviewed.

B156 Parsons, Louella. "Is Romance Out of Audrey Hepburn's Life?" *Los Angeles Examiner*. October 11, 1953.

Louella Parsons spills the beans on Audrey's broken engagement with James Hanson, and reports Audrey's denial of an affair with Gregory Peck.

B157 Parsons, Louella. "What's in a name?" *Pictorial Living* (the *Los Angeles Examiner* magazine). January 31, 1960.

A rare co-interview with Audrey and Mel conducted by Louella Parsons, in which the couple debate about names for their expected baby and discuss other upcoming productions.

B158 *People*. "The Voice, the Neck, the Charm: They Just Don't Make Movie Stars Like Audrey Hepburn Anymore." April 12, 1976.

"I wish I could spice this up with something shocking--really I do" says Audrey in this excellent cover story. Instead, she provides one of the best and simply eloquent explanations for her enduring popularity; "People associate me with a time when women wore pretty dresses in movies."

B159 *People*. "Our Fair Lady." February 1, 1993, pp 60-62, 64, 66-67.

An excellent, loving cover story and tribute, embellished with many photos from Audrey's films and private life.

B160 *People*. "Adieu To The Lady Next Door." February 8, 1993, pp 53-54.

Coverage of Audrey's funeral, noting the unpretentious nature of the ceremony and burial as "pure Hepburn." Those in attendance included Mel Ferrer, Dr. Andrea Dotti, Robert Wolders, Roger Moore, Hubert de Givenchy and Alain Delon.

B161 *People Extra.*"A Tribute to Audrey Hepburn." Winter 1993.

For the first time in its history, *People* Magazine devoted an entire 80-page special edition to remembering a single movie star. Despite two previous articles about Audrey's death in its weekly magazine, "it was soon apparent to the staff..that even a cover story couldn't do full justice to this extraordinary woman, " wrote publisher Ann Moore. The magazine was produced in just nine days, and Moore reports being amazed at the number of people who volunteered to work overtime on the project. The result is a treasure-trove of photos surrounding sections devoted to Audrey titled "The Enchantress," "The Girl," "The Stage," "The Movies," "The Woman," "The Look," "The Angel," "The Farewell," and "The Memories." Beautifully done, and an even more fitting tribute for its decision to donate the first $100,000 from newsstand sales to UNICEF.

B162 Pepper, Curtis Bill. "The Return of Audrey Hepburn." *McCalls.* January 1976, pp 94, 126-127.

One of the only detailed interviews of Audrey from the 1970's. She talks at length about her hiatus from Hollywood, her life in Rome, and the photographs of Dr. Dotti dancing in Italian nightclubs with other women; "It's his way of relaxing, and I think it's important for him to feel free. I don't expect him to sit in front of the TV when I'm not there."

B163 Perry, Hart. "Audrey Hepburn." *Seventeen*. January 1965, pp 79, 114.

A charming interview conducted by a starstruck sixteen-year-old. The article breaks no new ground, but is well-written and peppered with several amusing observations; "There was something tremendously aristocratic about her and all at once I was very glad that I had stopped to get a haircut before the interview."

B164 *Philadelphia Inquirer.* "Mindful of her past, Hepburn travels the world for UNICEF." February 8, 1990.

The Concert for Life is detailed (see S6).

B165 *Philadelphia Inquirer.* "Breakfast at UNICEF." May 13, 1990.

"Cinema goddess" Audrey discusses the origin of her relationship with UNICEF.

B166 *Photoplay.* August 1982.

B167 *Photoplay.* September 1986.

B168 *Photoplay.* February 1989.

B169 Pitt, Moya. "Audrey Hepburn: The 'Fair Lady' They Call the Iron Butterfly." *Uncensored.* June 1964, pp 20-21, 46.

With a title like that you know the tabloids are at it again. We are told that whether it's money, movies or men, Audrey gets exactly what she wants!

B170 *Pix.* "Audrey Hepburn: The new style in film stars." October 9, 1954, p.42.

A brief biography of Audrey, the heroine of "show business' greatest Cinderella story."

B171 Plaskin, Glenn. "Audrey Hepburn." *Us.* October 17, 1988, pp 43-46.

A two-hour interview produced the usual questions and answers-- "Whenever I hear or read I'm beautiful, I simply don't understand it"..."[World War II] made me resilient and terribly appreciative for everything good that came afterward"..."I always wanted lots of babies-- that's been a conducting theme in my life."

B172 Plaskin, Glenn. "She hardly goes lightly through life." *Richmond News Leader.* May 24, 1991.

Audrey discusses in surprisingly frank deatail her parents' divorce, the absence of her father, her own two failed marriages and her relationship with Robert Wolders.

B173 *Popular Photography.* "A Star In Motion." April 1957, pp 76-79.

A photo essay of Audrey by Ed Feingerish, taken in Paris. The text focuses on Feingerish and his photographic technique.

B174 *Postif.* May 1982.

A one-paragraph article, in French.

B175 *Premiere.* "Strike A Pose." January 1991.

Films about the fashion industry are the subject of this article, in which *Funny Face* figures prominently. It is listed as Audrey's "off-camera favorite," but this is not substantiated nor consistent with quotes in many other articles.

B176 Pritchett, Dolly. "Audrey Hepburn: The Dainty Dish That Hollywood Can't Digest." *Confidential*, April 1964, pp 38-39, 68.

Audrey's $1 million salary for *My Fair Lady* prompted this tabloid piece about her business sense. With Audrey, studio executives "come as supplicants to the Queen, bare their heads on entering her presence and sit down patiently while Audrey explains exactly what she wants, how much and when," according to this colorful concoction.

B177 Pryor, Thomas M.."Audrey Hepburn Home to Recover." *New York Times*. February 3, 1959.

Coverage of Audrey's recuperation from injuries she suffered after falling from a horse, on the set of *The Unforgiven* . "I'm fine, just fine," she tells reporters. "It doesn't hurt, except when I laugh."

B178 Putnam, Aaron. "But is it Really True What They're Saying about Little Audrey and William Holden?" *Whisper*. May 1963, pp14-16.

A rare tabloid article that is able to quote (slightly) more respectable sources for its allegations of an affair between Audrey and William Holden. "Everyone in the know has his fingers crossed that the romance between two big married stars is just a passing fancy that will be forgotten when the picture they're doing together is finished." wrote Hedda Hopper. A *New York Enquirer* item with the same gist is also reprinted. A tacky story graced by a gorgeous photo of Audrey.

B179 Queet, Henry. "Did Audrey Lose Mel to Sam?" *Confidential*. May 1968, pp 36, 72.

This tabloid article alleges that while Audrey had an affair with Albert Finney during production on *Two For the Road*, Mel Ferrer was romancing 22-year-old model Samantha Jones.

B180 *Rave*. "Audrey and The Lady from Dubuque." June 1954, pp 38-44.

A typical tabloid article, written with undeniable verve but questionable taste, which helps explain why Audrey would later shut herself off from the press; "The most sizzling actress in the United States these days is a gawky, flat-chested, saucer-eyed little English chick named Audrey Hepburn, whom not one person in a carload knew from Maisie Zilch just twelve months ago." A good palate-cleaner from the bouquets tossed by mainstream reporters.

B181 *Rave*. "Inside Audrey Hepburn." November 1954, pp 4-7.

More tabloid tripe, though this time Audrey emerges relatively unscathed. The article instead lambasts "balding, codfish-eyed, skull-headed" Mel Ferrer for latching on to Audrey to advance his own career. The same opinion was expressed by more respectable publications, but in less purplish prose.

B182 *The Reader*. "Audrey's Forgotten Classics." January 29, 1993.

While other publications recalled *Roman Holiday* and *My Fair Lady*, *The Reader* praised *Charade* as "the greatest Hitchcock pastiche ever made," and *They All Laughed*" as hilarious, ragged comedy."

B183 Reed, Rex. "Audrey Hepburn." *Vanity Fair*. March 1993, p.146.

Photo and brief obituary, written with affection by Rex Reed: "One look at the face of Audrey Hepburn and you knew that God made one of the ultimate impressions on earth, as perfect as a peony."

B184 Reynolds, Gordon. "The Startling Facts Behind Those Audrey Hepburn Blues." *Top Secret*. February 1959, pp 6-7, 42.

Another tabloid article, this time written with sympathy toward its subject rather than sarcasm. Audrey is depicted as miserable because she is unable to have a baby. Her son Sean was born the following year.

B185 Riding, Alan. "Audrey Hepburn Tribute After a 25-year Pause." *New York Times.* April 22, 1991.

More excerpts from interviews given during the Lincoln Center tribute (see B012).

B186 Ringgold, Gene. "Audrey Hepburn." *Films in Review*. December 1971. pp 585-601.

Superb biography, career review, analysis and filmography that provides an ideal introduction to Audrey Hepburn's career and mystique.

B187 Rosenblum, Anne. "Two For the Show." *Entertainment Weekly*. September 4, 1992, p. 30.

An article on stars and their designers. Audrey and Givenchy are listed with Sylvester Stallone and Gianni Versace and other pairs. "He defined elegance. She added the incandescence."

B188 *Salt Lake Tribune*. "Marion No Comeback, Insists Audrey." March 9, 1976

"I never retired. I'm not one of those people who retire and then come back year after year." said Audrey, who was faced with this question in every interview while promoting *Robin and Marian*.

B189 Sarris, Andrew. "Comedies With Bite." *American Film*. October 1986.

Film critic Andrew Sarris lists *Love in the Afternoon* as one of the top ten "Comedies with Bite," calling it "one of the romantic high points of the fifties."

B190 *Screen Stories*. December 1964.

Cover story on *My Fair Lady*.

B191 Seidenbaum, Art. "Audrey Hepburn; Making of My Fair Lady." *McCalls*. October 1964, pp 97-98, 182-186.

One of the very best articles ever written about Audrey, by a reporter who observed her at work for six months on the set of *My Fair Lady*. Journalist Art Seidenbaum begins by discussing her aversion to interviews, adding that "Pleased to meet you" was "the longest conversation we had for the next three months." What follows are several wonderful anecdotes about Audrey's friendly relationship with the film crew, the ongoing debate over her singing, and how the film set handled the announcement of President John F. Kennedy's assassination. When she finally did submit to an interview, Seidenbaum covers a variety of subjects, from her favorite films (*Camille* [1936] and *Waterloo Bridge* [1940]) to her homelife in Switzerland. First-rate.

B192 *Senior Scholastic*. "Audrey Scores Twice." April 7, 1954, p.64.

B193 Shawcross, Jim. "Is Audrey Hepburn Ashamed of her Burlesk Past?" *Revealed*. July 1957, pp 20-23.

More sordid details about Audrey's role in "that spicy French girlie show," *Sauce Piquante.* Old news by now, so the article also revealed that Audrey's father was carried for years on the suspect list of British counter-espionage because of his "pro-Nazi" sympathies.

B194 Shearer, Lloyd. "Showing Their Age." *Parade.* December 9, 1973, p.5.

Audrey and Ava Gardner both attended a society wedding in Austria, and reporter Lloyd Shearer took the opportunity to point out how old they looked. What a guy.

B195 *Sight and Sound.* "Gamine Against the Grain." March 1993, pp 30-32.

A fond remembrance of Audrey's stage and film career, with extensive coverage of her influence on sixties pop culture.

B196 *Silver Screen.* "Is Hollywood Shifting Its Accent on Sex?" July 1954, pp 24-29.

B197 Skolsky, Sidney. "Hollywood is my Beat." *Hollywood Citizen News.* July 16, 1959.

A disjointed piece about "a famous pair of He and She," Audrey and Mel, by columnist Sidney Skolsky.

B198 Smith, Liz. "The Gracious, Giving Hepburn." *Los Angeles Times.* January 22, 1993.

Columnist Liz Smith's lovely tribute to Audrey; "the ideal of chic, combined with vulnerability. Her voice, with its heartbreaking crack, was one of moviedom's most distinctive."

B199 *Sound Stage.* "Audrey Hepburn: Filmography." December 1964, p. 19.

A Hepburn filmography complete through *My Fair Lady.*

B200 Sragow, Michael. "The will of a Hollywood wisp." *San Francisco Examiner.* December 7, 1990.

Reviews of *Roman Holiday* and *Breakfast at Tiffany's,* presented in a double-bill at San Francisco's Castro Theater.

B201 *Stage & Cinema*. "It's all on with Audrey and Albie." December
29, 1967, pp 20-22.

Albert Finney is blamed for the divorce of Audrey and Mel Ferrer .

B202 *The Star*. "Brave Audrey Hepburn Vows: I Must Get Back to Work
For Starving Kids." November 17, 1992

"None of this changes anything, you know..the crusade goes on," said
Audrey when learning of her cancer, according to this tabloidarticle. She
remained determined to continue her work for UNICEF, and defied
doctor's orders to do so.

B203 *The Star*. "You've Made My Final Wish Come True." December
29, 1992.

The American Marines' mercy mission to feed the starving children of
Somalia fulfilled Audrey's dearest wish in her final days.

B204 Stein, Jeannine. "A Special Colleague." *Los Angeles Times*.
February 18, 1991.

Audrey is honored at a Valentine's Day luncheon and fashion show given
by the Colleagues.

B205 Stone, Melvin. "The Public Reason For Audrey Hepburn's
Private War." *Uncensored*. May 1958, pp 30-33.

Audrey's gradual retreat from publicity seemed to multiply those stories
that did not need her cooperation to be published. Though overstated,
there may be some truth to the article's statement that Audrey's brief
costume in *Ondine* did not cause the outcry it might have on another
actress, because "it's unthinkable that anyone would dare point a finger
at a girl who acts like a Queen every waking moment." However, reports
that critics "blasted" the play are erroneous.

B206 Swanson, Pauline. "Knee-Deep In Stardust." *Photoplay*. April
1954, pp 58, 102-103.

A relaxed, informal chat about family and friends, clothes and work, that
captures Audrey's still wide-eyed wonder at her success.

B207 Tallmer, Jerry. "Audrey's N.Y. Holiday." *New York Post*. April 22, 1991.

Brief interview and filmography.

B208 Taylor, Tom. "What 'Life' did not print about Audrey Hepburn," *Top Secret*. Spring 1954, pp 5-6

"Read and decide yourself how angelic she really is!" tempted this tabloid article, which described in lurid detail Audrey's appearance in "a risque French girlie show" called *Sauce Piquante* .

B209 Thompson, Frank. "Audrey Hepburn." *American Film*. May 1990, pp 54-56.

Nearly 30 years after *Roman Holiday*, Audrey continued to receive love letters from critics. "It's that face of hers that renders all critical distance null and void," writes Frank Thompson. "She is not an actress we judge, but a person we know and love." Thompson chooses the top ten Hepburn films available on videocassette: *Roman Holiday, Sabrina, Funny Face, Love in the Afternoon, The Nun's Story, Breakfast at Tiffany's, Charade, My Fair Lady, Wait Until Dark* and *Robin and Marian*. At the time *Two For the Road* was unavailable on video.

B210 *Time*. "Princess Apparent." September 7, 1953, pp 60-63.

Time's cover story on Audrey combined a rave review of *Roman Holiday* with an excellent in-depth interview; "Paramount's new star sparkles and glows with the fire of a finely cut diamond."

B211 *Time*. "Robin and Marian." March 22, 1976, pp 78-79.

An unfavorable review of *Robin and Marian*, and a nice sidebar piece on Audrey's return to the movies and her difficulty in adjusting to the faster-paced shooting schedule; "I've never made a film so fast and I would like to have had more time."

B212 *Time*. "Film's Fairest Lady." February 1, 1993, p. 63.

Obituary, and career overview.

B213 *Uncensored*. "The Secret Past of Audrey Hepburn." December 1954, pp 26-27.

Photos of Audrey in her *Sauce Piquante* costume, accompanied by surprisingly (for a tabloid) non-judgmental details of her performance.

B214 *U.S. News and World Report.* "Goodbye Fair Lady."
February 1, 1993, p.16.

Concise but well-written obituary, in which Audrey is again described as "the personification of true elegance and class." The article lauds her choices of family over career, and "political activism over photo opportunities and hype."

B215 Van Deusen, Charles. "Frail Dynamo." *Los Angeles Examiner.*
April 26, 1959.

An article that expresses surprise that Audrey and Mel Ferrer are still married. Nothing special.

B216 *Vanity Fair.* "Funny Face." July 1987.

"Suddenly the catwalks are thronged with Audrey Hepburns," noted this fashion article on how the look that "bewitched the 50's and 60's seems right for the 80's." Audrey's black dress in *Breakfast at Tiffany's* is singled out as a particularly prominent influence.

B217 *Variety.* Obituary. January 21, 1993.

B218 Viotti, Sergio. "Britain's Hepburn." *Films and Filming.* December 1954, p.7

When *Films and Filming* ran a negative review of Audrey's performance in *Sabrina* , the "violent discussion" that followed compelled them to run this opposing viewpoint. Writer Sergio Viotti defended Hepburn's performance, but expressed hope that she would play "stronger" parts that would "broaden the scope of her artistic possibilities."

B219 *Vogue.* February 15, 1954.

A two-page photo spread of Audrey and Mel Ferrer.

B220 *Vogue.* "Four Young Stars--Will They Be Great?" April 1, 1954, p. 123.

She had already been anointed by other publications, but *Vogue* was apparently still wondering if Audrey was the real thing. "More magic than any other young star. Her greatest weakness--a tendency to cuteness. Her greatest asset: her magnetism." The other three young stars were Julie Harris, Geraldine Page and Joan Greenwood, good choices all.

B221 *Vogue*. "Audrey Hepburn." November 1, 1954. pp 124-125.

A two-page photo spread of Audrey by Cecil Beaton, who would later design the sets and costumes for *My Fair Lady*.

B222 *Vogue*. August 15, 1964.

A photo layout by Cecil Beaton of Audrey in various Givenchy hats, inspired by the memorable headwear she wore in *My Fair Lady*. Audrey also confesses to being a hat-lover away from the set; "I feel that I am not completely dressed without one."

B223 *Vogue*. "Audrey and Andrea." March 15, 1969, p.153.

A two-page photo spread of Audrey and new husband Dr. Andrea Dotti, which mentions their intention to live in Rome.

B224 Waldman, Joyce. "Audrey's Fantastic Figure." *Cosmopolitan*. June 1959, pp 62-65.

Audrey demonstrates her exercise regimen in a series of photos.

B225 Warga, Wayne. "The Rapid Re-Rise of Audrey Hepburn." *Los Angeles Times*. April 11, 1976.

Another *Robin and Marian*-related interview, but also one of the few articles to make the observation that "Audrey's life would make a marvelous movie."

B226 *Washington Post*. "Audrey Hepburn, Will of the Wisp." August 5, 1985.

Basic interview following Audrey's contribution to a documentary on William Wyler (see F28).

B227 Waterbury, Ruth. "The Two Women Who Broke Up Audrey Hepburn's Marriage." *Photoplay*. December 1967, pp 72-76.

In the late sixties *Photoplay* began to resemble the more trashy tabloids with articles like this one, which dealt with Audrey's separation from Mel

Ferrer.

B228 Waterbury, Ruth. "Brides at 39--Mothers at 40?" *Photoplay.*
November 1969, pp 57,85.

A return to the more observant and interesting type of piece on Audrey
that *Photoplay* specialized in throughout the fifites. A new interview plus
some insightful points on how Audrey's life and personality changed
after marrying Dr. Dotti; "There seems to be a new Audrey emerging.
She is gay and outrightly careless. She is young andseems to have lots
of fun. Her phone number is listed in the Roman telephone book." The
article's title refers to Audrey and Jackie Kennedy.

B229 Weiler, A.H.. "Hepburn to Reign in Spain." *New York Times.* April
11, 1965.

Announcement that Audrey will play Queen Isabella in the film *The
Castles and the Crown*, directed by Mel Ferrer. The film was never made.

B230 Wesley, Lynn. "Is Audrey Hepburn A Homewrecker?"
Suppressed. September 1954, pp 19-21.

Typically trashy character assassination from perhaps the nastiest scandal
sheet of its day; "Is the Academy Award winner a dedicated young
thespian or a hard, calculating minx?"

B231 Whitcomb, Jon. "Dear Valentine." *Cosmopolitan.* February 1954,
p.91

Artist Jon Whitcomb selected his favorite 1954 heartthrobs. Of Audrey
he raved "I worship the celluloid you stand on."

B232 Wilson, Liza. "Audrey: the girl with the hop-skip-and-jump
marriage." *American Weekly (Los Angeles Examiner Magazine).*
September 29, 1957.

Audrey's habit of decorating hotel rooms with her personal possessions
is described.

B233 *Woman's Home Companion.*"Audrey Hepburn Plays a Classic
Heroine." September 1956, p. 83.

Coverage of Audrey's appearance in *War and Peace*.

B234 *Woman's Wear Daily.* February 27, 1987

B235 Woolridge, Jane. "At this stage of her life, Hepburn's still a fair lady." *Miami Herald.* December 3, 1989.

Coverage of a press conference held by Audrey to promote her tour with the New World Symphony to raise money for UNICEF (see S6).

B236 Wuntch, Phillip. "Audrey's Many Faces." *Dallas Morning News.* March 6, 1976.

Career review and preview of her "return" to movies in *Robin and Marian.* "Audrey Hepburn brings moviegoers a touch of sensuality, vulnerability, femininity and yes, a touch of class."

B237 Wuntch, Phillip. "Life imitates film art as Audrey meets press." *Dallas Morning News.* March 20, 1976.

Coverage of the premiere of *Robin and Marian* at Radio City Music Hall, where Audrey received a standing ovation from over 6000 fans outside the theater.

B238 Wuntch, Phillip. "Audrey Hepburn reminisces." *Dallas Morning News.* March 2, 1991.

Audrey receives the 1991 Master Screen Artist Award at the USA Film Festival.

B239 Zeitlin, David. "A Lovely Audrey in Religious Role." *Life.* June 8, 1959, pp 141-142.

Audrey is pictured in her Sister Luke attire from *The Nun's Story* on the cover, but the interview inside is with Louise Habetts, the real-life model for Audrey's character. Habetts said she was "delighted" with the film, which she saw three times. "I'm never going to see it again," she added, "because if I do I'm going to run right back to the convent."

BOOKS

B240 Affron, Charles. *Star Acting*. E.P. Dutton, New York, 1977.

A history of and homage to the careers of Greta Garbo, Lillian Gish and Bette Davis. Affron describes a scene in *The Unforgiven* when Gish combs out Audrey Hepburn's hair as one in which "two of the screen's most extraordinary faces are united."

B241 Anger, Kenneth. *Hollywood Babylon II*. E.P. Dutton, New York, 1984.

More shocking, gruesome photos and venomous stories in this sequel to *Hollywood Babylon*. Anger writes that Alfred Hitchcock's misogyny was "inflamed" by Audrey's backing out of *No Bail for the Judge* (see W12). Afterwards he began making films like *Psycho* (1960), which put the blame on women for stirring uncontrollable passions in men.

B242 Aylesworth, Thomas G. *The Best of Warner Bros*. Gallery Books, New York, 1986.

Coffee table book packed with color photos from Warner Bros. classics. One paragraph on *The Nun's Story*, and three pages on *My Fair Lady* and the country's preparation to resent Audrey for usurping the role of Eliza. But Aylesworth writes that she responded by "giving one of the greatest performances of her life." Reviewing *Wait Until Dark*, he offers more bouquets--"It would seem that Audrey Hepburn is incapable of giving a bad performance."

B243 Babington, Bruce and Peter William Evans. *Affairs to Remember*. Manchester University Press, Manchester, 1989.

In one chapter the authors analyze Julie Andrews' screen persona, and the complicated elements that are present "beneath her veneer of purity." They conclude that Andrews lost *My Fair Lady* to Audrey because she lacked "the kind of petite, fragile, pretty-pretty, gawky, Swiss Finishing School qualities so much in abundance in Hepburn."

B244 Balcon, Michael. *Michael Balcon Presents...A Lifetime of Films*. Hutchinson of London, London, 1969.

Balcon was the producer of *The Lavender Hill Mob*. "We all have our blind spots," he writes. "In the prologue and epilogue of *Lavender Hill Mob* we had a very pretty girl selling cigarettes to Alec Guinness in the airport lounge. I paid no particular attention to her. Her name was Audrey Hepburn."

B245 Bawden, Liz-Anne. *The Oxford Companion to Film*. Oxford University Press, New York, 1976.

Praise for Audrey in *Roman Holiday*, *Funny Face* and *My Fair Lady*, for which "she was justly acclaimed for the style and polish of her performance. This excellent reference volume also notes that with *Two for the Road*, she "progressed past the limits of the ingenue roles that initiated her success."

B246 Baxter, John. *King Vidor*. Simon & Schuster, New York, 1970.

Audrey, as Natasha in Vidor's *War and Peace*, is pictured on the cover of this scholarly assessment of Vidor's filmography. Baxter gives a mixed assessment of *War and Peace*, but adds that Audrey's Natasha "clearly outdistanced Henry Fonda' s languid, puzzled Pierre and Mel Ferrer's neutral Andrei."

B247 Beaton, Cecil. *Self-Portrait with Friends*. Times Books, New York, 1979.

Cecil Beaton was the set and costume designer on *My Fair Lady*. In these excerpts from his diary, he recalls his first meeting with Audrey, whom he describes as "chock-a-block with spritelike charm," and their instant friendship. But he expresses regret that she was often caught in the middle of his ceaseless arguments with director George Cukor.

B248 Brode, Douglas. *The Films of the 1960s*. Citadel Press, New Jersey, 1980.

Similar in style to Citadel's *Films of*...series, listing casts, credits, synopses and reviews of nearly 50 releases from the 1960s, including *Breakfast at Tiffany's* and *My Fair Lady*.

B249 Brown, Jared. *The Fabulous Lunts*. Atheneum, New York, 1986.

Brown discusses Alfred Lunt's direction of the play *Ondine*, and the problems he encountered with Mel Ferrer. "We bought Hepburn and the price was Ferrer," said one source, "it turned out to be much tooexpensive." Audrey spent rehersals torn between a loyalty to her director and her admiration of the man she would later marry.

B250 Brown, Peter M. and Jim Pinkston. *Oscar Dearest*. Harper & Row, New York, 1987.

An analysis of "six decades of scandal, politics and greed" involving the Academy Awards. *My Fair Lady*, dismissed as "a stylish, lovely film version of a hit Broadway play and little else," is on the authors' list of ten films that should not have won Best Picture honors. As for Audrey's performance-- "Nobody, not even her staunchest fans, believed for a moment that elegant Audrey Hepburn was a Cockney guttersnipe."

B251 Casper, Joseph Andrew. *Stanley Donen*. Scarecrow Press, Inc., New York, 1983.

The fifth in a series of books on prominent filmmakers. An excellent guide to the career and films of Stanley Donen, who directed Audrey in *Funny Face, Charade* and *Two for the Road*. Casper includes several Donen quotes about Audrey, all of which are complimentary--"Audrey, like Fred Astaire, makes my soul fly. She opens me up to beautiful feelings."

B252 Cawkwell, Tim. *The World Encyclopedia of Film.*. Galahad Books, New York, 1974.

A one-paragraph biography and an incomplete filmography.

B253 Chevalier, Maurice. *Bravo Maurice!* Julliard, Paris, 1968.

Chevalier recalls being "nervous" on the set of *Love in the Afternoon*, but warming quickly to co-stars Audrey Hepburn and Gary Cooper.

B254 Clarke, Gerald. *Capote: a biography*. Simon and Schuster, New York, 1988.

Capote wanted Marilyn Monroe to star in the film adaptation of his novella *Breakfast at Tiffany's*, saying she would have been "absolutely marvelous." "Audrey is an old friend and one of my favorite people, but she was just wrong for the part."

B255 Coward, Noel. *The Noel Coward Diaries*. Little, Brown & Co., Boston, 1982.

Three entries in Coward's diary mention Audrey. On April 26, 1952 he records his review of *Gigi*--"an orgy of overacting and a vulgar script. Audrey Hepburn was inexperienced and rather too noisy." On February 4, 1962 he thought the movie *The Children's Hour* was "not good enough in spite of Audrey and Shirley (MacLaine)." He writes about his supporting role in *Paris When it Sizzles* on October 1, 1962, and calls Audrey "unquestionably the nicest and most talented girl in the business."

B256 Crosland, Margaret. *Colette*. British Book Centre, Inc. New York, 1954.

There are many biographies of the famed French writer Colette, all of which make a passing allusion to her casting of Audrey in the title role of *Gigi*. The author's remark upon first seeing Audrey, translated and quoted in a variety of ways, appears here as "There is our Gigi for America!"

B257 Dallinger, Nat. *Unforgettable Hollywood*. William Morrow & Co., New York, 1982.

This wonderful collection of candid celebrity photos includes one of Audrey and William Holden at a Hollywood reception in 1953.

B258 Denis, Christopher.*The Films of Shirley MacLaine*. Citadel Press. New Jersey, 1980.

Basic *Films of...* book with synopsis, reviews and photos from *The Children's Hour*.

B259 Deschner, Donald. *The Films of Cary Grant*. Citadel Press. New Jersey, 1973.

Photos, synopsis and reviews of *Charade* in this typical *Films of* series entry.

B260 Dick, Bernard F. *Hellman in Hollywood*. Fairleigh Dickinson University Press, London, 1982.

Analysis of *The Children's Hour*, in which Dick credits the film with one intriguing twist on the original material--the possibility that Karen, played by Audrey, may also be a lesbian. But the idea "doesn't entirelywork, because Audrey Hepburn is so completely feminine."

B261 Dickens, Homer. *The Films of Gary Cooper*. Citadel Press, New York, 1970.

Cast and credit information, synopsis, reviews and photos from *Love in the Afternoon.*

B262 Donaldson, Maureen. *An Affair to Remember-My Life with Cary Grant.* G.P. Putnam's Sons, New York, 1989.

Donaldson was Cary Grant's steady from 1973-1977. She writes that Grant gave Audrey a custom-made chrome-plated photograph, "which he bestowed on only a privileged few of his 53 leading ladies."

B263 Drake, Nicholas. *The Fifties in "Vogue."* Holt, London, 1989.

A retrospective of post World War II fashion and culture, for which Audrey contributes the Foreward. She recalled the fifties as "a time of renewal and of regained security" after the war. *Vogue* referred to Audrey as its "wonder girl;" "She has so captured the public image and the mood of the time that she has established a new standard of beauty."

B264 Eames, John Douglas. *The MGM Story.* Crown Publishers, Inc., New York, 1975.

Describes Audrey's only MGM film, *Green Mansions*, as "a brave try," noting that Audrey and Anthony Perkins "brought an appropriately fey quality to their jungle dalliance."

B265 Englund, Steven. *Grace of Monaco* . Doubleday, New York, 1984.

Englund describes Audrey as having "a rare combination of refinement and pixie charm, (whose) acting set a standard for a certain kind of charm and loveliness."

B266 Eyles, Allen. *Rex Harrison.* W.H. Allen, Great Britain, 1985.

Harrison was always diplomatic when asked to compare his two *My Fair Lady* co-stars, Julie Andrews and Audrey Hepburn, but Eyles has elicited some interesting quotes on the subject. "Audrey is more delicate than Julie," said Harrison, "so I tempered my interpretation and was a more agreeable Higgins." He found Audrey "inadequate" as the unkemptEliza, but much better after being transformed into a lady. Harrison also called the dubbing of Audrey's songs "obvious and ridiculous," and viewed her snub by the Motion Picture Academy as a "public chastisement from the industry."

B267 Fisher, Eddie. *My Life, My Loves.* Harper & Row, New

York,1981.

Fisher writes of seeing Audrey on stage in *Ondine* and falling "hopelessly in love with everything about her. The next day I sat down and wrote her a letter, printing it out carefully like a schoolboy and sending it to her with some flowers. I have no idea what I said--something about being her number one fan, hoping she would suggest we meet. I received a formal, ladylike thank you note." Years later, Audrey and Mel Ferrer had dinner with Eddie Fisher and Elizabeth Taylor, and Audrey announced that she had just been given *My Fair Lady*. That night, Taylor demanded three times that Fisher "get her *My Fair Lady*." He recalls that he had always given her everything she wanted, "but that was one thing I would <u>not</u> do." At the premiere of *My Fair Lady*, Audrey remembered the note and asked Fisher "Are you still my number one fan?"

B268 Freedland, Michael. *Gregory Peck*. Michael Freedland. William Morrow & Co., New York, 1980.

Peck was one of the first to see Audrey's screen test for *Roman Holiday*, and he approved of her casting immediately. Later, as he watched the picture evolve into a vehicle for his neophyte co-star, he felt it would be "pretentious" of him to take top billing alone. He persuaded Paramount Pictures to bill Audrey on the same line. Years later, Peck commented that he wished Audrey's comic abilities had been further exploited; "she has a delicious sense of humor, yet the producers saw her mostly as a 'classy lady' and seldom gave her zaniness full expression."

B269 Gardner, Ava. *Ava--My Story*. Bantam, New York, 1990.

In this self-effacing autobiography, Gardner recalls being "relieved more than upset" when Audrey beat her out of the 1953 Best Actress Oscar.

B270 Geist, Kenneth L. *Pictures Will Talk*. Charles Scribner's Sons, New York, 1974.

A book on the life and films of Joseph Mankiewicz. Geist quotesthe director as saying he wanted very much to film Shakespeare's *Twelfth Night* with Audrey as both Viola and Viola's twin brother, and Danny Kaye as Aguecheek. "It was a question of availability. She wasn't available when I was."

B271 Giannetti, Louis. *Masters of the American Cinema*. Prentice-Hall, New Jersey, 1981.

Scholarly book that focuses on directors and their films. Photos of Audrey from *Roman Holiday, Sabrina* and *The Nun's Story*, plus a photo of Shirley MacLaine from *The Children's Hour* that is mislabelled as one of Audrey.

B272 Gill, Brendon and Jerome Zerbe. *Happy Times.* Harcourt Brace Jovanovich, Inc., New York, 1973.

A collection of Jerome Zerbe's candid photos, including one of Audrey and William Holden on the set of *Paris When it Sizzles*, and of Audrey at a party circa 1955.

B273 Gilliatt, Penelope. *Unholy Fools.* Viking, New York, 1973.

Gilliatt offers an enthusiastic review of *Breakfast at Tiffany's*, while pointing out the differences between the film and Truman Capote's original story; "The book observes the streak of cold brutality that is often present in the romantic; the film merely sees the vivacity and sweetness of Audrey Hepburn."

B274 Goldsmith, Warren. *Film Fame.* Fame Publications, Beverly Hills, California, 1966.

One hundred brief bios of Hollywood's greatest stars. Audrey made the cut. Nothing new.

B275 Goodman, Ezra. *The Fifty-Year Decline and Fall of Hollywood.* Simon & Schuster, New York, 1961.

Goodman, the one-time Hollywood correspondent for *Time* Magazine, includes in this series of job-related anecdotes an amusing transcript of an interview with Jack Benny and his wife Mary. They are asked about Audrey for an upcoming article, and offer a variety of comments which add up to almost nothing. Billy Wilder, however, provided some "rip-snorting" quotes, writes Goodman, including his oft-quoted line about Audrey "making bazooms a thing of the past."

B276 Graham, Sheila. *Hollywood Revisited.* St. Martin's Press, New York, 1985.

Graham writes about the traditional British tea times that were observed at Audrey' s insistence during production of *Wait Until Dark*. The studio grumbled about lost work time, but the breaks provided an opportunity for cast and crew to grow closer, and the result was a much more cheerful working environment.

B277 Granger, Stewart. *Sparks Fly Upward.* Putnam, New York, 1981.

Granger writes that his wife Jean Simmons was William Wyler's confirmed choice for the role of Princess Anne in *Roman Holiday*, but she became unavailable through the machinations of Howard Hughes, who had expressed an interest in buying the rights to the story. When that didn't happen and Audrey Hepburn was ultimately cast, Simmons swore never to see the film. However, she confessed to Granger that she sneaked into a theatre, and later telephoned Audrey; "Although I wanted to hate you, I have to tell you I wouldn't have been half as good. You were just wonderful." Audrey returned the compliment, saying that she had been a fan of Simmons for years.

B278 Green, Stanley. *Hollywood Musicals Year by Year.* Hal Leonard Publishing, Wisconsin, 1990.

Reference guide to musicals, but entertainingly written. Green praises *Funny Face* and *My Fair Lady*, and mentions that Audrey starred in both without critiquing her performance.

B279 Grobel, Lawrence. *The Hustons.* Charles Scribner's Sons, New York, 1989.

Grobel reports that Lillian Gish was critical of how John Huston handled Audrey in *The Unforgiven*. "She had great talent and he never used it."

B280 Halliwell, Leslie. *The Filmgoer's Companion.* Hill and Wang, New York, 1977.

The sixth edition of this venerable reference publication notes that Audrey Hepburn "rose rapidly to Hollywood stardom as an elegant gamine."

B281 Halliwell, Leslie. *Halliwell's Film Guide.* Scribner, New York, 1991.

Capsule reviews of every Audrey Hepburn film, except *Nederlands in 7 Lessen*.

B282 Harris, Radie. *Radie's World.* Putnam, New York, 1975.

Hollywood Reporter columnist Harris recalls first meeting Audrey at a 1952 dinner party, and later escorting her to a matinee of *Quadrille* with

Alfred Lunt and Joan Fontaine. Harris regrets not being able to see her more after stardom struck, but without any bittnerness. "To say anything against Audrey Hepburn is like talking against the church."

B283 Harrison, Rex. *A Damned Serious Business*. Bantam, New York, 1991.

Harrison's second set of memoirs offers more insight into the production of *My Fair Lady*; "Poor Audrey had the unenviable task of taking over Julie's part, and weathering a great deal of adverse press publicity about how much she was being paid," he writes. "In the end, Audrey gave an enchanting performance, [and] contributed greatly to the film's success and lasting popularity." Harrison calls Julie's Oscar win and Audrey's Oscar snub "a kind of rough justice, Hollywood style."

B284 Haskell, Molly. *From Reverence to Rape*. Holt, Rinehart and Winston, New York, 1973.

Haskell examines the treatment of women in the movies, and singles out Audrey and Grace Kelly as the public's favorite screen images of females in the 1950s. "Jennifer Jones, Ava Gardner and Marilyn Monroe were out--too voluptuous and sexy. Doris Day and Debbie Reynolds were all right--Audrey and Grace were dead-center 'in'. Boyish and invulnerable, aristocratic and independent. They never swallowed their pride, exploited their sexuality or made fools of themselves over men."

B285 Haver, Ronald. *David O. Selznick's Hollywood*. Bonanza Books, New York, 1980.

In this lavish coffee table book, Haver covers Selznick's desire to film Leo Tolstoy's novel *War and Peace*, at the same time that Dino De Laurentiis announced his plans for an adaptation, with a confirmation from Audrey to play Natasha. Selznick, not wishing to do a rush job or get into a competition, dropped the project.

B286 Higham, Charles. *Audrey: The Life of Audrey Hepburn*. Macmillan Publishing Company, New York, 1984.

Competent, servicable 228-page biography written in straightforward and predominantly objective prose by Higham. Best in its coverage of Audrey's life before stardom struck.

B287 Hirschhorn, Clive. *The Warner Bros. Story*. Crown Publishers, New York, 1979.

Capsule reviews of *The Nun's Story, My Fair Lady* and *Wait Until Dark*, each accompanied by one photo.

B288 Hirschhorn, Joel. *Rating the Movie Stars.* Publications International, Ltd., Skokie, Illinois, 1983.

Four hundred movie stars are judged on their acting ability and the quality of their respective filmographies. Audrey received 3.14 stars on a four star scale, the same rating as "the other Hepburn."

B289 Hobhouse, Penelope and Elvin McDonald. *Gardens of the World: the Art and Practice of Gardening.* Macmillan, New York, 1991.

Audrey contributes the Foreward to this book, which inspired the PBS television series that Audrey hosted (see T43).

B290 Holloway, Stanley. *Wiv A Little Bit O'Luck.* Leslie Frewn, London, 1967.

Holloway played Eliza's father in *My Fair Lady*, and first met Audrey on the set of her first film, *One Wild Oat* . He also appeared in the Broadway production of *My Fair Lady*, and recalls being drawn into the Audrey Hepburn vs. Julie Andrews brouhaha. "I don't think they can be compared sensibly," he writes. "Both rose to their occasions and coped with their respective problems. I just think I was lucky to have appeared with them both. I once told Rex (Harrison) that he should regard himself as lucky, too, to have two such brilliant and charming leading ladies."

B291 Holston, Kim. *Starlet.* McFarland, North Carolina, 1988.

Biographies and filmographies of 54 leading ladies of the 1960s, most of them 'B' players. An affectionate tribute to many familiar Hollywood faces, such as Yvette Mimieux, Pamela Tiffin and Susannah York, all of whom were compared to Audrey at one time by the media.

B292 Houseman, Victoria. *Made in Heaven.* Bonus Books, Inc., Chicago, 1991.

"Who was married to who and for how long" is the question answered by this unique reference volume. Lists the date of Audrey's marriage to Mel Ferrer, the birth of their son Sean, their divorce, her marriage to Dr. Andrea Dotti, the birth of Luca, and their subsequent divorce.

B293 Huston, John. *An Open Book*. Alfred A. Knopf, New York, 1980.

Huston remembers with regret his experiences filming *The Unforgiven*, particularly Audrey's fall from a horse. "I felt responsible. It was on my conscience." he writes.

B294 Hyams, Joe. *Bogie*. The New American Library, New York, 1966.

Recalls Humphrey Bogart's impatience with Audrey during production of *Sabrina*. "She's all right," he growled, "if you don't mind a dozen takes."

B295 *The International Motion Picture Almanac*. Quigley Publications, New York, 1993.

Lists Audrey's film and television credits, plus a few of the show business-related awards she received.

B296 Kael, Pauline. *Kiss Kiss Bang Bang*. Bantam, New York, 1969.

Positive reviews of *Laughter in Paradise*, incorrectly cited as the film which "introduces" Audrey Hepburn, and *The Lavender Hill Mob*.

B297 Kael, Pauline. *5001 Nights at the Movies*. Henry Holt & Co., New York, 1985.

A collection of capsule reviews by Kael. She raves about *Roman Holiday*, cheers *Funny Face* and *Breakfast at Tiffany's*, but has mixed feelings about *My Fair Lady* and *Two for the Road*. Kael did not enjoy *Sabrina* ("a horrible concoction"), *Love in the Afternoon* ("overextended and overproduced") and *The Children's Hour*.

B298 Kael, Pauline. *More Love*. Dutton, New York, 1991.

Criticism of Audrey's performance in *Always* spills over into some unflattering remarks about her off-screen persona; "People see her, rise to their feet and applaud. She's become a ceremonial icon, ravishing and hollow. Where has the actress gone? The one who gave a magnificent performance in *The Nun's Story*?"

B299 Kaminsky, Stuart. *Coop*. St. Martin's Press, New York, 1980.

Kaminsky writes that Gary Cooper was "bothered" by criticism of the age difference between himself and Audrey in reviews of *Love in the Afternoon*.

B 3 0 0 Kauffmann, Stanley. *World on Film.* Harper & Row, New York, 1966.

A collection of Kauffmann film reviews. He describes Audrey's performance in *The Nun's Story* as "better than her sheer ability as such could make it, because her personality is so right for the part. After she has done all she can with knowledge and design, her beauty speaks for her."

B 3 0 1 Kauffmann, Stanley. *Before My Eyes.* Harper & Row, New York, 1980.

Rave review of *Roman Holiday*, with particular praise for Audrey Hepburn; "Most of the world's filmgoers met Hepburn just about when Peck did in the film, the men in the audience tumbling, the women delegating...but it was the lusciousness of Hepburn's voice, in addition to the girlish-impish charm of her face, that ravished us."

B 3 0 2 Kobal, John. *Film Star Portraits of the 1950s.* Dover Publications, New York, 1980.

A beautiful collection of black and white portraits from the Kobal archives. Audrey is pictured in publicity stills from *Sabrina* and *The Nun's Story*.

B 3 0 3 Krull, Achim K., Eleanor Hendricks-Witmer and Murray Shukyn. *Video Movies to Go.* Grosvenor House Press Inc., Toronto, 1985.

Another video movie guide, less comprehensive than Leonard Maltin's similar *Movie and Video Guide* (see B311), however it does include adult films and serials. Only eight of Audrey's films are listed and rated, with the highest praise going to *My Fair Lady* (four stars).

B 3 0 4 Latham, Caroline. *Audrey Hepburn.* Proteus Publishing, London, 1984.

At just 127 pages, over half of which are devoted to photos, this is the least in-depth of the three biographies currently available. Latham covers the 18 years from Audrey's birth to her appearance in *High Button Shoes* in just three pages, and emphasizes her film career over her personal life. Not the best choice for the full story, but a solid overview with several anecdotes not found in the other bios.

B305 Learner, Laurence. *As Time Goes By: The Life of Ingrid Bergman*. Harper & Row, New York, 1980.

Bergman affectionately laughs at Cary Grant, her co-star in *Notorious* (1946) and *Indiscreet* (1958), making love on screen to Audrey, "a woman one-third his age" in *Charade*.

B306 Lees, Gene. *Inventing Champagne: the worlds of Lerner and Loewe*. St. Martin's Press, New York, 1990.

Capturing the appropriate "gutter quality" was the most difficult chore for both Audrey and Julie Andrews in their turns as *My Fair Lady*'s Eliza Doolittle, according to Lees. He writes that Alan Jay Lerner "hated" the film, but does not provide any details. Lerner wanted Audrey to star in the film *Gigi*, but she turned him down.

B307 Lerner, Alan Jay. *The Street where I live*. W.W. Norton, New York, 1978.

Lerner, who with Frederick Loewe composed the score to *My Fair Lady*, glosses over the film adaptation and the controversy surrounding Audrey's casting as Eliza in two brief paragraphs. He apparently harbored no animosity toward Audrey, however, as he later invited her to star in the film version of *Gigi*, another Lerner-Loewe musical.

B308 Likeness, George. *Oscar People*. The Wayside Press, Illinois, 1965.

A highly subjective reference guide to the Academy Awards, which covers the controversy over Audrey not being nominated for *My Fair Lady*. Likeness writes that a write-in campaign was started after her name was left off the ballot, but never got off the ground because Academy rules rendered such campaigns illegal.

B309 Logan, Joshua. *Movie Stars, Real People and Me*. Delacorte Press, New York, 1978.

Director Logan asked Audrey to star opposite Marlon Brando in his film *Sayonara* (see W7), but she passed. "I couldn't possibly play an Oriental. No one would believe me. They'd laugh." Logan respected her decision and remained a fan, describing her as "totally charming. She had the prettiest, sweetest, dearest valentine face."

B310 Madsen, Axel. *William Wyler*. Thomas Y. Crowell Co., New York,

1973.

Madsen vividly recounts the story of Audrey's *Roman Holiday* screen test, and Wyler's order to keep the cameras rolling after the scene was finished to capture a natural reaction. "She was absolutely delightful," was Wyler's response upon seeing the test. The book also compares the acting styles of Audrey and Shirley MacLaine in *The Children's Hour*, and recounts Wyler's disappointment in *How to Steal a Million.*

B 3 1 1 Maltin, Leonard. *Leonard Maltin's Movie & Video Guide 1992.* . Signet, New York 1992.

The most comprehensive paperback guide to films available on videocassette. In addition to listing all of Audrey's films plus the television movie *Love Among Thieves*, there is also a star index that lists her filmography, post-*Nederlands in 7 Lessen.*

B 3 1 2 Mancini, Henry. *Did They Mention the Music?* Contemporary Books, Chicago, 1989.

After Henry Mancini heard Audrey sing "How Long Has This Been Going On?" in *Funny Face*, he "felt strongly that she should be the one to sing the new song planned for *Breakfast at Tiffany's.*" He wrote "Moon River" in the same range so she could handle it, but regrets not using her version on the motion picture soundtrack. "There have been more than one thousand recordings of 'Moon River.' Of all of them, Audrey's performance was the definitive version." Mancini would also score *Charade, Two for the Road* and *Wait Until Dark.*

B 3 1 3 Marx, Groucho. *The Groucho Phile.* Wallaby, New York, 1977.

One photo from the mid-1950's of Groucho dancing with Audrey.

B 3 1 4 Maychick, Dlana. *Audrey Hepburn: An Intimate Portrait*. Carol Publishing, New York, 1993

The only complete popular trade biography, but Maychick's claims of personal interviews with Audrey have been disputed by Robert Wolders.

B 3 1 5 McGilligan, Patrick. *A Double Life: George Cukor.* St. Martin's Press, New York, 1991.

McGilligan reveals that Cukor almost became Audrey's director in *Gigi*, her American stage debut. Within his detailed coverage of the making of *My*

Fair Lady, he notes that Audrey was "devastated" after learning that her vocals would not be used, "but the actress carried on with her dignity intact, her chin up." Cukor's skill with actors was tested by the fact that "Hepburn got better as she rehearsed and redid scenes, [while] Harrison peaked on his first takes."

B316 Mellen, Joan. *Big Bad Wolves: Masculinity in the American Film.* Pantheon Books, New York, 1977.

According to Mellen all Hollywood product from the 1950's is pervaded by a male sense of values. One of the common scenarios features an infinitely desirable male who is portrayed as a prize to be won by a variety of eager women. She cites *Love in the Afternoon* as an example; "Were the male lead Audrey Hepburn's age and the female that of Gary Cooper, (the film) would hardly be as romantic" she argues.

B317 Michael, Paul. *The Academy Awards: A Pictorial History.* Crown Publishers, New York, 1978.

Photos from *Roman Holiday* and *My Fair Lady*. Michael describes Audrey's Oscar-winning performance in *Roman Holiday* as "a singular combination of guilelessness, refinement and savoir-faire."

B318 Monaco, James. *The Connoisseur's Guide to the Movies.* Facts on File, New York, 1985.

Critic Monaco chooses "the 1450 most significant movies in the world" in this very enjoyable book that is sure to cause arguments. Nine of Audrey Hepburn's films made the list, with "minor masterpiece" status awarded to *Roman Holiday, Breakfast at Tiffany's, My Fair Lady, Charade* and *Two for the Road.*

B319 Morino, Marianne. *The Hollywood Walk of Fame.* Ten Speed Press, Berkeley, California, 1987.

A listing of everyone who's received a star on the Walk of Fame. Morino includes the location of each star--Audrey's is at 1650 Vine--but she should have listed the year each star was awarded.

B320 Morley, Sheridan. *Tales from the Hollywood Raj: The British, the movies and Tinseltown.* Viking, New York, 1987.

Morley looks at the British influence on screen and off in Hollywood. Among the caricatures of prominent British stars on the cover is one of

Audrey as Eliza from *My Fair Lady*. The author believes that in the 1950s, Audrey's and Deborah Kerr's survival was based on their ability not to appear over-English on screen, "unless it is specifically requested by the script."

B 3 2 1 Morley, Sheridan. *James Mason: Odd man out*. Harper & Row, New York, 1989.

Morley writes that Audrey and James Mason almost starred together in a film version of *Jane Eyre*, but the project was dropped. In 1979 they did co-star in *Bloodline*, but the set was not a happy one. "Audrey had come with her own bodyguard, but decided after a while that she'd rather be kidnapped by the mafia than have to complete the picture."

B 3 2 2 Mosley, Leonard. *Zanuck: The Rise and Fall of Hollywood's Last Tycoon*. McGraw-Hill, New York, 1984.

Audrey is credited for introducing Darryl Zanuck to nightclub singer Juliette Greco during production of *The Sun Also Rises* (1957), starring Mel Ferrer. Greco received a part in the film, and began a stormy relationship with Zanuck that lasted for years.

B 3 2 3 Nash, Jay Robert and Stanley Ralph Ross. *The Motion Picture Guide*. Cinebooks, Inc., Chicago, 1985.

The most comprehensive encyclopedia of world cinema yet compiled. All of Audrey's films (except for *Nederlands in 7 Lessen*) are listed within its 18 volumes, with complete cast lists and credits, plus a plot synopsis and a rating from one to five stars.

B 3 2 4 Neal, Patricia. *As I am*. Simon & Schuster, New York, 1988.

In her autobiography, Neal recalls working with Audrey in *Breakfast at Tiffany's*; "She was quite friendly, and even invited me to her house for supper." Neal's opinion of Audrey changed drastically the night of the 1964 Academy Awards. As the previous year's winner for Best Actress she was invited to present the Best Actor award, but a severe stroke prevented her participation. Audrey did the honors, and Neal writes that "I couldn't wait to hear all the nice things she would say about me. But suddenly she was handing Rex Harrison his award, and she hadn't said a thing about me. I pounded on the table with my good hand. Someone asked if I was annoyed...I bloody well was." Audrey had indeed prepared some comments about Neal, but became caught up in the excitement of seeing her *My Fair Lady* co-star win.

B325 Nowlan, Robert and Gwendolyn Wright Nowlan. *Movie Characters of the Leading Performers of the Sound Era.* American Library Association, Chicago, 1990.

A paragraph of background and biography of over one hundred stars, followed by a list of the characters they portrayed in motion pictures.

B326 Osborne, Robert. *Fifty Golden Years of Oscar.* ESE California, La Habra, California, 1979.

The best of the many Academy Award reference guides. Osborne lists Audrey's Oscar win and four nominations, plus her eight appearances (through 1976) as a presenter.

B327 Palmer, Laura Kay. *Osgood and Anthony Perkins.* McFarland, North Carolina, 1991.

A reference guide to the work of Osgood and Anthony Perkins. Parker writes that Anthony Perkins was "disappointed" in *Green Mansions*; "Audrey Hepburn as Rima failed to be half-bird, but any other actress would have had trouble with that critical aspect of Rima's character."

B328 Parish, James Robert and Dan E. Stanke. *The Glamour Girls.* Arlington House, New York, 1975.

Biographies of nine famous actresses who peaked during and just after Hollywood's golden age. The 70 pages devoted to Audrey Hepburn provide detailed coverage of her every professional endeavor through 1974.

B329 Parish, James Robert and Michael R. Pitts. *The Great Hollywood Musical.* The Scarecrow Press, Inc., Metuchen, New Jersey, 1992

Cast, credits, plot synopses, review excerpts and commentary on *Funny Face* and *My Fair Lady.* "The fact that Fred Astaire, at fifty-seven, was nearly twice Audrey Hepburn's age seemed magically unimportant in the course of their lyrical *Funny Face* courtship," the authors write. *My Fair Lady* is criticized for "casting flaws," but the authors do not name names.

B330 Peary, Danny. *Cult Movies.* Delacorte, New York, 1989.

Peary devotes a chapter to *Two for the Road*, and offers insightful analysis into its storytelling technique, and the reason for its lukewarm reception. Peary felt that critics and audiences "could not get beyond the image of [Albert] Finney, the young cinema upstart, mistreating their princess. It was an imbalance that haunted the film from the beginning."

B331 Peary, Danny. *Alternate Oscars.* Delta, New York, 1993.

Peary second-guesses the Motion Picture Academy in this provocative book. Though he "can't really argue" with Audrey's victory in 1953 for *Roman Holiday,* he would award that year's Oscar to Gloria Grahame for *The Big Heat.* However, Peary would also recall Katharine Hepburn's 1967 Oscar for *Guess Who's Coming to Dinner* and give it to Audrey for her performance in *Two for the Road.*

B332 Phillips, Michael. *7 Poems for Audrey Hepburn.* Flowers
Publishing Corp., New York, 1968.

Just what it says--seven poems, all of which could fit on one page, dedicated to Audrey Hepburn. There is a similarity in style to the "Beat" poetry that was in vogue during the late sixties, but Phillips seems to have worried more about the creative arrangement of his words on the page than the words themselves. You either get it or you don't. Not really a book, though it is listed as one in some reference publications.

B333 Plaskin, Glenn. *Turning Point: Pivotal Moments in the lives of
America's Celebriites.* Birch Lane Press, New York, 1992.

"Nobody makes an entrance like Audrey Hepburn" begins the chapter devoted to Audrey's turning point. She chose to discuss her first meeting with Robert Wolders at a 1981 dinner party; "...eventually we did fall in love. When that happened, nobody was more surprised than I."

B334 Quinlan, David. *British Sound Films: the studio years 1928-1959*
Barnes & Noble Books, Totowa, New Jersey, 1985.

One of the few sources for information on Audrey's UK films *One Wild Oat, Laughter in Paradise, Young Wives Tale* and *The Secret People.* Audrey's name is included in the credits, but there is no commentary on her respective appearances.

B335 Quirk, Lawrence J. *The Films of William Holden.* Citadel Press.
New Jersey, 1973.

Quirk says the title role in *Sabrina* was "tailor-made" for Audrey Hepburn, and that she "did her best to salvage" *Paris When it Sizzles* "via her unique personality."

B336 Ragan, David. *Who's who in Hollywood.* Arlington House, New Rochelle, New York, 1976.

An incomplete filmography. More complete information is available from a variety of other sources.

B337 Riodon, Walter. *The Biographical Encyclopedia & who's who of the American Theatre.* J.H. Heineman, New York, 1966.

A brief biographical sketch, incorporating Audrey's stage and film credits through 1966.

B338 Robertson, Patrick. *Guinness Book of Movie Facts and Feats.* Guinness Publishing, Great Britain, 1991.

Audrey $1 million salary, plus her agreement to keep the $100,000 wardrobe she modeled in *Bloodline* was worthy of inclusion in this compilation of unusual movie feats. Robertson also credits Audrey's blond-streaked brunette hairstyle in *Breakfast at Tiffany's* with inspiring a trend.

B339 Rogers, Henry C. *Walking the Tightrope: the private confessions of a public relations man.* Morrow, New York, 1980.

Rogers, one of Hollywood's top publicists, met Audrey on the set of *War and Peace* and was "enchanted" by the warm greeting and embrace he received. He became Audrey's American publicist, but they parted company later when Rogers began to disagree with Mel Ferrer over career decisions involving his client.

B340 Rollvson, Carl E. *Lillian Hellman: her legacy and her legend.* St. Martin's Press, New York, 1988.

Hellman was not happy with William Wyler's film *The Children's Hour*, an adaptation of her play. She called the movie "outdated in its attitudes and treatment."

B341 Rosen, Marjorie. *Popcorn Venus.* Coward, McCann and Geoghegan, New York, 1973.

Rosen praises Audrey as one of the most "intriguing and individualistic heroines" in fifties cinema. "A constantly surprising and modern screen personality, she offered women a positive alternative beyond Leslie Caron's Lili, or Debbie Reynolds' bumptious tomboy who grew up and calmed down with love."

B342 Russo, Vito. *The Celluloid Closet.* Harper & Row. New York, 1985.

A provocative look at the treatment of homosexuality in the movies. *The Children's Hour* is grouped with other films that view homosexuality as an awful disease. Russo quotes Shirley MacLaine saying (with Audrey's support) that she wanted a more explicit development of her character's growing sexual awareness, but director William Wyler did not believe middle America was ready for such frankness. Most intriguing is a photo from a scene that was cut from the movie, in which the two teachers are found guilty in court of "sinful sexual knowledge of one another."

B343 Sackett, Susan. *The Hollywood Reporter Book of box office hits.* Hollywood Reporter, Los Angeles, 1988.

Credits, synopses and reviews of the top five movies of every year from 1939 to 1988. *My Fair Lady* grossed enough for the number four spot in 1964. Sackett's commentary is adequate, but her statement that Marni Nixon was brought in because Audrey Hepburn "couldn't sing a note" will ring false to anyone who's seen *Funny Face* or *Breakfast at Tiffany's.*

B344 Sarris, Andrew. *Confessions of a Cultist.* Simon & Schuster, New York, 1970.

In this collection of erudite film reviews, *Village Voice* critic Sarris mildly praises *Charade* ("consistently better than ordinary without ever being extraordinary"), but criticizes Audrey's performance in *My Fair Lady.* Sarris judged her as "not technically qualified" for the role, and was dismayed that she did not perform her own songs.

B345 Sayre, Nora. *Running Time: Films of the Cold War.* Dial Press, New York, 1978.

It isn't easy to find truly scathing criticism of Audrey Hepburn as an actress or public persona, but Sayre lets her have it with both barrels. Adolescent girls in the 1950s were "tyrannized" by her, according to the author, because she "blended cuteness and elegance with a sham innocence that almost insulted human nature. The innocence seemed false because no one over fifteen could have remained so sheltered as her screen personae--not even in the fifties." Sayre writes that if Audrey had "been a better actress" her style would not have been as oppressive; "but her ability was meager; beyond batting her eyelids with regal authority or dispensing sudden grins and bursts of overanimation, she didn't exert herself at acting." Sayre concludes that the public's adulation of Audrey Hepburn "seemed to tell us that young women ought to be well-heeled, submissive and sexually spotless."

B346 Sennett, Ted. *Hollywood Musicals.* H.N. Abrams, New York, 1981.

Huge, photo-laden coffee table book with color pictures of Audrey in *Funny Face* and *My Fair Lady.* Sennett praises both films and Audrey's performances.

B347 Shipman, David. *The Great Movie Stars: the International Years.* Hill and Wang, New York, 1980.

Surprisingly thorough four-page career overview, with photos from *Roman Holiday, War and Peace, Funny Face* and *Two for the Road.*

B348 Shipman, David. *Movie Talk.* Bloomsbury Publishing Ltd., London, 1989.

An immensely enjoyable compilation of quotes by stars about other stars. There are twelve devoted to Audrey, from such performers as James Mason, Fred Astaire, David Niven and Lucille Ball, who lauded Audrey's comedic talent; "You'd never think of her being able to do my type of comedy, but she can. But she's so beautiful, so ethereal, that it would be sacrilege to put her through it."

B349 Sinclair, Marianne. *Hollywood Lolitas.* Henry Holt & Co., New York, 1988.

Sinclair analyzes Hollywood's recognition and exploitation of a sexual taboo--the attraction of older men to young girls. Audrey is cited as a *gamine*, a type of nymphet that emerged in the 1950s, with "youthfulness so deliberately exaggerated that it was calculated to bring out incestuous-father longings in an adult male, rather than straightforward boy-girl feelings of mutual attraction." *Sabrina* and *Love in the Afternoon* are listed as examples.

B350 Sinyard, Neil. *The Films of Richard Lester.* Barnes & Noble, New Jersey, 1985.

High praise for Audrey's only collaboration with director Lester on *Robin and Marian*. Sinyard writes that the performances of Hepburn and Connery "are among the finest either of them has accomplished on screen."

B351 Speck, Gregory. *Hollywood Royalty*. Birch Lane Press, New York, 1992.

A series of direct quotes from dozens of celebrities, weaved into the conversation of a fictional dinner party. The presentation is not entirely effective, though many of the quotes are memorable. There are several quotes from Audrey on a variety of subjects, including *Roman Holiday*, Henry Fonda, William Wyler and John Huston.

B352 Spoto, Donald. *The Dark Side of Genius*. Little, Brown & Co., Boston, 1983.

Of the many Alfred Hitchcock biographies, this one gives the most details about the director's abandoned movie *No Bail For the Judge*, and his anger toward Audrey. Hitchcock prepared for the project in his usual meticulous way, and was glad when Audrey agreed to play the lead role. When asked about his usual penchant for blondes, Hitchcock said "I'm quite prepared to try a cool brunette if I come across one." But Spoto writes that after Audrey read the final script, which included a brutal rape scene involving her character, the film "was virtually cancelled from that minute." Hitchcock registered "shock, with a rare burst of anger" when he heard that she had pulled out, citing pregnancy.

B353 Springer, John. *All Talking! All Singing! All Dancing!: A pictorial history of the movie musical*. Citadel Press, New York, 1969.

Photos from *Funny Face*, *My Fair Lady* and *Breakfast at Tiffany's*. According to Springer, Audrey was at "her most entrancing" in *Funny Face*, and can "point to her inspired antics in (the film) as one of her real career high spots." He also praised her performance in *My Fair Lady*, but believed she was too elegant to be a guttersnipe.

B354 Thomas, Bob. *Golden Boy: The Untold Story of William Holden.* St. Martin's Press, New York, 1983.

The most detailed account of Holden's love for Audrey Hepburn, though it is not able to conclude if their relationship was consummated. "Most of Holden's romances with his leading ladies ended with the completion of their movies together. Not so with Audrey Hepburn. To

Holden she embodied everything that he admired in a woman." According to Thomas, Audrey was "entranced by his manly charm and gentle humor, and had agreed to marry Holden once he divorced his wife Andis, but she backed out after learning that Holden could no longer have children. When they were teamed a second time for *Paris When it Sizzles*, Holden told Ryan O'Neal how he felt like a condemned man when he arrived in the City of Lights. "I realized I had to face Audrey Hepburn and I had to deal with my drinking. And I didn't think I could handle either situation." At one point production shut down when Holden checked into the Chateau de Garche, a hospital for alcoholics.

B355 Thompson, Howard. *Fred Astaire: A Pictorial Treasury of his Films*. Falcon Enterprises, New York, 1970.

Very little text accompanying a rich selection of photos from Fred Astaire's movies, including two of Audrey and Fred from *Funny Face*.

B356 Thomson, David. *A Biographical Dictionary of film*. William Morrow and Co., Inc., New York, 1981.

An unflattering biographical sketch that judges many of Audrey's performances as "dated." "Because she seemed to bring the idea of innocence to her films, rather than the prospect of character, it is likely that, past youth, she will not make many movies."

B357 Trescott, Pamela. *Cary Grant*. Acropolis Books Ltd., Washington D.C., 1987.

Audrey and Cary Grant developed a close friendship and rapport during production of *Charade*. Grant wanted Audrey for his co-star in *Father Goose* (1964), but the role went to Leslie Caron.

B358 van Gelder, Peter. *That's Hollywood*. Harper Perennial, New York, 1990.

A behind-the-scenes look at the "sixty greatest films of all time," according to the author. *The Lavender Hill Mob* made the list, and Audrey is mentioned as having a bit part.

B359 Vance, Malcolm. *The Movie Ad Book*. Control Data Publishing. Minneapolis, Minnesota, 1981.

Interesting collection of movie ads and posters. Audrey's filmography is represented by *Roman Holiday, War and Peace, Green Mansions* and

The Nun's Story.

B360 Vermilye, Jerry. *Burt Lancaster*. Falcon Enterprises, New York, 1971.

A pictorial history of Burt Lancaster's films, with two photos of Burt and Audrey from *The Unforgiven*.

B361 Vickers, Hugo. *Cecil Beaton*. Little, Brown and Co., Boston, 1985.

Vickers includes in his enjoyable biography a note Audrey wrote to Cecil Beaton after seeing his photos of her in various *My Fair Lady* costumes: "Dearest C.B., Ever since I can remember I have always so badly wanted to be beautiful. Looking at those photographs last night I saw that, for a short time at least, I am, all because of you. Audrey." She would later send Beaton a letter of congratulations after his double-Oscar victory for the same film.

B362 Warner, Alan. *Who Sang What on the Screen*. Angus & Robertson Publications, London, 1984.

Fun to read, but inconveniently organized guide to movie songs and the stars who performed them. It is thorough enough to remember not only Audrey's performance of "Moon River" in *Breakfast at Tiffany's*, but also her renditions of "La Vie En Rose" and "Yes we Have no Bananas" in *Sabrina*. However, it also credits Audrey with singing "I Could Have Danced All Night" in *My Fair Lady*, which was actually performed by Marni Nixon.

B363 Weaver, John T. *Forty Years of Screen Credits*. Scarecrow Press, Metuchen, New Jersey, 1970.

Weaver compiled two volumes of screen credits from films released between 1929 and 1969. With the exception of *Nederlands in 7 Lessen*, Audrey's films through *Wait Until Dark* are listed.

B364 Webb, Michael. *Hollywood Legend and Reality*. Little, Brown and Co., New York, 1986.

Published in conjunction with a traveling exhibit on Hollywood compiled by the Smithsonian Institute. Two Audrey items: a Cecil Beaton sketch of Audrey in her *My Fair Lady* cockney flower girl outfit, and a breathtaking photo of Audrey and Grace Kelly from 1956.

B365 Wiley, Mason and Damien Bona. *Inside Oscar.* Ballantine Books, New York, 1986.

A fascinating account of Academy Award ceremonies from their humble beginnings to 1992. Several Audrey Hepburn anecdotes, and the best coverage available of the *My Fair Lady* controversy.

B366 Windeler, Robert. *Julie Andrews: a biography.* W.H. Allen, London, 1982.

Recounts Julie's disappointment at losing the role of Eliza in *My Fair Lady* the movie. "If it had been anyone but Audrey Hepburn, she would have been blazing mad," according to Windeler. But Andrews praised Audrey's work, and Audrey returned the compliment after seeing *Mary Poppins* (1964). The feud that the press tried to fuel between the two stars never came to pass.

B367 Woodward, Ian. *Audrey Hepburn.* St. Martin's Press, New York, 1984.

Extensive use of quotes from friends, associates and previous articles, vivid descriptions of important people and places in Audrey's life, and excellent documentation help make this 312-page biography the best of the 1984 crop (see B286 and B304), though like the others it is impaired by its date of publication.

B368 Zolotow, Maurice. *Billy Wilder in Hollywood.* G.P. Putnam's Sons, New York, 1977.

Zolotow analyzes Wilder's treatment of women in film, noting that Audrey "twice played innocent girls who studied to be sophisticated, independent women so they could manifest their true beings to the man they loved (*Sabrina, Love in the Afternoon*)." The author also chronicles the near-daily battles on the set of *Sabrina* between Wilder and Humphrey Bogart.

Appendix A: What Might Have Been

Audrey Hepburn appeared in 30 films, which represent only a fraction of the projects that were offered to her from the 1950's up to her death in 1993. These are just some of the scripts that she turned down. Most were made with other actresses, but for some of them her rejection signaled the end of the project.

W 1 *Laughter in Paradise* (Associated British Films, 1951).

Audrey was offered the lead role of Lucille Grayson, but refused to ignore her prior commitment to *Sauce Piquante* (1950--see S3). The lead went to Beatrice Campbell, but Audrey does appear in a bit part as a cigarette girl.

W 2 *Quo Vadis?* (MGM, 1951).

Alec Guinness, who worked with Audrey in *The Lavender Hill Mob* (1951--see F5) introduced her to director Mervyn LeRoy, then in the process of casting his next film *Quo Vadis?*. LeRoy wanted Audrey for the lead role of Lygia, which would have been her breakthrough performance in Hollywood. MGM vetoed the decision, preferring a "name" actress in the part, which ultimately went to Deborah Kerr.

W 3 *Lady Godiva Rides Again* (London/Carroll, 1951).

Audrey was in the running for the lead role of Marjorie Clark, a beauty contest winner who tries repeatedly to launch an acting career, but is only successful after agreeing to play a nude stage role. Pauline Stroud was cast when Audrey was deemed too thin.

W 4 *Brandy For the Parson* (Associated British Films, 1952).

Audrey was offered the role of Petronilla, girlfriend of the lead. When Associated British Films couldn't agree on a start date, Audrey left to make *Monte Carlo Baby* (1953--see F7). Jean Lodge played Petronilla. It was on the set of *Monte Carlo Baby* that Audrey was discovered by the author Colette and cast in the Broadway play *Gigi*, her star-making performance.

W 5 *The Beggar's Opera* (Warner Bros., 1953).

When Audrey was "too busy" to play Polly Peachum opposite Sir Laurence Olivier as Macheath, the role went to Dorothy Tutin.

W 6 Untitled (1957).

Audrey was approached to play Maria Von Trapp in a film biography. She turned the role down citing a need for rest and her hope to start a family with Mel Ferrer. Two years later, Rogers & Hammerstein turned the Von Trapp story into the Broadway musical *The Sound of Music.*

W 7 *Sayonara* (Warner Bros., 1957).

Director Joshua Logan asked Audrey to play Marlon Brando's Japanese lover Hana-ogi in this story of interracial romance reminiscent of *Madame Butterfly*. Though she liked the part, she told Logan "I couldn't possibly play an Oriental. No one would believe me. They'd laugh." An Oriental actress, Miiko Taka, played the role.

W 8 *Look Homeward, Angel, The Lark, L'Aiglon* (Paramount, 1957).

After starring opposite her husband Mel Ferrer in the television movie *Mayerling* (see F10), Audrey suggested to Paramount that they collaborate again for film versions of either Thomas Wolfe's *Look Homeward, Angel* or Jean Anouilh's *The Lark*. She also expressed willingness to be directed by Ferrer in *L'Aiglon*, playing the son (!) of Napoleon and Marie Louise. Paramount declined all three projects. *L'Aiglon* was almost revived with William Wyler at the helm, but did not materialize.

W 9   *Twelfth Night* (1957).

Cosmopolitan magazine announced that Audrey's next film after *Love in the Afternoon* (1957--see F12) would be a production of Shakespeare's *Twelfth Night* directed by Joseph Mankiewicz. The film was never made.

W 1 0   *Saint Joan* (United Artists, 1957).

Audrey turned down the title role, which made a star out of Jean Seberg, during one of her self-imposed hiatuses from the movies.

W 1 1   *Gigi* (MGM, 1958).

"I would have loved to have done it but I'm glad Leslie Caron did it," said Audrey in a 1967 interview. "At the time, Billy Wilder had asked me to do *Love in the Afternoon* with Gary Cooper and I wanted to do something new rather than doing *Gigi* again." According to *Films In Review* magazine, however, it was MGM's refusal to take Audrey and Mel Ferrer as a package deal that kept her from reprising the role (see S4). *Gigi* turned out to be the last great MGM musical, and the recipient of eight Academy Awards including Best Picture.

W 1 2   *A Certain Smile* (20th Century-Fox, 1958).

Audrey's one year off from movies in 1958 prevented her from appearing as Francoise Ferrand in this adaptation of Francoise Sagan's novella. The role was played by Joan Fontaine.

W 1 3   *The Diary of Anne Frank* (20th Century-Fox, 1959).

"I just could not deal with it. There were floods of tears. I became hysterical," said Audrey of the role that in many ways paralleled her own experiences of growing up in war-torn Arnhem. When director George Stevens asked her to play the role, she actually met with Anne Frank's father to discuss the project, but Audrey ultimately decided the experience would be too painful. In 1989, however, she would read excerpts from Anne's diary on a UNICEF tour with the New World Symphony Orchestra (see S6). "The difference," she said, "is I'm not playing Anne Frank. I'm just reading her thoughts. I still wouldn't play her. It would be like putting me back into the horrors of that war." The film role was played by newcomer Millie Perkins.

W14 *No Bail For the Judge* (1959).

Alfred Hitchcock planned to direct this story of a London barrister whose father, a judge, is wrongly accused of murder. Audrey agreed to play the barrister, who investigates the case and uncovers the actual murderer. Her interest waned, however, after reading the final script, which had her character being victimized in an explicit rape scene. Audrey backed out, citing her pregnancy as an excuse. An outraged Hitchcock refused to continue the project with another actress, so the film was abandoned.

W15 *The Cardinal* (Columbia, 1960).

As a new mother enjoying her baby, Audrey was not interested in returning to work in *The Cardinal.* Instead, Carol Lynley played the lead female role of Mona in this Otto Preminger film about one priest's difficult rise to the College of Cardinals.

W16 *West Side Story* (United Artists, 1961).

One can only speculate how effective Audrey, the regal European princess, would have been as Maria, a Hispanic poverty-stricken New Yorker. And would she have done her own singing, after vowing to do so if given another chance after *My Fair Lady* (1964--see F21)? As it was, the role went to Natalie Wood, who was nominated for an Oscar and whose singing was dubbed by Marni Nixon. Nixon also contributed Audrey's singing vocals in *My Fair Lady.*

W17 *A Taste of Honey* (Continental Distributing, 1962).

Audrey never had the chance to take or leave this British working class drama, but American financiers wanted her for the lead role of Jo and would only back the film if she were cast. Director Tony Richardson turned down the Yankee cash and cast unknown Rita Tushingham.

W18 *Cleopatra* (20th Century-Fox, 1963).

Both Audrey and Elizabeth Taylor expressed interest in playing the legendary Queen of the Nile, but Audrey's pregnancy and Paramount's refusal to release her to Fox helped Taylor win the role. The result became one of Hollywood's most famous--and expensive--flops. Taylor, however, received a $1 million contract plus $50,000 a week for overtime, which grew over the course of shooting the four-hour epic into a salary fit for a queen.

W19 *Man's Favorite Sport* (Universal, 1964).

Director Howard Hawks wanted Audrey and Cary Grant to play Abigail Page and Roger Willoughby in this screwball comedy, but instead they decided to make *Charade* (1963--see F19). The roles went to Rock Hudson and Paula Prentiss.

W20 *The Umbrellas of Cherbourg* (Madeleine-Parc-Beta/Landau,1964).

This French production, an homage to classic American musicals, told its story entirely through dialogue that was sung instead of spoken. Audrey, on hiatus after *My Fair Lady*, turned down the lead role of Genevieve Emery, which went to Catherine Deneuve.

W21 *Peter Pan* (??).

Audrey's name has been mentioned in connection with both stage and screen versions of James Barrie's classic tale almost since she arrived in America to star in *Gigi*. The idea came closest to becoming reality when George Cukor, for whom *Peter Pan* was a lifelong dream project, directed Audrey in *My Fair Lady* (1964) and saw in her the ideal Pan. Unfortunately, the film never emerged from the discussion stage. Two years later Mel Ferrer tried to revive the idea, but Walt Disney secured an injunction to stop the project, fearing it would conflict with its animated version.

W22 *The Castles and the Crown* (1965).

Mel Ferrer acquired the movie rights to *The Castles and the Crown*, a historic novel about Columbus's voyage to America. Ferrer hoped that Audrey would play Queen Isabella, but the film was never made.

W23 *Romeo and Juliet* (British Home Entertainments-Verona/Paramount,1968).

Audrey, then 34 years old, was offered the part of Juliet in Franco Zeffirelli's exquisite film of the Shakespeare tragedy. But she was still on her *My Fair Lady* hiatus, so the role went to 15-year-old Olivia Hussey.

W24 *Goodbye, Mr. Chips* (MGM, 1969).

In a packaging deal remarkable for its time, MGM offered Richard Burton and Audrey Hepburn $1 million against 10 percent of the gross profit to star in a musical remake of the classic 1939 Robert Donat-Greer Garson film, based on James Hilton's novel. According to the *New York Times*, "If Mr. Burton and Miss Hepburn wind up on the 'Mr. Chips' marquee, it would mark one of the few times that such a large percentage of the immediate income of a picture was allocated to the co-stars." They didn't, and the roles were played by Peter O'Toole and Petula Clark.

W25 *Nicholas and Alexandra* (Columbia, 1971).

Audrey turned down countless scripts in the ten years between *Wait Until Dark* (1967--see F24) and *Robin and Marian* (1976--see F25). One of them offered her the role of Russia's last Czarina in this lavish historical drama. Janet Suzman played Alexandra.

W26 *Forty Carats* (Columbia, 1973).

An adaptation of the hit Broadway play about a forty-year-old divorcee who is pursued by a twenty-year-old suitor. Audrey expressed interest if the film could be made in Rome, where she was enjoying married life. Such a move would have made the project far more expensive than estimated, so the film was made in Hollywood with Liv Ullman.

W27 *The Survivors* (??).

A proposed adaptation of Anne Edwards's 1969 novel, about a girl who survives the mass murder of her family by psychotics, was turned down by Audrey, who felt herself too old to play the girl. The film was never made.

W28 *Conversation Piece* (Rusconi/GAU, 1977).

Audrey was offered the role of Bianca in Luchino Visconti's esoteric story of decadence. The staid professor whose life is disrupted by Bianca was played by Burt Lancaster. Audrey was not comfortable with the sexual escapades in the script, so Silvana Mangano played the role.

W29 *A Bridge Too Far* (United Artists, 1977).

"When I read that book (by Cornelius Ryan) I was destroyed. The same as when I first read Anne Frank's diary," said Audrey in a 1991 interview. The story of an ill-fated allied invasion of the Netherlands in World War II became a star-studded movie, but painful childhood memories contributed to Audrey's refusal to play Kate ter Horst. Liv Ullman stepped in.

W30 *The Turning Point* (20th Century-Fox, 1977).

At one point, Audrey and Grace Kelly, the two actresses who most symbolized class and elegance in the 1950's, were touted to star in this drama about two friends and former ballet dancers who are reunited after many years. Kelly, who was then Princess Grace of Monaco, had not made a film since 1956, and though Audrey had appeared in *Robin and Marian* one year earlier she remained uninterested in resuming her acting career full time. Given these facts, it is probable that the speculation was more a hoped-for dream of the producer and studio than a serious possibility. The roles of Deedee Rodgers and Emma Jacklin went to Shirley MacLaine and Anne Bancroft.

Jean Hersholt presents Audrey with the 1953 Best Actress Academy Award for her performance in *Roman Holiday*.

Appendix B: Awards, Honors, Tributes

A1 **Best Actress** (1953). Presented by the Academy of Motion Picture Arts & Sciences for Audrey's performance in *Roman Holiday* (see F8), her first starring role.

A2 **Best Actress** (1953). Presented by the British Academy Awards for *Roman Holiday*.

A3 **Picturegoer Gold Medal** (1953). Another "Best Actress" honor for *Roman Holiday*, this one from the British moviegoers.

A4 **Best Actress** (1953). Audrey was also the New York Film Critics choice for *Roman Holiday*.

A5 **Best Actress in a Drama** (1953). A Golden Globe award from the Hollywood Foreign Press Association for *Roman Holiday*.

A6 **Look Movie Award** (1953). Audrey was named Best Actress of the year by the editors of *Look* Magazine.

A7 **The Find of 1953** (1953). Awarded by *Film Daily* Magazine

A8 **Best Actress of the Broadway Season 1953-54**. (1954). Audrey's performance in *Ondine* tied with Deborah

Kerr's performance in *Tea and Sympathy*. Both actresses received this award from the New York Drama Critics Circle.

A7 **Mademoiselle Merit Award** (1954). Presented by *Mademoiselle* magazine. Audrey is lauded for "her incomparable technique, her mobile face and her combination of wistfulness and hauteur."

A8 **World's Favorite Film Player** (1954). From the Foreign Press Association (Golden Globe).

A9 **Distinguished Performance in a Dramatic Play by a Female Star** (1954). Audrey received the Antoinette Perry (Tony) Award for *Ondine* (see S5).

A10 **Best Actress nomination** (1954). From the Motion Picture Academy for her performance in *Sabrina* (see F9) The Oscar went to Grace Kelly for *The Country Girl.*

A11 **Our Girl of the Year** (1958). Presented by *Picturegoer Film Annual*, voted on by British moviegoers.

A12 **Best Actress** (1959). From the British Academy for Audrey's performance in *The Nun's Story* (see F13).

A13 **Best Actress** (1959). For *The Nun's Story*, presented by the New York Film Critics.

A14 **Actress of the Year** (1959) From *Film Daily* magazine-- *The Nun's Story.*

A15 **Best Actress nomination** (1959) Audrey's third Oscar nomination, this time for *The Nun's Story*. The award was given to Simone Signoret for *Room At the Top.*

A16 **Best Foreign Actress** (1959-1960). Audrey received the David Di Donatello Prize, Italy's highest film honor, for *The Nun's Story.*

A17 **Mr. Blackwell's Fashion Independents** (1960). Audrey's association with designer Givenchy was noted and applauded by fashion-watcher Mr. Blackwell.

A18 **Best-Dressed Hall of Fame** (1961). The New York Couture Group bestowed its highest status on Audrey.

A19 **Best Actress nomination** (1961). Audrey's fourth nomination in eight films, for her performance in *Breakfast at Tiffany's* (see F17). She lost to Sophia Loren in Two *Women*.

A20 **Best Foreign Actress** (1961-1962). Audrey received her second David Di Donatello Prize for *Breakfast at Tiffany's*.

A21 **Best Actress** (1964). British Academy Award number three for Audrey, for her work in *Charade* (see F19).

A22 **Best Foreign Actress** (1964-1965). For *My Fair Lady* (see F21), Audrey's third David Di Donatello Prize.

A23 **Academy Award nomination** (1967). Audrey's fifth and final Oscar nomination, for *Two For the Road* (see F23). The Oscar went to Katharine Hepburn in *Guess Who's Coming To Dinner?*

A24 **Special Tony Award** (1968). Despite starring in only two Broadway plays, Audrey was one of five performers to receive a Tony Award for her contribution to the New York stage. Other honorees included Pearl Bailey, Carol Channing, Marlene Dietrich and Maurice Chevalier.

A25 **Life Legend Award** (1986). Audrey was one of twelve recipients whose life and career received significant coverage in the pages of *Life* Magazine (see T28)

A26 **Museum of Modern Art Film Preservation Fund Tribute** (1987). Among the guests who paid a minimum of $1000 to attend this dinner-dance honoring Audrey were Gregory Peck, Hubert de Givenchy, Ralph Lauren and Princess Yasmin Aga Khan. All proceeds were donated to the MOMA's Film Preservation Fund.

A27 **Prix d'Humanite'** (1989). For her work with UNICEF, Audrey received this honor from the Lions Club Circles of the

Netherlands.

A28 Institute of Human Understanding Award for an Individual of International Fame (1989). Audrey and Bob Geldof were recipients.

A29 The Cecil B DeMille Prize (1990). The Hollywood Foreign Press Association's lifetime achievement award was presented to Audrey by former co-stars Gregory Peck (*Roman Holiday*), George Peppard (*Breakfast at Tiffany's*) and Richard Crenna (*Wait Until Dark*).

A30 Child Survival Medal (1990). Presented to Audrey by President Jimmy Carter, for her work as UNICEF Goodwill Ambassador.

A31 Hall of Fame (1990). Presented by the International Women's Forum, a by-invitation-only organization whose members include Margaret Thatcher, Corazon Aquino and Justice Sandra Day O'Connor. It's Hall of Fame inductees must "be prominent in their field and must exert influence beyond their own sphere of endeavor."

A32 Master Screen Artist Award (1991). This award was the culmination of a salute to Audrey at the USA Film Festival in Dallas, Texas.

A33 Tribute of the New York Film Society at Lincoln Center (1991). Audrey is the recipient of testimonials from Gregory Peck, Alan Arkin (*Wait Until Dark*), Anthony Perkins (*Green Mansions*), Billy Wilder (*Sabrina, Love in the Afternoon*), Stanley Donen (*Funny Face, Charade* and *Two for the Road*) and Harry Belafonte (UNICEF).

A34 Golden Plate Award (1991). Presented by the American Academy of Achievement, to honor America's outstanding leaders.

A35 BAMBI Prize (1991). Presented at the UNICEF Gala in Wiesbaden, Germany.

A36 New York Fashion Industry Tribute (1991).

A37 Screen Actors Guild Award (1992). For lifetime achievement in film, awarded to those who foster "the finest ideals of the acting profession."

A38 George Eastman Award for Distinguished Contribution to the Art of Film (1992). From the International Museum of Photography, presented for "distinguished contribution to the art of film." In 1987 Audrey presented the same award to old friend Gregory Peck.

A39 Special Award (1992). Presented by the British Academy of Film and TV Arts.

A40 Variety Clubs International Award (1992). Audrey's achievements as an actress and a humanitarian are saluted.

A41 Medal of Freedom (1992). Audrey received the United States' highest civilian honor from President George Bush, but illness forced her to miss the ceremony.

A42 Lifetime Achievement Award (1992). From the international nursing society Sigma Theta Tau, who decided that Audrey "personified the sense of caring, which is an integral component of nursing."

A43 Jean Hersholt Humanitarian Award (1993). A special honor awarded by the Academy of Motion Picture Arts and Sciences to Audrey for her work with UNICEF and to Elizabeth Taylor for her work in AIDS research. Audrey died two weeks after learning of the award, which was presented to her son Sean at the 65th Annual Academy Awards, accompanied by a tribute to her life and career.

A44 UNICEF dinner (1993). Charles Champlin emceed a dinner at the Restaurant Bikini in Los Angeles, that was co-chaired by Gregory Peck and Billy Wilder. Guest speakers included Peter Bogdanovich, who directed Audrey in *They All Laughed* (see F26) . During the festivities, a life-size bronze portrait sculpture of Audrey by Finnish artist Eino was unveiled. The dinner and an auction of Eino's work raised $50,000 for the U.N. Children's Fund.

A45 Day of Tribute (1993). The New York Metropolitan Committee for UNICEF sponsored a tribute to Audrey on what would have been her 64th birthday. A memorial service at the Fifth Ave. Presbyterian Church was followed by a three-film retrospective at the Angelika 57 Theater. All proceeds supported UNICEF's Audrey Hepburn Memorial Fund.

A46 Hal Roach Entertainment Award (1993). Presented "to an individual whose life and work exemplify the kind of family entertainment for which movie producer Hal Roach always stood."

A47 Tiffany's display (1993). The New York jewelry store honored its most famous customer with a special display.

A48 Grammy Award (1994). Presented posthumously to Audrey in the category of Best Children's Spoken Word Recording, for her narration of *Audrey Hepburn's Enchanted Tales*.

Index

About the Author

DAVID HOFSTEDE is a freelance writer, presently working on a book about Hollywood heroes.

Titles in
Bio-Bibliographies in the Performing Arts